Social Media Marketing Management

This book responds to calls for a systematic approach in understanding the transformations in the social media marketing landscape. To narrow the focus, the book takes a developing economy perspective and presents a comprehensive understanding of social media practices and how these can be integrated in firms' operational activities to create a competitive advantage.

In emerging markets and developing economies (EMDEs), social media provides a technological solution to the economic challenges faced by governments, firms, and people at the bottom of the economic pyramid. Social media is often considered to be fundamentally changing the business paradigm and is increasingly integrated into the marketing function, and EMDEs seem to be quickly finding out that it offers them a relatively low-cost opportunity to potentially leapfrog the competition in developed markets.

By using social technology to reach users in different market segments in ways that were impossible before, social sites such as Facebook and X (formerly Twitter) create tremendous new growth opportunities for businesses. As businesses embrace social media solutions however, some challenges emerge in the adoption, utilisation, integration, and implementation of social media systems and tools in EMDEs— hence the need to provide pathways to better integrate social media into the marketing activities of emerging market institutions.

This book provides practical guidance on the use of social media in marketing management. It provides contemporary perspectives on social media marketing, and while it is aimed primarily at practitioners, it could also serve as teaching text for undergraduate and postgraduate teaching programmes.

Social Media Marketing Management

How to Penetrate Emerging Markets and Expand Your Customer Base

Robert E. Hinson, David Mhlanga,
Kofi Osei-Frimpong, and Joshua Doe

Routledge
Taylor & Francis Group

A PRODUCTIVITY PRESS BOOK

First published 2025
by Routledge
605 Third Avenue, New York, NY 10158

and by Routledge
4 Park Square, Milton Park, Abingdon, Oxon, OX14 4RN

Routledge is an imprint of the Taylor & Francis Group, an informa business

ISBN: 978-1-032-30964-4 (hbk)
ISBN: 978-1-032-30963-7 (pbk)
ISBN: 978-1-003-30745-7 (ebk)

DOI: 10.4324/9781003307457

Typeset in Garamond
by Deanta Global Publishing Services, Chennai, India

Contents

Foreword by Dr Alistair Mokoena

Social Media Marketing: Engaging and Winning in Africa and Other Emerging Markets

One of the most profound effects of the digitalisation of the marketing and communications disciplines is the proliferation of media channels which has been driven by the explosion of social media touchpoints such as YouTube, Facebook, X, and Tik Tok, amongst others. As a result, social media marketing has become the de facto route to market strategy for many marketers.

Another key aspect to the evolution of marketing and communications is the growth of e-commerce and social commerce across Africa, which was accelerated by the COVID-19 pandemic. This is the new battleground for a consumer's mind space.

As the war for share of wallet intensifies, consumers are bombarded with many competing messages. With the average consumer being exposed to at least 10,000 messages a day, finding the right consumer to target with the right message at the right time in way that maintains data privacy has never been harder.

The good news is that this book delivers a wealth of insights into winning the hearts and minds of consumers through social media marketing. It is packed with fantastic case studies from successful brands, as well as easy-to-apply principles that will set you apart from the competition. Whether you are a marketing or communications practitioner, a student or an entrepreneur, this book will set you up for success.

This book presents a fantastic treatise on customer service as a secret weapon for brands. What we have observed is that innovation that is fuelled by advances in technology has narrowed the product efficacy gap between brands, resulting in the need to identify other differentiators. One of the most potent differentiators in a marketer's arsenal is customer service. Done right, customer service can be a game changer.

In this book, you will find a practical guide on how to design winning service products, which are underpinned by strong product delivery and delivered by passionate, insightful service-oriented employees. You will find all the ingredients that you need to help you nurture customer relationships, resulting in superior customer lifetime value.

As Maya Angelou once famously said, "I've learned that people will forget what you said, people will forget what you did, but people will never forget how you made them feel." The case studies contained in this book confirm that exceptional customer service leads to loyalty and advocacy, which is the ultimate goal of marketers. Keep this handbook close as you navigate the highly contested waters of marketing.

About Dr Alistair Mokoena

Dr Alistair Mokoena is an Extraordinary Professor of Practice in the field of Digital Marketing at the North-West University Business School, and a member of Council at the University of Johannesburg. He is the Country Director for Google in Southern Africa and an award-winning Chartered Marketer. He is the best-selling author of the book *Servings of Self-Mastery.*

Author Biographies

Robert E. Hinson is Professor of Marketing and Pro-Vice-Chancellor at the Ghana Communication Technology University, Ghana. Prior to his current position, he served as Deputy Vice-Chancellor Academic at the University of Kigali and also as Director of Institutional Advancement at the University of Ghana.

Apart from being a Chartered Marketer, Professor Hinson holds a Bachelor's, Master's, and Doctorate Degree in Marketing from the University of Ghana. He holds a second doctorate degree in International Business from the Aalborg University Business School in Denmark. He is also a Distinguished Visiting Professor at the University of Johannesburg in South Africa.

Professor Hinson delivered the keynote at the inauguration of the African Marketing Confederation (AMC) in Victoria Falls, Zimbabwe, in October 2022, and the keynote at the 26th Annual Zambia Institute of Marketing Conference and Awards Gala Dinner held from 19 to 22 April 2023 in Zambia. Professor Hinson also delivered the keynote at the 2nd African Marketing Confederation Conference held in September 2023, in Uganda.

Professor Robert Hinson holds honorary professorial positions in South Africa and the UK and has been ranked as the leading African marketing scholar by the Alper-Doger Scientific Index (2021–2023) and the leading Business and Management Scholar in Ghana, by the same global research ranking.

He delivered the keynote at the launch of the Durban University of Technology Business School in Durban in 2022 and has spoken at the Harold Pupkewitz Graduate School of Business in Windhoek, Namibia. He is a globally sought-after speaker who has made presentations in five continents of the world.

With 35 originally authored books and monographs to his credit, Professor Hinson is the author of *Sales Management: A Primer for Frontier Markets, Business-to-Business Marketing, How to Understand and Succeed in Business Marketing in An Emerging Africa,* and *Customer Service Essentials: Lessons for Africa and Beyond.*

Professor Hinson avers that his belief in Jesus Christ constitutes the central driver of his business and professional accomplishments to date.

David Mhlanga is a Senior Research Fellow at the University of Johannesburg, South Africa, specialising in Economics, Business, and Finance. Conducts impactful research on, Sustainable Development, Fintech, Financial Inclusion, the Fourth Industrial Revolution and the application of artificial intelligence, machine learning, and blockchain technology in business, finance, economics, and education. With expertise in complex data analysis, curriculum development and effective communication, delivering excellent presentations. Published extensively in several peer-reviewed academic journals and recognised with research Excellence and Postdoctoral Research Excellence Awards and top researcher in the College of Business and Economics in 2021 and 2022 from the University of Johannesburg, South Africa. Notable achievements include published books on digital financial inclusion, FinTech and AI for Sustainable Development, and Responsible Industry 4.0 for Development: A Framework for Human-Centered Artificial Intelligence and three published edited books focusing on sustainable development and economic inclusion and the Fourth Industrial Revolution in Africa.

Joshua Kofi Doe was a senior lecturer at Central University, currently a lecturer and the Acting Head of Marketing Department at the University of Media Arts and Communications (UniMAC), as well as a teacher by profession.

He holds a certificate in education in 1995, qualifying to be a professional teacher. He also holds bachelor's first-class honours degree in marketing (one of the only two persons who had first class in marketing, 2002), and a Master of Philosophy degree in marketing, all from the University of Ghana. He also holds a Ph.D. in marketing innovations from the Open University of the Netherlands in 2020. His Ph.D. thesis birthed the Firm Level Technology Adoption Model (F-TAM) which proposes an eco-systems interactive view of examining factors that engender the firm-level adoption of digital innovations.

Dr. Joshua Doe had worked in the tourism industry to become the general manager of a tour company, in which he spearheaded the establishment of a virtual office where marketing and transactions could be completed online, as far back as 2006.

His research focus has been on the adoption and application of digital innovations and virtualization of marketing activities for institutional growth and efficiency. He has twelve journal publications, five book chapters, and six conference papers. He is winner of two best paper awards to his credit – one from *"the 12th IADIS International Conference Information Systems 2019"* and the other from *"The 17th International Conference on Web Based Communities and Social Media 2020"*.

Kofi Osei-Frimpong is an Associate Professor of Marketing at the Africa Business School, University Mohammed VI Polytechnic, Rabat, Morocco. Prior to joining Africa Business School, Kofi was an Associate Professor of Marketing and Deputy Director of Research and Consultancy at the University of Professional Studies, Accra (UPSA), Ghana. He also served as Coordinator of Doctoral Studies at UPSA. He has also served as Coordinator of Postgraduate programs at the Ghana Institute of Management and Public Administration (GIMPA), and a Research Fellow at the Vlerick Business School, Belgium. He holds a PhD in Marketing from the University of Strathclyde, Glasgow, United Kingdom. Kofi has over 10 years of experience in higher education and combines research and teaching. His research interest includes value co-creation in healthcare service delivery, customer engagement practices, social media brand engagement, artificial intelligence voice assistants and customer engagement, and service design and experience. He has also regularly presented competitive papers at reputable international service research and marketing conferences in several countries. His research works are published in leading international academic journals including *Technological Forecasting & Social Change*, *Journal of Business Research*, *Information Technology & People*, *International Journal of Contemporary Hospitality Management*, *European Journal of Work and Organizational Psychology*, etc. In addition to consulting for firms in the area of marketing, strategic business planning, and management strategies, Kofi develops and runs business workshops for middle and senior managers in various industry sectors ranging from the regulatory agencies, services firms, and manufacturing companies.

Chapter 1

Social Media Marketing in Africa and Other Emerging Economies

Chapter Outline

- Introduction to social media marketing in emerging markets and developing economies (EMDEs)
- Africa's social media landscape
- What is social media marketing?
- Successful social media marketing campaigns from the Global North
- Successful social media marketing campaigns from Africa
- Structure of the book
- Review questions

Chapter Outcome

By the end of this chapter, the reader will be able to:

Gain insight into how social media marketing influences marketing success:

- Analyse the specific ways in which social media marketing strategies impact overall marketing success.

DOI: 10.4324/9781003307457-1

Explore Africa's social media landscape:
- Conduct a comprehensive analysis of Africa's social media platforms, user demographics, and engagement trends.
- Map out the key players and influencers within Africa's social media ecosystem.

Examine best-case social media marketing campaigns:
- Scrutinise successful social media marketing campaigns to identify actionable strategies and tactics.
- Deconstruct the elements contributing to the success of top-performing campaigns.

Introduction

In the dynamic landscape of global business, the intersection of social media and marketing has become a transformative force, reshaping the ways in which brands engage with audiences. Africa has recently seen growth in technology adoption and utilisation, which is also reflective in the active use of social media among various actors. Accordingly, social media and utilisation of the internet, particularly social networking websites and platforms such as Facebook, Instagram, Messenger, and WhatsApp for marketing, have gained momentum as the most popular and effective medium of marketing communication in the 21st century (Prasad & Saigal, 2019). In 2019, social media advertising spending accounted for 13% of total global ad spending and was ranked the third-largest advertising channel, behind TV and paid search. Social media advertising spending increased from $4.1 billion in 2013 (Johansson & Zhu, 2023) to $84 billion in 2019 (Ashley & Tuten, 2015). Again, over 140 million businesses are currently using social media, not only to hire employees or engage with their communities but also to find new customers and reach existing ones. Additionally, the use of social media to engage with existing and prospective customers has resulted in improved brand loyalty and purchase intention (Almohaimmeed, 2019).

In emerging markets and developing economies (EMDEs), social media offers a technological solution to the economic issues that are encountered by governments, corporations, and people at the bottom of the economic pyramid. This is the case since social media allows for easier communication without boundaries. EMDEs appear to be quickly realising that social media provides them with a very low-cost opportunity to leapfrog the competition in developed markets. This is despite the fact that social media is often seen as having the potential to fundamentally change the business paradigm and is becoming an increasingly integrated part of the marketing function.

Marketing through social media can be an extremely efficient means of connecting with an audience on a worldwide scale, fostering engagement with clients, and propelling growth in a firm. Nevertheless, it necessitates careful planning, persistent work, and a profound comprehension of both the intended audience and the dynamics of each social media platform that is employed. It should not come as a surprise to learn that numerous companies operating in EMDEs are integrating metrics derived from social media platforms into their marketing communications and customer relationship management endeavours in an effort to better communicate with and interact with their target audiences.

In view of this, the level of creativity demonstrated in producing the content (e.g., messages, pictures, videos), coupled with the perceived understanding of the shared content, are more likely to elicit varying experiences among participants. For instance, Boateng and Okoe (2015) are of the view that features of contents advertised or shared on social media in relation to brands are likely to result in behavioural responses on the part of the customer. Further, Hinson et al. (2019) found that consumer engagement with brands on a firm's social media platform is more likely to influence positive user-generated content on the part of the customer. Such practices could drive and enhance customer–brand relationships. As a result, it is essential for firms and scholars to gain deeper consumer insights on why they use social media, their motivation for participating in online social media engagement practices, and the potential effects of such practices on enhancing brand performance. In this vein, the potential role of social media in marketing management is essential to understand.

In addition, Ashley and Tuten (2015) advocate for a need to extend research on social media to shed more light on how branded social content influences consumer engagement behaviours. Further, Osei-Frimpong (2019) calls for a need to deepen our understanding of the effects of contextual support of firms' social media platforms on consumer motivations in consuming, searching, sharing, participating, contributing, and playing. Also, as businesses embrace social media solutions, new challenges have emerged in the corporate adoption, utilisation, integration, and implementation of social media in EMDEs. Hence, there is a need to provide solutions to tackle the challenges of social media in EMDEs. This book responds to calls for a systematic approach to understanding the transformations in the social media marketing landscape. To narrow the focus, the book takes a developing economy perspective and presents a comprehensive understanding of social media practices and how these could be integrated into firms' operational activities to create a competitive advantage. This book seeks to provide practical guidance on the use of social media in a firm's operations. While it provides practical perspectives by addressing contemporary issues in relation to social media marketing practices, this book will also serve as a relevant teaching text in social media marketing in both undergraduate and graduate programmes, as well as executive training for practitioners.

Unique Characteristics of Social Media Marketing in EMDEs

The growth and usage of social networking sites (SNSs) have increased significantly in EMDEs in recent times. For instance, daily time spent on SNSs since the COVID-19 pandemic has significantly increased, which creates an opportunity for firms to enhance their competitive advantage through social media brand engagement. This allows the utilisation of social media functionalities to disseminate a firm's brand-related information in the form of posts to consumers (Osei-Frimpong et al., 2023). As a result, while more people in these regions gain access to the internet and social media platforms, businesses can tap into a growing and potentially lucrative market. Whereas social media marketing in emerging economies presents opportunities to firms and individuals, there are some challenges worth considering. These challenges are context-specific; hence, it is essential to understand the unique dynamics and considerations of social media marketing in the EMDE context. These unique characteristics define social media marketing in emerging economies:

1. **Rapid growth of internet and mobile users:**

Emerging economies often experience a rapid increase in internet and mobile phone usage. This provides a vast and growing user base for social media platforms.

2. **Mobile-first approach:**

In many emerging economies, people primarily access the internet through mobile devices. Therefore, social media marketing strategies should be mobile-friendly, including mobile-optimised websites and responsive content. This book places a very strong emphasis on concepts such as mobile commerce and mobile marketing.

3. Localised content:

Local culture and language make it imperative that marketers understand cultural nuances and customs to maximise the potential of both brick-and-mortar and social media marketing campaigns.

4. Connectivity challenges:

Access to reliable internet may be limited in some areas, and so marketers must carefully consider issues around bandwidth and connectivity that users may face when designing content and campaigns. The July 2023 "Change their Borla Style" Zoom Lion Private Services Limited campaign in Ghana, for instance, uses an Unstructured Supplementary Service Data (USSD) code, a communications protocol that allows GSM telephones to communicate directly with mobile network operator's computers, to encourage Zoom Lion customers to pay for environmental management services. Zoom Lion Private Services Limited, a leading waste management company in Sub-Saharan Africa, has launched a digital payment platform that will help the company and its customers transact business through an efficient and cashless system. The digital payment options are strategically aimed at easing payment for customers and leveraging the power of technology to deliver improved services based on a deep understanding of their clients across the country. This platform is also focused on promoting responsible waste management practices in the serviced communities (https://www.myjoyonline.com/zoomlion -goes-digital-launches-payment-platform-to-improve-customer-service/).

5. Diverse social media landscape:

Different countries may have their own preferred social media platforms. Marketers must research and choose the platforms most popular among their target audiences in the specific emerging markets they are operating in.

6. Affordable smartphones:

The affordability of smartphones in emerging economies means that more people can access social media. This opens up opportunities for reaching a wider audience.

7. E-commerce potential:

Social media is a powerful platform for e-commerce in emerging economies. Many businesses use platforms like Facebook and Instagram to sell products directly to emerging markets.

8. Payment solutions:

In some emerging markets, digital payment methods like mobile wallets are widely used. Integrating these into your social media marketing efforts can facilitate transactions for firms operating in emerging markets.

9. Data privacy concerns:

Marketers must be mindful of data privacy concerns and ensure that their data collection and usage practices comply with local regulations.

10. Market research:

Marketers must conduct thorough market research to understand consumer behaviour, preferences, and the competitive landscape in the specific emerging economy they are operating in.

Africa's Social Media Landscape

Africa's social media landscape is dynamic and rapidly evolving. While the continent faces unique challenges, such as limited internet access in some areas and varying levels of infrastructure development, it also presents significant opportunities for social media growth and innovation. The use of social media has become an integral part of the daily lives of people on the continent. While it appears to be dominated by individual activism in interacting with family, friends, and others, it creates a social space for firms to leverage to connect with target customers. In particular, small- and medium-sized enterprises (SMEs) in Africa with limited resources are able to easily engage in brand communications with target customers at a minimal cost (Karikari et al., 2017; Odoom et al., 2017). Efforts are taken to ensure technologically sparse communities in EMDEs are connected to the internet to enhance access to information. Africa's social media landscape is marked by its diversity, with each country having its own unique characteristics and preferences. As infrastructure continues to improve, internet access becomes more widespread, and as social media platforms adapt to local needs, the social media landscape in Africa will likely continue to evolve and grow. By tailoring your strategies to the unique dynamics of these markets, marketers can leverage the opportunities presented by the growing digital landscape in emerging economies.

Given the growth of internet and social media usage within the EMDEs, there is a need to shed light on some key features and trends in Africa's social media landscape:

1. **Mobile-first usage:** Africa is often referred to as a "mobile-first" continent, as many people access the internet and social media primarily through mobile devices. The affordability of smartphones has fuelled this trend. This book focusses heavily on issues around mobile marketing and mobile commerce.
2. **Facebook dominance:** Facebook remains the most popular social media platform across Africa, with a strong presence in many countries. However, its dominance is being challenged by other platforms.
3. **WhatsApp and Messenger:** WhatsApp and Facebook Messenger are widely used for communication and sharing content, including news and information. WhatsApp is particularly popular for group chats and business communication.
4. **Twitter engagement:** Twitter is a popular platform for news, politics, and public discourse. African Twitter users actively engage in conversations on a wide range of topics, making it a valuable platform for social and political discussions.
5. **Instagram growth:** Instagram is gaining popularity among younger users and urban populations. Its visual appeal makes it a platform of choice for sharing photos and stories.
6. **YouTube's influence:** YouTube is a significant platform for video content, with many African creators and influencers building substantial followings. Educational and entertainment content performs well on this platform.
7. **Local platforms:** Some African countries have their own social media platforms tailored to local languages and cultures. Examples include Eskimi (Nigeria), MXit (South Africa), and M-Pesa (Kenya).
8. **E-commerce and social commerce:** Social media platforms are increasingly used for e-commerce and social commerce in Africa. Businesses and entrepreneurs leverage platforms like Facebook Marketplace to sell products and services.

9. **Political activism and social change:** Social media has played a crucial role in political activism and social change movements across Africa. It provides a platform for citizens to voice their concerns and mobilise for various causes.
10. **Challenges:** Internet access remains a challenge in some rural and underserved areas. Additionally, limited access to affordable data and inconsistent electricity supply can hinder online participation.
11. **Privacy and data concerns:** Data privacy and security are growing concerns. Some African countries are enacting data protection regulations to address these issues.
12. **Content regulation:** Content regulation and censorship vary from country to country. Some governments have imposed restrictions on social media platforms and internet access during political events or protests.
13. **Language diversity:** Africa is linguistically diverse, with thousands of languages spoken. Social media content often reflects this diversity, with content available in multiple languages.
14. **Youth demographic:** Africa has a youthful population, and social media platforms are popular among young people. This demographic trend contributes to the vibrant social media landscape.

What is Social Media Marketing?

Social media marketing is a digital marketing strategy that involves using social media platforms and websites to promote products, services, or brands. It leverages the reach and engagement potential of social media to connect with target audiences, build brand awareness, drive website traffic, and achieve various marketing and business goals. Successful social media marketing in emerging economies requires adaptability, cultural sensitivity, and a deep understanding of the local context. Social media provides enormous opportunities and challenges; the platforms can help users share personal thoughts and experiences with friends, relations, and business partners instantly (Karikari et al., 2017; Odoom et al., 2017). For instance, this could provide users, including owners of small or large businesses, with unlimited opportunities to attract new customers, maintain existing customers more efficiently, create innovative business models, and spur economic development (Arora & Rahman, 2017; Loiacono & McCoy,

2018). Firms in EMDEs are using social media to influence consumers and expand.

Social media marketing is also a multi-faceted concept and encompasses various tools and platforms like:

1. **Social media platforms:** Social media marketing encompasses the utilisation of several social media channels, as exemplified in Figure 1.1:

Social media marketing includes promotional activities conducted across diverse social media channels, as exemplified by the platforms illustrated in Figure 1.1. These platforms include Facebook, Instagram, Twitter, LinkedIn, YouTube, Pinterest, TikTok, Snapchat, WhatsApp, and WeChat. There are many others, depending on the target audience and objectives.

By using social technology to reach users in different market segments in ways that were impossible before, social sites such as Facebook and Twitter create tremendous new growth opportunities for businesses. Powered by social media, the public and private sectors in emerging markets can find leapfrogging solutions and work together to reduce poverty and inequality while boosting economic mobility and prosperity (Andrews et al., 2019).

2. **Content creation and sharing:** Marketers create and share content on social media platforms to engage their audience. This content can include text posts, images, videos, infographics, blog articles, and more.

Content creation and sharing are at the core of social media marketing. High-quality, engaging content is what attracts and retains the attention of your target audience on social media platforms. Here are key considerations for content creation and sharing in social media marketing for marketers looking to leverage social media for business advantage:

a. Your audience

Understanding your audience is crucial to content creation. It involves delving into the demographics, interests, challenges, and preferences of your target audience. This information is essential in tailoring your content to effectively resonate with them. For instance, content aimed at teenagers will significantly differ from that for professionals in their 30s. Recognising these differences helps in crafting messages that are more likely to engage and

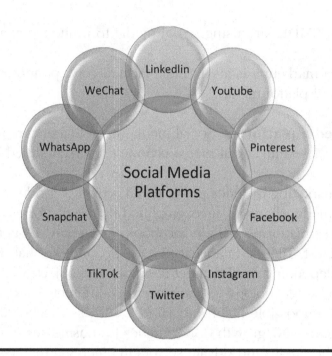

Figure 1.1   Social media platforms. Source: Authors (2024)

influence your audience, ensuring that your content is not just seen but also appreciated and acted upon.

b. Your goals

Setting clear objectives is a foundational step in content creation. Determine the purpose of your content—whether it's increasing brand awareness, driving traffic to your website, generating leads, or boosting sales. These goals will serve as the guiding light for your content strategy, influencing the kind of content you produce, the tone you adopt, and the metrics you use to measure success. Aligning content with your business objectives ensures that every piece of content contributes towards the broader goals of your organisation.

c. Content strategy

A comprehensive content strategy is like a roadmap for your content creation efforts. It should outline what types of content you will create, how often you will post, and which platforms you will use. Importantly, it should take into account the buyer's journey, creating tailored content for each stage—awareness, consideration, and decision. This ensures that your content meets potential customers where they are in their journey, providing them with the information and engagement they need at the right time.

d. Content Formats

Diversity in content formats can significantly enhance audience engagement. Experimenting with various formats like text posts, images, videos, infographics, live streams, stories, and polls can cater to different preferences within your audience. Each format has its own strengths and can be used to convey your message in the most effective way. For example, videos may be more engaging for tutorials, while infographics are great for presenting data.

e. Consistency

Consistency in terms of your posting schedule is key to building trust and keeping your audience engaged. It's not just about the frequency of your posts but also the consistency in the quality and style of the content. This regularity helps in establishing a brand voice and keeps your audience anticipating your next post. A consistent schedule also aids in building a habit among your audience, making your content a regular part of their digital consumption.

f. Storytelling

Storytelling is a powerful tool in content creation. It involves crafting narratives that resonate with your audience, making your content more engaging and memorable. Good storytelling can turn mundane information into compelling content. It helps build emotional connections with the audience, making your brand more relatable and memorable.

g. Visual appeal

In the visually driven world of social media, high-quality visuals are essential. This means investing in good photography, graphic design, and video production. Visual content, including graphics, charts, and animations, should not only be eye-catching but also relevant and informative. Such content tends to get more engagement on social media and can help break through the clutter.

h. User-generated content (UGC)

UGC is content that members of your audience have created that relates to your company or its goods. It can be a powerful tool in building trust and authenticity, as it provides a real-life perspective of your brand from the user's point of view. Encouraging UGC can also foster a sense of community among your audience and provide you with a wealth of content to share.

i. Hashtags

Hashtags are a strategic tool for increasing the visibility of your content. Using relevant and targeted hashtags can help your content reach a wider audience and encourage them to participate in relevant conversations. It's important to research and identify both popular and niche hashtags within your industry to maximise the discoverability of your content.

j. Caption and copywriting

Captions and copy play a crucial role in complementing your visuals. They provide context, tell stories, ask questions, and encourage interaction. Good copywriting can captivate the audience, convey your message clearly, and prompt engagement. It's an opportunity to show your brand's personality and connect with your audience on a deeper level.

k. Engagement

Engagement is a two-way street. Responding to comments, messages, and mentions promptly shows that you value your audience's input and are willing to engage in conversations. This not only helps in building relationships but also encourages further interaction, increasing the visibility and reach of your content.

l. Shareable content

Creating content that is easily shareable can significantly increase your reach. Shareable content often includes humour, inspirational quotes, or timely and relevant information. Such content resonates with a broad audience and encourages them to pass it along, thereby amplifying your message.

m. Content calendar

A content calendar is a planning tool that helps you organise and schedule your content. It ensures a consistent flow and allows for aligning your content with relevant events, holidays, and promotions. This foresight in planning helps in maintaining a steady stream of content and avoids last-minute rushes, ensuring quality and relevance.

n. Analytics and optimisation

Using analytics tools to track the performance of your content is crucial for understanding what resonates with your audience. This data allows you to identify successful content and areas for improvement. Regular analysis and optimisation of your strategy based on these insights can enhance the effectiveness of your content over time.

o. Platform-specific content

Different social media platforms cater to different audiences and have unique characteristics. Tailoring your content specifically to each platform can increase its effectiveness. For instance, what works on LinkedIn may not work on TikTok. Understanding these nuances and customising your content accordingly can lead to better engagement and reach.

p. Paid promotion

Paid promotion, such as boosting posts or advertising, can be an effective way to extend the reach of your best-performing content. It allows you to target a wider or more specific audience, potentially increasing your visibility and impact. This should be a strategic choice, focusing on content that has proven to resonate with your audience.

q. Test and iterate

Experimenting with different strategies and measuring their impact is essential for continuous improvement. Don't be afraid to try new approaches and see how they perform. Based on the results, refine and iterate your strategy to find what works best for your audience and goals.

r. Stay informed

The social media landscape is constantly evolving. Staying informed about the latest trends, algorithm changes, and best practices is crucial for adapting and updating your content strategy. This ensures that your approach remains relevant and effective in the ever-changing digital environment.

Effective content creation and sharing on social media require a combination of creativity, strategic planning, and a deep understanding of your audience. By consistently delivering valuable and engaging content, you can build a loyal following, increase brand visibility, and achieve your social media marketing objectives.

3. **Audience targeting:** Social media marketing allows for precise audience targeting based on factors such as demographics, interests, behaviour, location, and more. This helps ensure that content reaches the most relevant audience.
4. **Paid advertising:** Many social media platforms offer paid advertising options, allowing businesses to promote their content to a wider or more specific audience. This can include sponsored posts, display ads, and more.
5. **Engagement and interaction:** Social media marketing encourages engagement with the audience through likes, shares, comments, and direct messages. Building relationships with followers is a key aspect of this strategy.
6. **Analytics and insights:** Social media platforms provide analytics tools that allow marketers to measure the performance of their campaigns. Metrics like engagement rates, click-through rates, and conversion rates help assess the effectiveness of marketing efforts.
7. **Community building:** Brands often focus on creating a loyal and engaged community of followers who advocate for the brand and contribute to user-generated content and discussions.
8. **Influencer marketing:** Collaborating with social media influencers (individuals with a substantial and engaged following) is a common tactic in social media marketing to expand reach and credibility.
9. **Customer support:** Many brands use social media platforms as channels for providing customer support and addressing inquiries, complaints, and feedback from customers.
10. **Virality and shareability:** Social media marketing aims to create content that is shareable and has the potential to go viral, spreading quickly through social networks.
11. **Brand reputation management:** Social media marketing allows brands to monitor and manage their online reputation by addressing negative comments or reviews promptly and positively.
12. **Campaign planning and strategy:** Successful social media marketing campaigns are often part of a broader marketing strategy. Marketers

plan their campaigns, set objectives, create content calendars, and allocate resources accordingly.

13. **Cross-platform integration:** Brands may integrate their social media efforts with other marketing channels, such as email marketing, content marketing, and influencer partnerships, for a more comprehensive approach.

Social Media Influencer Marketing

Social media influencer marketing is on the rise, with African influencers partnering with brands for sponsored content and promotions. Influencer marketing is a digital marketing strategy that involves collaborating with individuals who have a significant and engaged following on social media platforms or other online channels. Social media influencer marketing is defined as a "strategy in which a firm selects and incentivizes online influencers to engage their followers on social media in an attempt to leverage these influencers' unique resources to promote the firm's offerings, with the ultimate goal of enhancing firm performance" (Leung et al., 2022, p. 228). These individuals, known as influencers, can impact the opinions, behaviours, and purchasing decisions of their followers. Influencer marketing leverages the influencers' credibility and influence to promote products, services, or brands. Here are key aspects of influencer marketing:

1. **Types of influencers:**
   - **Macro-influencers:** Celebrities or well-known figures with a large following.
   - **Micro-influencers:** Individuals with a smaller but highly engaged and niche-specific audience.
   - **Nano-influencers:** Individuals with a very small but highly dedicated and localised following.
   - **Industry experts:** Influential figures within a specific industry or niche.
2. **Benefits of influencer marketing:**
   - **Credibility:** Influencers are seen as trustworthy sources of information by their followers.
   - **Reach:** Influencers can help your brand reach a larger and more targeted audience.

– **Engagement:** Influencers often have highly engaged followers, leading to higher interaction rates.
– **Content creation:** Influencers can create authentic and relatable content that resonates with their audience.
– **Brand awareness:** It can significantly boost brand awareness and visibility.

3. **Steps in influencer marketing:**
   – **Identify and research influencers:** Find influencers who align with your brand and target audience.
   – **Set objectives:** Clearly define your goals for the influencer marketing campaign.
   – **Negotiate and collaborate:** Reach out to influencers, discuss terms, and establish a collaboration agreement.
   – **Content creation:** Work with influencers to create content that aligns with your brand and campaign objectives.
   – **Promotion:** The influencer shares the content with their followers, typically in a way that feels authentic.
   – **Monitoring and analytics:** Track the performance of the campaign using metrics like engagement, reach, and conversions.
   – **Compensation:** Influencers are often compensated with monetary payments, free products, or other incentives.

4. **Choosing the right influencers:** Consider factors such as their niche, audience demographics, engagement rates, content quality, and alignment with your brand values.

5. **Disclosure and transparency:** It's essential for influencers to disclose their partnerships and sponsorships transparently to maintain trust with their audience and adhere to legal regulations.

6. **Measuring success:** Use key performance indicators (KPIs) to measure the effectiveness of your influencer marketing campaign. Common KPIs include reach, engagement, conversion rates, and return on investment (ROI).

7. **Regulatory compliance:** Be aware of advertising regulations and guidelines in your region, as well as those that may apply to influencers. Ensure that all sponsored content complies with these regulations.

8. **Long-term relationships:** Building long-term relationships with influencers can be beneficial, as it can lead to ongoing collaborations and a deeper understanding of your brand.

9. **Authenticity:** Successful influencer marketing campaigns feel authentic and align with both the influencer's persona and your brand's values.

10. **Ethical considerations:** Be ethical and responsible in your influencer marketing efforts, and avoid any deceptive or manipulative practices.

Influencer marketing has become a powerful and influential component of digital marketing. When executed effectively, it can help businesses connect with their target audience, increase brand awareness, and drive customer engagement and conversions. However, selecting the right influencers and maintaining authenticity are critical factors in achieving success in influencer marketing.

Successful Social Media Marketing Campaigns from the Global North

It is important to note that all social media marketing campaigns evolve around what is referred to as the DRIP factors:

D: Differentiate a product, service, or brand.
R: Remind or reassure prospects and consumers about a product, service, or brand.
I: Inform prospects about a product, service, or brand.
P: Persuade prospects and consumers to buy a product, service, or brand.

Here are some real-world examples of successful social media campaigns that have garnered attention and engagement and achieved some or all of the DRIP marketing communications objectives:

1. **ALS Ice Bucket Challenge (2014):**
   a. Objective: Raise awareness and funds for amyotrophic lateral sclerosis (ALS) research.
   b. Success: The campaign went viral, with millions of people participating, including celebrities. It raised over $115 million for the ALS Association.

2. **Dove's "Real Beauty" Campaign:**
   a. Objective: Promote body positivity and redefine beauty standards.
   b. Success: The campaign featured real women instead of models and encouraged discussions on self-esteem and body image. It received widespread praise and increased brand loyalty.

3. **Old Spice's "The Man Your Man Could Smell Like" (2010):**
   a. Objective: Rebrand and appeal to a younger audience.
   b. Success: The humorous and viral videos featuring the "Old Spice Guy" generated millions of views, increased sales, and reinvigorated the brand.

4. **Red Bull's Stratos Jump (2012):**
   a. Objective: Showcase Red Bull's association with extreme sports and energy.
   b. Success: Felix Baumgartner's historic skydive from the edge of space, live-streamed on YouTube, generated immense global attention and engagement.

5. **Oreo's "Dunk in the Dark" (2013):**
   a. Objective: Capitalise on real-time marketing during the Super Bowl blackout.
   b. Success: Oreo quickly tweeted a clever image saying, "You can still dunk in the dark," which went viral and received widespread praise for its timeliness and creativity.

6. **Airbnb's #WeAccept (2017):**
   a. Objective: Promote Airbnb as an inclusive platform after criticism of discrimination.
   b. Success: Airbnb's Super Bowl ad and social media campaign highlighted its commitment to acceptance and diversity, resulting in positive media coverage and an improved brand image.

7. **Coca-Cola's "Share a Coke" (2014):**
   a. Objective: Boost sales and engagement by personalising Coke bottles.
   b. Success: Coca-Cola replaced its logo with popular names on its bottles, encouraging people to share photos with their personalised bottles on social media. The campaign led to a significant increase in sales and social media mentions.

8. **Starbucks' "Unicorn Frappuccino" (2017):**
   a. Objective: Create buzz and boost sales for a limited-time product.
   b. Success: Starbucks' colourful and Instagram-friendly Unicorn Frappuccino went viral, with social media users sharing photos

and videos of the drink. It resulted in a significant sales boost during its limited run.

9. **Nike's "Dream Crazy," featuring Colin Kaepernick (2018):**
   a. Objective: Take a stance on social issues and reinforce brand values.
   b. Success: Nike's ad featuring Colin Kaepernick generated both praise and controversy, but it ultimately led to increased brand loyalty and sales while reinforcing its commitment to social justice.

10. **Burger King's "The Whopper Detour" (2018):**
    a. Objective: Drive traffic to Burger King locations.
    b. Success: The campaign used geofencing technology to offer customers a one-cent Whopper when they were near a McDonald's. It generated a significant increase in app downloads and foot traffic to Burger King stores.

These examples demonstrate the power of creative and strategically executed social media campaigns to drive brand awareness, engagement, and business outcomes in various industries. Successful campaigns often leverage timeliness, creativity, and an understanding of their target audience's preferences and interests.

AI and Social Media Marketing

Artificial intelligence (AI) has had a significant impact on social media marketing in recent years, revolutionising the way businesses and marketers engage with their audience and optimise their strategies. Here are some ways AI is used in social media marketing:

1. **Content recommendation:** AI algorithms analyse user data and behaviour to recommend personalised content. On platforms like Facebook and Instagram, AI suggests posts, ads, and pages to follow based on a user's interests, interactions, and demographics.
2. **Chatbots and virtual assistants:** On platforms like Facebook Messenger, real-time customer service and engagement are possible

with chatbots powered by AI. They can answer frequently asked questions, assist with purchases, and provide information 24/7.

3. **Content generation:** AI can generate content, including text and images. For instance, it can create social media posts, product descriptions, or even articles. This is particularly helpful for businesses that need to maintain an active online presence.

4. **Predictive analytics:** AI algorithms analyse vast amounts of social media data to predict trends and user behaviour. Marketers can use this information to adjust their strategies and create content that is more likely to resonate with their target audience.

5. **Ad targeting and optimisation:** AI helps advertisers target their ads more effectively. It can analyse user data to identify potential customers and deliver ads to the right people at the right time. AI also optimises ad campaigns by adjusting parameters like bidding strategies and ad placements.

6. **Social listening:** AI-powered tools can monitor social media platforms for mentions of a brand, product, or industry keyword. This enables businesses to track their online reputation and gather insights into customer sentiment.

7. **Image and video recognition:** AI can automatically analyse and categorise images and videos shared on social media. This is useful for identifying user-generated content related to a brand or tracking the use of brand logos and products in social media posts.

8. **Competitive analysis:** AI can analyse competitors' social media strategies, identifying their top-performing content, engagement tactics, and audience demographics. This information can help businesses refine their own strategies.

9. **Sentiment analysis:** AI can assess the sentiment of social media conversations around a brand or topic, providing insights into customer opinions and allowing for timely responses to negative feedback or emerging trends.

10. **Content scheduling and posting:** AI-powered social media management tools can suggest optimal posting times based on historical data and user activity patterns. They can also automate the scheduling and posting of content across multiple platforms.

11. **Ad fraud detection:** AI algorithms can detect fraudulent activity in digital advertising, helping businesses avoid wasting ad spend on fake clicks and impressions.

12. **Content moderation:** AI can be used to automatically moderate user-generated content for inappropriate or harmful material, ensuring a safe and positive online environment.

Incorporating AI into social media marketing can lead to more efficient and data-driven campaigns, improved customer engagement, and better targeting. However, it's important for businesses to use AI responsibly, respecting user privacy and ensuring compliance with relevant regulations, such as General Data Protection Regulation (GDPR). Additionally, AI should complement human expertise, not replace it, as human creativity and strategic thinking remain essential in crafting compelling social media marketing campaigns.

Case Study 1

Cussons Baby Brand Challenge

In 2014, PZ Cussons wanted to increase its brand affinity, customer loyalty, and market share in three key markets in Africa (Ghana, East Africa, and Nigeria).

Social media marketing intervention: We created an online trusted resource, a community. This community was built as a one-stop online resource with parenting and mom-related content. The community was made up of new, rookie, and veteran moms, as well as midwives and paediatricians. We used Facebook and a blog as the main channels for the community to connect, share, and learn about the mom and parenting journey from the first trimester through until the baby is 24 months old. (See https://www.facebook.com/cussonsbaby.gh and https://www.cussonsbaby.com.gh/blog/.). Similar channels were created for the East Africa and Nigeria markets.

One key activity was the use of Facebook Live for weekly virtual consulting room sessions. We also used the blog to share expert content on pregnancy and baby care and shared excerpts from the blog content on Facebook to drive conversation. Wherever relevant, the content featured Cussons baby products (powder, lotion, gel, etc.) and the proper way of using them for baby skincare needs.

Quantifiable Outcomes

In the first year, the Facebook page or community in each of the three countries had over 100,000 passionate moms. Today (September 2023), there are over 1.3 million active moms in the three communities in the three markets (Ghana, East Africa, and Nigeria).

- Brand affinity grew by 7.3% in year 1.
- Customer loyalty grew by 10.21% in year 1.
- Cussons Baby increased its market share and consolidated its number 2 position in all the markets.

Stephen Boadi (former head of Digital Marketing, PZ Cussons Africa, January 2013–July 2017).

Successful Social Media Marketing Campaigns from Africa

African countries have witnessed several successful social media campaigns that have achieved their objectives, whether it's raising awareness, promoting causes, or driving social change. Here are a few notable examples:

1. **#BringBackOurGirls (Nigeria):**
   a. Objective: Raise awareness about the kidnapping of over 200 schoolgirls by the extremist group Boko Haram.
   b. Success: This hashtag campaign gained global attention and support, with celebrities and activists joining in. While the girls' full recovery remains a challenge, it puts pressure on the Nigerian government to act.

2. **#KenyaChat (Kenya):**
   a. Objective: Promote Kenya as a tourist destination.
   b. Success: The Kenya Tourism Board initiated this Twitter chat campaign, encouraging users to share their experiences and travel stories about Kenya. It resulted in increased tourism and a positive perception of Kenya as a travel destination.

3. **#RhinoCharge (Kenya):**
   a. Objective: Raise funds and awareness for rhino conservation.
   b. Success: The Rhino Charge, an off-road motorsport event, used social media to attract sponsors, participants, and donors. The campaign successfully raised funds for rhino conservation efforts.

4. **#FeesMustFall (South Africa):**
   a. Objective: Advocate for free and accessible higher education in South Africa.
   b. Success: This student-led movement used social media to mobilise supporters and coordinate protests. It eventually led to significant discussions and policy changes regarding higher education fees.

5. **#MyAfricanPortrait (various African countries):**
   a. Objective: Challenge stereotypes and showcase African diversity.
   b. Success: This social media campaign encouraged people across Africa to share photos and stories that challenge stereotypes and showcase the continent's rich cultural diversity.

6. **#HeForShe (global, initiated by UN Women with African participation):**
   a. Objective: Promote gender equality and engage men in the fight for women's rights.
   b. Success: African celebrities and activists actively participated in the global #HeForShe campaign, sparking discussions and actions around gender equality.

7. **#StopXenophobia (South Africa):**
   a. Objective: Raise awareness about xenophobic attacks and promote tolerance.
   b. Success: During periods of xenophobic violence in South Africa, this hashtag campaign garnered international attention and condemnation, putting pressure on the government to address the issue.

8. **#FreeBobiWine (Uganda):**
   a. Objective: Raise awareness and advocate for the release of opposition politician and musician Bobi Wine.
   b. Success: This campaign gained traction on social media, drawing international attention to human rights abuses in Uganda and the plight of political prisoners.

These African social media campaigns demonstrate the power of social media as a platform for advocacy, awareness, and social change. They have been instrumental in rallying support, influencing public opinion, and catalysing positive action in various social, political, and environmental spheres.

Structure of the Book

Social Media Marketing: Engaging and Winning in Africa and Other Emerging Markets is laid out as follows:

Chapter 1 Social Media Marketing in Africa and Other Emerging Economies
Chapter 2 Social Media Marketing Strategy
Chapter 3 Social Commerce
Chapter 4 Mobile Ecosystems and Apps in Social Media Marketing
Chapter 5 Social Networking Sites: A Focus on Mobile Marketing Strategies
Chapter 6 Introduction to Mobile Commerce
Chapter 7 Ethical, Social, and Legal Issues in M-commerce
Chapter 8 Socio-Cultural and Ethical Aspects of Social Media
Chapter 9 Social Media Marketing Management: How to Penetrate Emerging Markets and Expand Your Customer Base

Review Questions

1. What is social media marketing and what key considerations should you take cognizance before breaking a social media campaign in Africa?
2. Share some successful social media marketing campaigns you are privy to.

3. What key social media campaign lessons can be drawn from the Cussons Baby case study?

References

Almohaimmeed, B. M. (2019). The effects of social media marketing antecedents on social media marketing, brand loyalty and purchase intention: A customer perspective. *Journal of Business and Retail Management Research, 13*(4), 146–157.

Andrews, S., Ayers, S., Bakovic, T., et al. (2019). *Reinventing business through disruptive technologies: Sector trends and investment opportunities for firms in emerging markets* (IFC Report). Retrieved April 4, 2020, from https://www.ifc .org/wps/wcm/connect/8c67719a-2816-4694-91877de2ef5075bc/Reinventing -business-through-Disruptive-Techv2.pdf?MOD=AJPERES&CVID=mLo6cfr

Arora, B., & Rahman, Z. (2017). Information technology capability as competitive advantage in emerging markets. *International Journal of Emerging Markets, 12*, 447–463.

Ashley, C., & Tuten, T. (2015). Creative strategies in social media marketing: An exploratory study of branded social content and consumer engagement. *Psychology & Marketing, 32*, 15–27.

Boateng, H., & Okoe, A. F. (2015). Consumers' attitude towards social media advertising and their behavioural response: The moderating role of corporate reputation. *Journal of Research in Interactive Marketing, 9*, 299–312.

Hinson, R., Boateng, H., Renner, A., & Kosiba, J. P. B. (2019). Antecedents and consequences of customer engagement on Facebook: An attachment theory perspective. *Journal of Research in Interactive Marketing, 13*, 204–226.

Johansson, A. C., & Zhu, Z. (2023. Reputational assets and social media marketing activeness: Empirical insights from China. *Electronic Commerce Research and Applications, 61*, 101305.

Karikari, S., Osei-Frimpong, K., & Owusu-Frimpong, N. (2017). Evaluating individual level antecedents and consequences of social media use in Ghana. *Technological Forecasting & Social Change, 123*, 68–79.

Leung, F. F., Gu, F. F., & Palmatier, R. W. (2022). Online influencer marketing. *Journal of the Academy of Marketing Science, 50*, 226–251.

Loiacono, E., & McCoy, S. (2018). When did fun become so much work: The impact of social media invasiveness on continued social media use. *Information Technology & People, 31*, 966–983.

Odoom, R., Anning-Dorson, T., & Acheampong, G. (2017). Antecedents of social media usage and performance benefits in small- and medium-sized enterprises (SMEs). *Journal of Enterprise Information Management, 30*, 383–399.

Osei-Frimpong, K. (2019). Understanding consumer motivations in online social brand engagement participation: Implications for retailers. *International Journal of Retail & Distribution Management, 47*, 511–529.

Osei-Frimpong, K., Appiah Otoo, B. A., McLean, G., Islam, N., & Soga, L. R. (2023). What keeps me engaging? A study of consumers' continuous social media brand engagement practices. *Information Technology & People, 36*(6), 2440–2468.

Prasad, P., & Saigal, P. (2019). Social media marketing: Tools and techniques. In *Application of gaming in new media marketing*, Pratika_ Mishra & Swati Oberoi Dham, (eds.), (pp. 202–214). IGI Global.

Chapter 2

Social Media Marketing Strategy

Chapter Outline

- Introduction
- Review of the social media space
- Channels of social media
- The value of social media to marketing
- Defining social media marketing
- Core marketing concepts and social media
- Marketing objectives of firms incorporating social media in their marketing mix
- Social media value chain and marketing management
- Firm orientation towards social media
- Social media marketing management tasks
- Conclusions

Chapter Outcome

By the end of this chapter, the reader will be able to:

Integrate social media marketing planning into organisational strategy:
- Analyse and apply how social media marketing planning aligns with and contributes to an organisation's overall planning framework.

DOI: 10.4324/9781003307457-2

Identify and navigate phases of social media marketing maturity:

- Analyse case studies on how social media marketing contributes to different company growth phases.
- Develop a roadmap for advancement through the various stages of social media marketing maturity.

Design organisational structures to support social media marketing:

- Formulate organisational structures that effectively support and integrate social media marketing initiatives.

Construct an effective organisational social media policy:

- Develop and articulate the relevance of a comprehensive organisational social media policy for organisational success.

Introduction

Social media has emerged as a dynamic and influential platform that connects billions of individuals around the globe. As a result, businesses and organisations have recognised the importance of social media as a platform to engage with their customers, shape brand perception, drive sales, and foster meaningful relationships in both the business to consumer (B2C) and business-to-business (B2B) segments. Given this development, the need to craft an effective social media marketing strategy has become imperative as far as firms' competitiveness is concerned. It should be noted that a well-defined social media marketing strategy is more than a mere presence on these social networking platforms; it involves a thoughtful and strategic approach to content creation, audience targeting, community engagement, and data analysis. This chapter explores the key components that make social media strategy successful, taking into account the unique dynamics of the platform and the ever-changing trends in the digital space.

Irshad and Ahmad (2019) reported that marketers are faced with challenging issues of identifying consumers' motivations that affect subsequent trust in social media retailers and the attitudes of consumers with respect to social media marketing. To this extent, Odoom et al. (2017) note that the burgeoning nature of social media calls for more studies across several business levels, sectors, and contexts examining the adoption, usage, strategies, and outcomes of social media with the aim of developing theories. To succeed, it is indispensable for marketers to have a thorough understanding of the tools and techniques required to attract different clusters of customers using social media because different social media platforms have different target audiences. This chapter is therefore designed to provide comprehensive coverage of a wide range of social media marketing issues to effectively address the dearth of literature regarding social media from an emerging economy perspective. The chapter introduces and defines social media marketing, identifies core marketing concepts in social media, reviews the social media space in emerging economies, identifies channels of social media, explains the value chain in relation to social media marketing, justifies firms' orientation towards social media adoption and usage, and discusses the social media marketing tasks.

Strategic Planning and Social Media Marketing

Strategic planning for the utilisation of social media in a firm's operational activities and competitiveness is considered imperative. Honda is considered one of the active companies that incorporates social media platforms into their marketing activities. The company has strategically utilised several different social media channels and vehicles in recent years and has coordinated these with more traditional tactics like paid broadcast media to maximise impact. The company has an active presence in social communities, including YouTube, Facebook, Instagram, and Twitter, but also runs targeted campaigns on niche community networks like Snapchat and Pinterest. Honda partnered with Salesforce to manage its social media activity and ensure it could be responsive to fans around the world who use social media to reach out to the brand. It also uses Adobe Marketing Cloud to facilitate local adaptations of its social media content for different world regions and ensure consistency by providing social media tools for dealers to use in local and regional communications. This chapter brings to light Honda's approach to social media marketing.

For marketers like those at Honda, strategic planning is the process of identifying objectives to accomplish, deciding how to accomplish those objectives with specific strategies and tactics, implementing the actions that make the plan come to life, and measuring how well the plan met the objectives. The process of strategic planning is three-tiered, beginning at the corporate level, then moving to the business level, and lastly moving to the functional areas of the organisation, including marketing. Planners first identify their overall objectives (e.g., "raise consumer awareness of our brand by 10% in the next year") and then develop the specific tactics they will use to reach those goals (e.g., "increase our spending on print advertising in targeted publications by 15% this year"). A marketing plan is a written, formalised plan that details the product, pricing, distribution, and promotional strategies that will enable the brand in question to accomplish specific marketing objectives. Table 2.1 provides a sample of an overall marketing plan's structure.

Table 2.1 The Structure of a Typical Marketing Plan

The Marketing Plan Outline	Questions the Plan Addresses
A. PERFORM A SITUATION ANALYSIS 1. Internal Environment	• How does marketing support my company's mission, objectives, and growth strategies? • What is the corporate culture and how does it influence marketing activities? • What has my company done in the past with its: Target markets? Product? Pricing? Promotion? Supply chain? • What resources including management expertise does my company have that make us unique? How has the company added value through its offerings in the past?
2. External Environment	• What is the nature of the overall domestic and global market for our product? How big is the market? Who buys our product? • Who are our competitors? What are their marketing strategies? • What are the key trends in the economic environment? The technological environment? The regulatory environment? The social and cultural environment?
3. SWOT Analysis	• Based on this analysis of the internal and external environments, what are the key strengths, weaknesses, opportunities, and threats (SWOT)?
B. SET MARKETING OBJECTIVES	• What does marketing need to accomplish to support the objectives of my firm?

C. DEVELOP MARKETING STRATEGIES 1. Select Target Markets and Positioning	• How do consumers and organisations go about buying, using, and disposing of our products? • Which segments should we select to target? If a consumer market, what is the relevant demographic, psychographic, and behavioural segmentation approaches, and the media habits of the targeted segments? If a business market, what are the relevant organisational demographics? • How will we position our product for our market(s)?
2. Product Strategies	• What is our core product? Actual product? Augmented product? • What product line/product mix strategies should we use? • How should we package, brand, and label our product? • How can attention to service quality enhance our success?
3. Pricing Strategies	• How will we price our product to the consumer and through the channel? • How much must we sell to break even at this price? • What pricing tactics should we use?
4. Promotional Strategies	• How do we develop a consistent message about our product? How do we best generate buzz? • What approaches to advertising, public relations, sales promotion, and newer forms of communication (such as social networking) should we use? • What role should a sales force play in the marketing communications plan? How should direct marketing be used?
5. Supply Chain Strategies	• How do we get our product to consumers in the best and most efficient manner? • What types of retailers, if any, should we work with to sell our product? • How do we integrate supply chain elements to maximise the value we offer to our customers and other stakeholders?
D. IMPLEMENT AND CONTROL THE MARKETING PLAN 1. Action Plan (for all marketing mix elements)	• How do we make our marketing plan happen?

2. Responsibility	• Who is responsible for accomplishing each aspect of implementing the marketing plan?
3. Timeline	• What is the timing for the elements of our marketing plan?
4. Budget	• What budget do we need to accomplish our marketing objectives?
5. Measurement and Control	• How do we measure the actual performance of our marketing plan and compare it to our planned performance and progress towards reaching our marketing objectives?

Source: Authors (2024)

Why Should We Take the Time to Plan?

Although it is tempting to just follow our instincts, it turns out that there is tremendous value in planning. Planning ensures that an organisation understands its markets and its competitors. It helps to ensure that organisations are aware of the changing marketplace environment. When organisational partners participate in the planning process, they are better able to communicate and coordinate activities. Planning requires that objectives be set and agreed upon, which improves the likelihood of those objectives being met. It enhances the ability of managers to allocate limited resources using established priorities. Perhaps most of all, planning enables success to be defined. Success, or the lack thereof, becomes a measurable outcome that can guide future planning efforts. It's increasingly common for organisations to include a heavy dose of social media in their marketing plans. The annual Social Media Marketing Industry Report provides data on the use of social media marketing by B2B and B2C marketers around the world (Stelzner, 2012). The report further revealed that 90% of marketers feel social media is important to their marketing initiatives. Whether large or small, B2B or B2C, most businesses recognise that social media should be integrated into their marketing plans.

Due to this upward trend, it makes sense to include social media marketing in a brand's marketing plan. Social media marketing has many applications for marketers. Social media can be a delivery tool to build buzz and word-of-mouth communication. They can efficiently deliver coupons and other special promotional offers. Social platforms can be the primary venue for the execution of contests and sweepstakes. They can collect data to build databases and generate sales leads. Social media can also serve as efficient channels to manage customer service relationships and conduct research for new product development. Not to mention, social media are relatively inexpensive ways to increase the reach and frequency of messages that are otherwise delivered via more traditional, big media methods. Because the creative applications related to social media are somewhat unique, we suggest an approach for developing an in-depth social media marketing strategy much as advertising plans (also known as integrated marketing communications (IMC) plans or marcom plans) provide in-depth detail on the execution of the (traditional) promotional portion of a brand's marketing plan. In the early days of social media marketing, many plans were developed for standalone campaigns that were not fully integrated into the brand's promotional mix. Today, social media marketing campaigns may serve as standalones and/or be a fully integrated media choice in the brand's marketing plan. For simplicity, we approach the sample plan from the perspective of planning a standalone campaign. Table 2.2 provides the structure of a social media marketing plan. We will begin this process as we explore the strategic

Table 2.2 A Social Media Marketing Plan Outline

I. Conduct a situation analysis and identify key opportunities.
• Internal environment
1. What activities exist in the overall marketing plan that can be leveraged for social media marketing? 2. What is the corporate culture? Is it supportive of the transparent and decentralised norms of social media? 3. What resources exist that can be directed to social media activities? 4. Is the organisation already prepared internally for social media activities (in terms of policies and procedures)?
• External environment
1. Who are our customers? Are they users of social media? 2. Who are our competitors? What social media activities are they using and how are social media incorporated in their marketing and promotional plans? 3. What are the key trends in the environment (social, cultural, legal and regulatory, political, economic, and technological) that may affect our decisions regarding social media marketing?

• SWOT analysis
1. Based on the analysis, what are the key strengths, weaknesses, opportunities, and threats (SWOT)?

II. State objectives
1. What does the organisation expect to accomplish through social media marketing (promotional, objectives, service objectives, retail objectives, research objectives)?

III. Gather insight into target audience
1. Which segments should we select to target with social media activities? 2. What is the relevant demographic, psychographic, and behavioural characteristics of the segments useful in planning a social media marketing strategy? 3. What are the media habits, and especially the social media habits of the segments?

IV. Select social media zones and vehicles
1. Which mix of the four zones of social media will be best to accomplish our objectives within the resources available?

• Social community zone strategies
a. What approach to social networking and relationship building should we use? How will we represent the brand in social networks (as a corporate entity, as a collection of corporate leadership, as a brand character)? What content will we share in the space?

• Social publishing zone strategies
a. What content do we have to share with audiences? Can we develop a sufficient amount of fresh, valuable content to attract audiences to consume content online? b. What form should our blog take? c. Which media sharing sites should we use to publish content? How should we build links between our social media sites, owned media sites, and affiliates to optimise our sites for search engines?

• Social media entertainment zone strategies
a. What role should social entertainment play in our social media plan? Are there opportunities to develop a customised social game or to promote the brand as a product placement in other social games? Is there an opportunity to utilise social entertainment sites such as Myspace as an entertainment venue?
• Social commerce zone strategies
a. How can we develop opportunities for customer reviews and ratings that add value to our prospective customers? b. Should we develop retail spaces within social media sites? If we socially enhance our own e-retailing spaces, what applications should be used? c. How can we utilise social commerce applications like group deals to increase conversions?
V. Create an experience strategy encompassing selected zones
1. How can we develop social media activities that support and /or extend our existing promotional strategies? 2. What message do we want to share using social media? 3. How can we encourage engagement with the brand in social spaces? 4. How can we encourage those who engage with the brand socially to act as opinion leaders and share the experience with others? 5. In what ways can we align the zones used as well as other promotional tools to support each other? Can we incorporate social reminders in advertising messages, in store displays, and other venues?
VI. Establish an activation plan
1. How do we make the plan happen? 2. Who is responsible for each aspect of implementing the plan? 3. What is the timing of the elements in the plan? 4. What budget do we need to accomplish the objectives? 5. How do we ensure that the plan is consistent with the organisation's overall marketing plan and promotional plan?
VII. Manage and measure
1. How do we measure the actual performance of the plan?

Source: Authors (2024)

development of social media marketing plans. Then we'll cover the steps in strategic planning for social media marketing. Finally, we'll discuss structural approaches organisations can take to be prepared to execute their plans.

The Phases of Social Media Marketing Maturity

If you keep up with industry news, you might be tempted to think that every brand has a social media strategy. Each day seems to bring new stories about a marketing campaign with social media elements, on ads, storefronts, and business cards.

Although it seems everyone is talking about social media, it is one thing to claim you use social media and quite another to say you have a strategy that incorporates social media. In the former case, a group can turn to social media activities to stage *stunts* (one-off ploys designed to get attention and press coverage) or as *activation tools* to support other marketing efforts. For example, when Skittles let its social media presence take over its website, that was a stunt. But when Starbucks runs social media promotions, it integrates these promotions with the overall campaign in place. The most engaging brands using social media for marketing will ensure that all communications are consistent with the brand's image while using social media as an element for experimentation and engagement with short-term campaigns as well as use in omni-channel marketing campaigns. As organisations mature in terms of their social media marketing, they plan systematically to ensure social media marketing activities are consistent with their marketing and marketing communications plans and are capable of meeting specific marketing objectives.

By this, we mean that, as a result of time and experience, we tend to see that applications that start as one-time "experiments" often morph into more long-term and carefully thought-out elements that the organisation integrates with all the other communication pieces it uses to reach customers. Nevertheless, many marketers currently use social media marketing tactics without that level of maturity. A major study of marketers in both Europe and North America found huge differences in the level to which respondents use social media and integrate it with other initiatives. Many still just experiment with baby steps (like creating a Facebook page) rather than including social media as a fundamental component of their marketing strategy. Companies are eager to benefit from social media, but many are still figuring out just how these approaches can go beyond the novelty stage and actually help them meet their objectives. Companies can be thought of in terms of their level of maturity in social media marketing, of which there are three phases: trial, transition, and strategic. Let's take a closer look at each phase.

Trial Phase

The trial phase is the first phase of the adoption cycle. Organisations in the trial phase test out social media platforms, but they do not really consider how social media can play a role in their overall marketing plan. In these early days, most groups focus on learning to use a new form of communication and exploring the potential of social media as a venue. It is not necessarily a bad thing to test the waters of social media. Companies need, especially early on, to experiment—to play in the sandbox, so to speak. Doing so helps them brainstorm ideas for using social media and understand what it takes to succeed in this brave new world. However, the problem with the trial phase is that many companies do not treat it as an exploratory stage of what is really a multi-stage process. Instead, they just jump right in and focus only on cool new ways to communicate. Think this couldn't happen? According to the 2016 Social Media Marketing Industry Report, 41% of marketers have been using social media for less than 2 years.

British Airways is an example of a brand in the transition stage of social media marketing. It uses Twitter (now X) as a brand presence and customer support channel but doesn't consistently manage complaints. How do we know? Consider this example. A customer of British Airways, frustrated about his lost luggage (using his Twitter handle @hvsvn), posted a "promoted tweet" (that's paid media in a social vehicle) advising people to avoid flying with British Airways due to its horrendous service. The company didn't respond for 8 hours! When it did, it tweeted that customer service hours were standard business hours (9 am–5pm) and asked that the customer direct message (DM) his baggage claim information to them. What would you think? You got it. Twitter is available 24/7. Brands don't have the option of working only 8 hours per day. Influencers have the power to amplify problems like this. We tend to think of brands partnering with influencers to increase the reach and spread of positive content. But if influencers have a negative experience, their complaints will spread as well. British Airways (BA) learned this the hard way when television star Phillip Schofield documented the delays and lack of support from BA employees during a computer system failure that left thousands stranded at Heathrow. Schofield posted a selfie to Instagram with the crowded chaos in the background and

Figure 2.1   The transition stage of social media marketing. Source: Authors (2024)

tweeted what some called an "epic rant" to @britishairways too. Schofield wasn't the only BA customer using social media to complain to BA that day, but his activity is especially relevant because of his multi-million-person fan base (Lawrence, 2022).

Transition Phase

When an organisation matures in their use of social media marketing, they enter a *transition phase*. During this phase, social media activities still occur somewhat randomly or haphazardly, but a more systematic way of thinking starts to develop within the organisation. In the transition stage, brands are on the right track but may not have fully formed a strategic approach. For instance, the brand may have established social media profiles and be using them regularly but still make mistakes. A common one is the use of automation to schedule social media posts and replies. This means that some of the responses to tweets or Facebook posts (or other social media comments) are programmed. In the industry, these automated responses are useful for workflow management, but users view automation as fake, referring to the practice as *social media zombies*. In and of itself, that's not bad. Automation can help brands be responsive. But if it is overused or used ineffectively, people will know. And they will resent it.

Strategic Phase

When a business reaches the final phase of its strategic planning, it employs a systematic procedure to plan actions related to social media marketing with the goal of establishing defined metrics and targets. In the organisation's entire marketing strategy, social media will be incorporated as an essential component from this point forward. There are advantages to making a strategic commitment to social media marketing, despite the fact that it takes time to create such a commitment. Marketers have reported that social media marketing has led to greater brand visibility, brand attitudes, and even sales. Naturally, this is not something that is going to be simple, especially for marketers who have a significant amount of expertise with social media. 40% of respondents believe that marketing using social media is more challenging now than it was in the past. A fluid social media landscape, in conjunction with the requirement to demonstrate the return on investment (ROI) of marketing operations, causes obstacles.

Critical Reflection

Bots Among Us

Bots are algorithms acting on social media networks. Their capabilities offer potential value to marketers and consumers. For instance, bots can make recommendations, provide information, facilitate purchases, and interact in conversations with surprising authenticity. Automation provides efficiency for marketers. Many of us have interacted with bots. There are already thousands of them on Facebook Messenger, WeChat, and other social channels. Some are clearly labelled, particularly when used as a branded app like the one TripAdvisor offers on Facebook Messenger. Research on consumer attitudes towards chatbots suggests that people are open to using chatbots but want their accuracy to improve security measures to protect credit card data and other personal information bots may have access to. That's not the whole story, though. Some bots are distinguished, and to the average social media user, the bots seem like real people. In fact, 30% cannot identify bots from real users on social networks. The risk? Bots can influence perceptions and sentiment, impact the spread of information, and cause all kinds of trouble. A simple example? Barack Obama is frequently praised for his strong Twitter following. But estimates suggest that more than 50% of Obama's followers are actually bots! Bots can send spam, make bogus offers, deliver messages with malware, and more. Scammers are well aware of this phenomenon. Security research firm Cloudmark has documented the rise of a flirtatious bot called "TextGirlie." After obtaining a victim's name and telephone number from their social media profile, TextGirlie would send the victim a personalised message asking them to continue the conversation in an online chatroom. A few coquettish exchanges later, and the victim would be asked to click on a link to an adult dating or webcam site. Bots can be programmed to post fake messages to sway public opinion. It's a problem known as "astroturfing," in which a seemingly authentic swell of grassroots opinion is in fact manufactured by a battalion of opinionated bots. The ramifications of astroturfing are in fact so serious that the US Department of Defence has developed an app called BotOrNot, which can determine whether a Twitter account is run by a bot: https://twitter.com/Botometer. The application provides a predictive analysis, based on account activity and tweet semantics, that suggests whether the account operator is likely to be a human or a bot (Souce: Baraniuk, n.d.).

The threat is that real estimates suggest that 15% of Twitter accounts are bots. To put that in perspective, that's about 50 million Twitter "users." Bots stay busy too. One study found that bots generate more than 60% of all Internet traffic. Richard Wallace, a creator of bots for customer service and other marketing uses, explains that the most realistic bots can convince people that they are humans. Bot designers compete for the Loebner Prize, a contest in which chatbots try to convince judges that they are humans. Twitter and other social networks have detection systems to identify bots, but the systems are no match for well-designed bots. A group of researchers showed just how easy it is to infiltrate Twitter if the bots look and act like real Twitter users (Zhang et al., 2023). They created 120 bot accounts, making sure each one had a convincing profile complete with a picture and attributes such as gender. After a month, they found that almost 70% of the bots were left untouched by Twitter's bot detection mechanisms. What's more, the bots were pre-programmed to interact with other users and quickly attracted thousands of followers. Another problem with bots? As artificial intelligence (AI) programmes, bots learn from their surroundings and interactions. This is meant to be an advantage, but there are risks too. Savvy trolls can manipulate what bots learn. That's what happened with the Microsoft bot Tay. Tay was a conversation bot created for Twitter. She was designed to learn from conversations and then use what she learned. Trolls began to converse with the programme in ways to trick it into becoming racist, ignorant, and even cruel. Within a day, the programme was tweeting out offensive posts, and Microsoft shut the bot down (Barbaschow, 2019).

Social Media Campaigns: The Strategic Planning Process

Those organisations that have moved beyond the trial and transition phases of social media marketing maturity develop strategic plans for social media that incorporate components of the social media mix as channels to accomplish marketing objectives. As we saw in Table 2.2, the process consists of the following steps:

- Conduct a situational analysis and identify key opportunities.
- State objectives.
- Gather insight into and target one or more segments of social consumers.
- Select the social media channels and vehicles.
- Create an experience strategy.
- Establish an activation plan using other promotional tool (if needed).
- Execute and measure the campaign.

Situation Analysis

The first step in developing the plan is much the same as it is in the creation of traditional strategic plans: research and assessing the environment. Good social media planning starts with research on the industry and competitors, the product category, and the consumer market. Once this research is compiled, strategists try to make sense of the findings as they analyse the data in a situational analysis. The situation analysis details the current problem or opportunity the organisation faces. It will typically include a social media audit. In addition to the standard things marketers need to know, the social media audit ensures the team understands the brand's experience on social media.

The audit will assess the brand's past social media activity, including whether profiles are consistent with the brand image, frequency of activity, types of activity, responsiveness, engagement, and other measures of effectiveness. Free tools that are useful for auditing social media activities are LikeAlyzer, Fan Page Karma, and AgoraPulse. Audit reports can also be created using paid vendor services like those from Sprout Social, Sysomos, and others.

In addition, a review of the brand's SWOT analysis will highlight relevant aspects of the firm's internal and external environment that could affect the organisation's choices, capabilities, and resources. This acronym refers to the strengths, weaknesses, opportunities, and threats that the firm should consider as it crafts a strategy. The internal environment refers to the strengths and weaknesses of the organisation—the controllable elements inside a firm that influence how well the firm operates. The external environment consists of elements outside the organisation's opportunities and threats that may affect its choices and capabilities. Unlike elements of the internal environment that management can control to a large degree, the firm can't directly control these external factors, so management must respond to them through its planning process.

A key aspect of the external environment is the brand's competition. Analysing competitive social media efforts and how the target market perceives those efforts is a must-do in social media marketing planning. It can be done in much the same way as the social media audit, except the focus is on the competing firms. You can use an internal system or a cloud service such as RivalMap (www.rivalmap.com) to organise competitive information and monitor news and social activity. When you use RivalMap, you can maintain a search of competitive activity and news mentions online for a small fee. A competitive social media analysis should answer the following questions:

- On which social media channels and specific vehicles are competitors active?
- How do they present themselves through those channels and vehicles?
- Include an analysis of profiles, company information provided, tone, and activity.
- Who are their fans and followers? How do fans and followers respond to the brand's social activity?

Social Media Audit Template

- How many likes do we have?
- How often do we post?
- What is our push/pull mix?
- What types of media do we use?
- Does our Facebook link to our website?
- Do we have updated cover and profile?
- Do we respond to comments?
- Do we have a rating? What is it?
- What is our social media voice?
- What do the comments on our page and photos typically say?
- Do we share articles? How often?

- How many followers do we have?
- What is our media mix for posts?
- What kind of hashtags do we use?
- Does our profile link to our website?
- What is our social media voice?
- Who do we follow?
- Do we respond to comments?
- What are the comments on our photos saying?

■ What is our push/pull mix?

■ How many followers do we have ?
■ What is our media mix for posts?
■ What is our social media voice?
■ Have we claimed their Google business listing?
■ Does our profile link to our website?
■ Do we respond to comments?
■ What is our push/pull mix?

■ What type of content do we post?
■ Do we drive consumers to our website based on our content?
■ What is our pull/push mix? Do we interact with users?
■ Do we post stories often?

■ Do we use YouTube?
■ What types of video content do we post ?

- Are these videos shared on our other social channels?
- How many subscribers do we have?
- What are the comments on our videos saying?
- Do we respond to comments?
- Does our profile link to our websites?
- How many likes do we receive, on average, for a video?
- How many views do we receive, on average, for a video?

Importantly, marketers have many approaches to solving problems and taking advantage of opportunities. Here we are concerned with the organisation's use of social media, but still, the planner should ask the question, "Given the situation and the problem identified, is social media marketing the appropriate approach?" Especially for organisations that are still in the trial phase, it's tempting to focus on social media "gimmicks," even if other less trendy tactics might in fact be more effective. So, a word of caution: social media often provides effective solutions to marketing problems, but beware of blindly using these tools. To see how the early stages of the strategic planning process work in the real world, let's return to the example of Honda. Honda uses social media as part of its integrated marketing campaigns for Honda and each sub-brand (e.g., CRV, Civic, and Ridgeline) and also creates independent social media initiatives. It does so in a way that resonates with specific social media vehicles like Twitter, Instagram, YouTube, Pinterest, and Tumblr. Honda is one of the most well-known brands in the world, named 20th on the Forbes most valuable brands list. That's not all; the brand has won awards for most trusted car brand, best value brand, and best overall brand! But Honda faces stiff competition online and offline.

Identify Social Media Marketing Objectives and Set Budgets

In this stage of the process, the planner elaborates on what is expected of the social media campaign and what financial and human resources are available to meet those objectives. An objective is a specific statement about a planned social media activity in terms of what that activity intends to accomplish. The content of the objective will vary based on the situation and the problem at hand. For instance, the campaign may be designed to amplify other marketing communication efforts the organisation uses. Let's say, for example, that the brand co-sponsors a concert series. This series is an event marketing strategy built into the overall marketing communications plan. But the organisation realises that promoting the event using social media can build pre- and post-event buzz. In this case, the objective (to create heightened awareness of the event among target customers) relates to other activities in the organisation. The basic assumption is that the campaign can accomplish the desired marketing objectives. What are some examples of the basic marketing objectives social media marketers are pursuing? Here are some important ones:

■ Increase brand awareness.
■ Improve brand or product reputation.
■ Increase website traffic.
■ Amplify or augment public relations work.

Table 2.3   Honda's Social Media SWOT Analysis

Strengths:	Weaknesses:
• Loyal customers	• Difficulty standing out in a highly competitive marketplace
• High brand equity	• Reputation issues due to recalls
• Affordability	• Reputation issues related to being an old-school brand
• Quality products	
• High levels of coverage across all forms of media	
• Financial resources for marketing and social commerce options	
Opportunities:	**Threats:**
• Social media as a cost-efficient channel	• Strong brand competition from competitors
• Affiliations with causes and lifestyle passions	• Economic concerns may slow spending on high-price purchases
• Growth in social entertainment and social commerce options	• Environmental concerns over gas consumption and pollution

Source: Authors (2024)

- Improve search engine rankings.
- Improve perceived customer service quality.
- Generate sales leads.
- Reduce customer acquisition and support costs.
- Increase sales revenue.

In this stage, it's important to state the objectives in a way that will help the planner make other decisions in the planning process and eventually measure the extent to which the objective was accomplished at specific points in the campaign. A well-stated, actionable objective should include the following characteristics:

- Be specific (what, who, when, where).
- Be measurable.
- Specify the desired change (from a baseline).
- Include a timeline.
- Be consistent and realistic (given other corporate activities and resources).

Here's an example of an actionable objective: To increase site stickiness in the retail areas of our site by 100% (from 5 minutes of browsing to 10 minutes per site visit) with the addition of social commerce sharing applications by the end of the third quarter. The statement of the objective should include specific elaboration on the individual goals the brand wishes to achieve over the course of the campaign, taking care to state these goals such that they are specific, measurable, realistic, and time-lined. With Honda's precise objectives (*"serve people worldwide with the joy of expanding their life's potential"*), we can gauge that through this objective, Honda seeks to generate engaging, precise objectives to build its fan base in social communities, build brand equity, and increase top-of-mind awareness.

There should be a focus on resources. You've probably heard people say that the main benefit of social media marketing is that it's free. When brand managers work with agencies to plan traditional advertising campaigns, the cost of media placement can seem overwhelming. With that as a point of comparison, one can see why many might think of social media marketing as a free alternative to advertising. Even for brand participation on social networking sites, social media is not free. In planning a social media campaign, a budget must be allocated that ensures sufficient resources to accomplish the goals—just like in a traditional ad program. Granted, the media costs are often much lower compared to, say, a national television campaign. But there are other costs associated with social media. Charlene Li, a leading social media strategist, once said, "Social media trades media costs for labour costs."

What does Li's comment mean? The social communities in which brands largely engage consumers are indeed free-to-play spaces in terms of media costs. But there are other costs we must consider. Content must be generated, shared, and managed, and the time this takes requires funding. Strategies in some social media channels of our social media framework require development costs (in-house or with a vendor or agency), such as customising profiles and developing social games, branded applications and widgets, and microsites. Organic reach is increasingly difficult for brands to achieve as well. The result is an increase in the use of advertising (paid media) on social networking sites (SNS). At the end of the day, there's no such thing as a free lunch!

To date, most organisations have allocated only a small portion of their marketing budgets to social media. Though that budget is expected to nearly double in the next 5 years, where will this money be spent? Primarily, organisations are staffing for content management, ensuring that time is available for content development, blogging, monitoring social channels, and paying for social advertising. The job of social media manager, akin to that of a brand manager, is becoming more commonplace. This person has the role of overseeing, managing, and championing the social media strategy internally. Most organisations now have a dedicated team for social media marketing, but 80% of teams have fewer than four people. Typical roles include those of social media strategist, community manager, social media analyst, and social media associate. In addition, organisations may budget for software and services to manage social media accounts, manage projects, analyse effectiveness, automate tasks for efficiency, host content, monitor social conversations and collect data, and facilitate content creation.

Agencies and other providers can supplement the work of the social media manager (or team) with ideas, ways to integrate social media brands with the rest of the brand's marketing plan, technical expertise, and measurement. As with everything else in business, the budget is critical; without funding, the organisation can't initiate or maintain the campaign. How much should it allocate? When it comes to social media campaigns, budgets run the gamut from a few hundred to hundreds of thousands of dollars. For instance, Honda reportedly shifted its budget for communications on cable television networks to fund its social entertainment initiative. Many businesses calculate their social media marketing budgets as a percentage of their advertising expenditures, which planners within the company then allocate using one of several formulas. The method referred to as percentage of ad spend assigns a set portion of the overall advertising budget for the organisation to social media activities. Some use a variation where they allocate a percentage of online marketing funding to social media.

Two other methods are used by companies. The competitive parity method uses competitors' spending as a benchmark. Like advertiser share of voice, competitive parity is based on the belief that spending the same or more on social media marketing will result in a comparable change in share of attention for the brand. When it comes to social media, though, the share of voice takes on a new dimension; social media includes conversations about the brand from other sources. In contrast, increasing the share of voice in advertising involves simply purchasing more media time

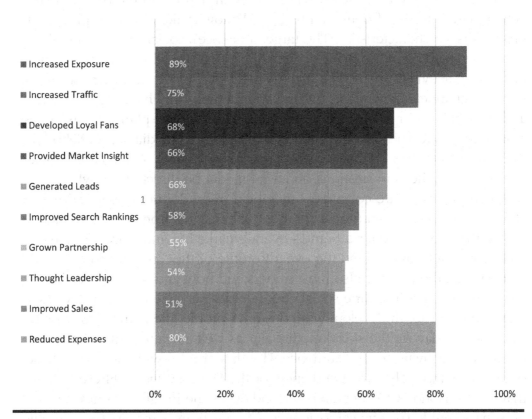

Figure 2.2   Top objectives marketers pursue using social media. Source: Stelzner, 2016 Social Media Marketing Industry Report, p. 17 Reproduced with kind permission of the Social Media Examiner

for advertisements. With social media marketing, the costs of different approaches and platforms vary widely, and even a large spend may not result in widespread buzz, or content sharing, or viral spread. The resulting share of voice depends in part on the extent to which fans and friends share the message with their own networks. Lastly, the objective-and-task method considers the objectives set out for the campaign and determines the cost estimates for accomplishing each objective. This method builds the budget from a logical base, with what is to be accomplished as the starting point.

Profile the Target Audience of Social Consumers

Social media marketing plans, like any marketing plan, must target the desired audience in a meaningful and relevant manner. To do this, it requires the development of a social media profile for the target audience. The target market for the brand will have been defined in the brand's marketing plan in terms of demographic, geodemographic, psychographic, and product-usage characteristics. The target audience's social profile will take this understanding of the market one step further. It will include the market's social activities and styles, such as their level of social media participation, the channels they utilise and the communities in which they are active, and their behaviour in social communities. The strategic planner must assess what it means to speak to the audience in the social media space. Who is the core target? How can we describe the key segments of that core target? To whom will the conversations on social media be directed? Of which social communities are consumers members? How do they use social media? How do they interact with other brands? The insights from the consumer profile that were done for a brand's overall marketing and marcom plans will be useful to understand the overall profile of the target market.

However, the planner also must understand how and when his or her customers interact in online social communities, as well as which devices they use to do so. In developing a consumer profile, the planner may plot out a typical day for the social media user as well as gather information on the Internet activities of the audience. Honda's profiles will align with those of its sub-brands. The target audience for the Honda Civic is different than that for the Honda CRV, and so on. Honda uses the insights about each persona to guide specific campaigns and interactions across its social media activities.

Select social media channels and vehicles once the organisation understands who it wants to reach, it's time to select the best social media mix to accomplish this. The zones of social media make up the channel and vehicle choices available for a social media mix. Similar to a more traditional marketing mix, the social media mix describes the combination of vehicles the strategy will include to attain the organisation's objectives. The social media mix options lie among the four zones we've already discussed: relationship development in social communities, social publishing, social entertainment, and social commerce. Within each zone, there are many specific vehicles that may be best suited to reach a certain audience. For instance, to meet the desired objectives and the social media patterns of a target audience that includes college students, the planner may determine that the campaign should include social networking, social publishing, and social games. The media vehicles might include Facebook, YouTube, and Flickr. Social publishing may utilise a corporate blog and document sharing sites such as Scribd. Brands can leverage the popularity of games, music, and videos in the zone of social entertainment. It's also a good idea at this stage of planning to map out how the campaign will build earned media and utilise paid and owned media synergistically.

Exhibit 1

Honda's experience strategy invited fans to design stunt tracks to promote the newest Civic Coupe. Honda created a user-generated context (UGC) campaign for Instagram. Instagram's user profile matches the persona of the Honda Civic's target audience, and UGC campaigns inspire engagement. The experience? Fans helped design the world's first crowdsourced stunt track, the Dream Track. Filled with obstacles like bowling pins, pinball bumpers, and—strangely—donut cannons, the track was the culmination of suggestions from Honda fans all over the world. Fans could submit ideas using Facebook, Twitter, and Instagram. Fans whose ideas were picked for the stunt track got a shout-out from Honda. Once the Dream Track was finalised, Honda created photos and videos featuring a professional stunt driver showing off the Civic's capabilities on the Dream Track. The content was shared on Instagram. The concept aligned with Honda's marketing campaign, "The Power of Dreams," while effectively engaging the Civic target audience. Not only was the choice of experience and social vehicles appropriate given the target persona, but the campaign was also designed for propagation. Fans who contributed ideas were invested in the campaign and likely to share the campaign content with their friends.

Honda utilises many of the social media zones and multiple vehicles within each zone. The choice of zone and vehicle is based on the nature of the marketing objective and the persona characteristics, as well as how best to bring the experience strategy to life. Figure 2.4 shows a summary of Honda's zone activity.

Create an Experience Strategy

If we were planning an advertising campaign, the next step would be to identify a creative message strategy. The message strategy refers to the creative approach we will use throughout the campaign. This should flow from the brand's positioning statement, a single written statement that encapsulates the position the brand wishes to hold in the minds of its target audience. Positioning statements succinctly capture the heart of what the brand is and what the sponsor wants it to become. Reviewing the position is a necessary step in preparing a social media marketing strategy because the social media activities the campaign plans and executes need to consistently support the desired message. Can you identify the brands that go with these positioning statements?

1. "The computer for the rest of us"
2. "Networking networks"
3. "The world's information in one click"
4. "Personal video broadcasting network"

The message strategy should also be appropriate to meet the campaign's objectives. It is developed from a creative brief document that helps creatives channel their energy towards a sound solution for the brand in question. In planning for social media marketing campaigns, the design process works similarly; the planners create a brief to guide the development of the campaign. But because, unlike traditional media, social media focuses on interactive experiences, social sharing, and engagement, the brief has a somewhat different structure and goes by a different name. Some planners call this document an *experience brief.* The concept of an experience brief evolved from the work of website developers, who consider the direct impact on users when they design site architecture, imagery, copy, and other site features. Griffin Farley, a strategy planner, uses a different term. He

Figure 2.3   An example of a user generated vehicle. Source: Authors (2024)

1. Active participation in sns,

sharing content with hastags,   replying to fans, and interracting with influecial profiles,

2. In naddition to the Honda Autos social media accounts, there are additional accounts for the corporate brand, accura, racing, power sports, power equipment, and Honda marine

3. Profiles on facebook, X, instatram, YouTube, Snapchat, Pinterest, Google+

1. Edutaianment Video Content (eg. Always thinking about tomorrow films) to YouTube

2. Demonstrate Video and Photo content to Instragram

3. Sponsorship of social content (eg. Sponsor of Buzzfeeds, Tasty social video channel featuring shopable video recipes)

4. Image content published to Pinterest

Reviews and ratings for dealers on Yelp

1. Social Gaming (eg. Integration with songpop social game, including branded playlist).

2. Social music and video on YouTube (eg. concerts associated with Honda tags,

3. Oroginal branded entertainment videos (eg. Making a Dream Web series on YouTube)

4. Social television (eg. Interrctions with Fox Stars)

Figure 2.4   Honda's zones of social media marketing. Source: Authors (2024)

describes the planning document for social media as a *propagation brief.*
He explains that propagation planning means to plan not for the people
you reach but for the people that they will reach. In other words, the audience produces more audience. Traditional advertising promotes a message
to a passive audience, and that audience is the target. Social media invite an
interactive experience with an audience of influencers who will then share
the brand's message and invite others to the experience.

Researchers conceptualise brand experience as the sensations, feelings,
thoughts, and behaviours evoked by brand-related stimuli when consumers
interact with brands, whether during exposure to brand messaging, shopping and service interactions, or product consumption. The four dimensions
of brand experience point to important elements in experience design:

- To trigger the sensory dimension, the experience should engage the
  senses, especially the visual.
- To evoke the affective dimension, the experience should be emotional.
- To activate the behavioural dimension, the experience should enable
  physical action.
- To stimulate the cognitive dimension, the experience should stimulate
  curiosity, problem-solving, or other intellectual motives.

Based on the brand experience dimensions, social media marketing strategies should use visual elements like video, emotional creative appeals (like
humour, love, guilt, nostalgia, and fear), and interactive features. Surprisingly,
research suggests that brands have focused on functional messages in social
media marketing far more than on emotional messages. In one study of top
brands using social media, nearly 90% of the brands studied used functional
messages, but only 57% used interactivity and 43% used emotional appeals.
The study found that engagement and influence were both positively influenced by emotional appeals and interactivity, while functional appeals
had no effect at all. To develop a social experience worthy of participation
and sharing, social media planners ask and answer several questions. The
answers become the basis for the brief:

- What are the campaign goals and/or communication tasks? Objectives
  have been set for the campaign, and the use of social media has been
  identified as a possibility. Here, the planner reviews these decisions and
  provides a succinct overview of the goals.

■ How is the brand positioned? What is unique and special about its position in the marketplace? As in a traditional creative brief, any campaign work should leverage the brand's positioning strategy and build on the brand's strengths.

■ Who is the target audience? You've profiled the target already. Now consider what you want the audience to do. Do you want them to talk to the brand? Create and share content. Spread the message to their network. On what devices (e.g., iPad, smartphone, desktop) will they interact with your brand? What could you offer of value in exchange for their cooperation?

■ Is there another group of people who can persuade the target audience to follow them? This group is your influence—the people who will propagate your message. Why would these people want to share your message with others? What's in it for them?

■ What are the existing creative assets? How can the brand's creative assets foster a social experience? Most brands already have some creative assets that drive their paid and owned media. For example, a well-known and popular brand spokescharacter such as the GEICO Gecko is a creative asset that the GEICO insurance company has developed in its traditional advertising, so he might be employed in a social media campaign to give the company a head start in terms of consumer recognition as it tries to break through the clutter of competing messages. The planner should list the creative assets that already exist and identify the assets he or she still needs to extend the brand's story. How can the creative assets already available be used and/or leveraged in a social media context?

■ How can we integrate with the organisation's other branded media, and how long do we have to execute? This is a question that refers to how the campaign can best integrate with the brand's paid and owned media.

■ What experiences are possible given the target market's needs and motives, the available channels, and the creative assets? How can we design these experiences to maximise device portability and access? Creative assets used in social media campaigns should inspire activity and interactivity. These questions ask what types of activities could be engaging for the target audience on multiple devices and worth sharing with their network.

- What content will be needed? Social media is content-driven. What content will be relevant to the campaign, and what will be the source? Comments? Questions and polls? Video? Images? Stories? Apps?
- How will engagement be extended and shared throughout the social channels? For instance, will engagement activity auto-post to status updates (e.g., "Tracy created a Honda playlist on Songpop")?

After the planner goes through the process of discovery and briefing to provide these "must-knows" to the creative team, the creative team will then enter the stage of ideation or concepting. *Discovery* is the term used to describe the research stage of the plan. Planners may rely on secondary and primary research as they seek to discover insights that will be useful to the creative team. These insights will be presented to the team during the briefing. The creative team will spend time brainstorming ideas and developing possible concepts for the campaign. Eventually, the chosen ideas will be further refined and designed, and prototypes or mock-ups will be developed. These preliminary executions can then be used for internal review, usability testing, and other pre-testing.

Additionally, the makeup of the brand's social persona may vary. Other brands, such as Zappos, utilise different employee voices in social communities, so the online retailer's persona is the sum of its employees. Still others have represented the brand with a person, but with a single individual charged with the brand's social reputation. The brand's mascot may take the social stage, as Travelocity has done with its Roaming Gnome. Some brands present themselves as funny, comedic, thought leaders, and friends. There is no right or wrong social persona—it should ultimately be a social representation of the brand's position and, of course, be consistent with how the brand presents itself in other contexts.

Exhibit 2

Honda's Brand Personality shines on social media

Honda's brand personality is reflected in its social media banter. In addition to brand fans, Honda's presence in Zone 1—the social community—also includes engaging in conversations with other popular brands on Twitter. Honda sent antagonistic remarks to 15 powerful brands in a humorous way designed to spark engagement and conversation. Take a look at a message Honda tweeted to Oreo. This was a smart engagement! The tweet was clever, funny, and relevant! What car owner hasn't felt the frustration of crumbs left over from an in-transit snack? Plus, because the brands Honda teased all have large, active fan bases on Twitter, Honda was able to reach a large audience—but without the cost of paying influencers.

Integrate with Other Promotional Components and Establish Activation Plan

Traditional media campaigns typically have a designated lifespan, with timing tied to the accomplishment of specific objectives. For social media, though, campaigns are not necessarily events with fixed start and stop dates. Conversations in communities continue over time, and a brand's social media marketing presence should do this as well. This is particularly true for brands that rely on social media for customer service and customer relationship management.

Some of the most famous social brands, like Dell and Zappos, are "always on" with their social media campaigns. They aim to project a constant presence in the communities in which they participate. Honda uses a mix of short-term campaigns and an ongoing presence. Other organisations have also done this.

Exhibit 3

Honda Makes Social Community Meaningful

Brand-created experiences are one of the most effective tactics for building consumer engagement. Honda connects with its loyal customers through its "Honda Loves You Back" social media strategy by rewarding them with perks like sports tickets, massages, and food giveaways. Once the Honda Facebook page reached 1 million followers, the company began searching the Facebook pages of brand fans, looking for unique stories. They soon discovered Joe, a Honda owner who was approaching 1 million miles on his 1990 Honda Accord. Working with RPA, its Los Angeles-based ad agency, Honda devised a native video campaign to introduce Joe to the Honda community—with a unique twist. RPA posted its first video, "Meet Million Mile Joe," on Honda's Facebook and YouTube pages, where fans could track Joe's mileage and encourage him along the way. The second video captured a great surprise for Joe: a hometown parade in his honour, culminating with a gift of a new Accord. News stations across the country began carrying the story that night, creating earned media impressions on and offline. The campaign earned more than 44 million unique impressions in earned media, achieved several hundred thousand views of the YouTube videos, and drove positive sentiment and social conversations about Honda.

Execute and Measure Outcomes

In the final stage of the strategic planning process, we implement the plan and measure the results. The data gathered on all aspects of the social media plan is used to provide insight for future campaigns.

Case Study

Honda's Social Media Strategy Featuring Storytelling

Honda's social media marketing strategy encompasses multiple campaigns across zones and channels, supporting integrated marketing communications initiatives and executing unique social experiences. Best practices recommend brands develop content for social media that is authentic, engaging, valuable for the audience, creative, and experiential. Ultimately, brands must inspire the audience to participate and to share the experience with others. Honda's "Serial One" campaign accomplished all this and more. In 1969, Honda made its first entry into the American car market with the compact N600 two-door sedan. The N600 remains a storied piece of Honda's history, with a firm tie to Americana and the heyday of muscle cars. But those first vehicles were thought to be lost until just a few years ago, when a mechanic named Tim Mings discovered the last N600. Dubbed "Serial One" for its unique model number N600—1000001, the car was a lime-green, undriveable wreck. Mings' restoration of Serial One became a rare opportunity for Honda to tell the story of its humble beginnings, protect a historical artefact, and connect with Honda fans, restoration enthusiasts, and classic car buffs. Camera crews documented every step of Mings' work to restore Serial One, a year-long process that captured pivotal moments from Serial One's first engine start since being rebuilt to the revelation of Serial One fully restored at the Japanese Classic Car Show. The story of Serial One's restoration was shared in a 12-part video documentary series, published at a dedicated microsite, www.serialone.com, and on Honda's YouTube channel and Facebook page. The hero content was promoted across Honda's other social channels using the hashtag #HondaSerialOne, and augmented with GIFs, interview clips, and other shareable story elements. In sharing the story of Serial One, Honda also told the story of Honda's renegade spirit. The N600 was Honda's very first automobile and the granddaddy of every Honda on the road today. The American market didn't believe Honda could make a car, but the N600 was, ultimately, the reason Honda became the household name that it is today. When all was said and done, Honda not only got to tell the story of the N600 over the course of a year, but also launched a brand movement that social fans everywhere fell in love with. Serial One's success was built on an authentic experience in zone 2—the zone of social publishing—that was activated with posts and conversations in zone 1—the zone of social community.

Results and Outcomes

Honda's "Serial One" initiative was truly one-of-a-kind. The sentiment was overwhelmingly positive. The launch video alone received 48.7 million impressions across Honda's social platforms, with a total of 206 million PR impressions and features from online publications such as Motor Trend, Jalopnik, and Yahoo! Autos. A completion rate of 81% indicates that the videos captured the audience's attention. Week by week, people followed along to check in on Serial One's progress, as indicated by the project's average engagement rate of 4.8%. Over the yearlong restoration, the Serial One content kept fans interested and engaged all the way to the final video, which received more than 39 million PR impressions. Now that Serial One is complete—with a new ceramic white paint job—it has taken a place of honour at the Honda Museum, where admirers can check out Mings' handiwork in perpetuity—and hopefully occasionally rev its engine.

As we've seen, many organisations are still "social media wannabes." They're at an early stage in the process and feeling their way in a new environment. So perhaps we can forgive them for the common mistakes they tend to make. Here are some of the biggest offenders:

■ Staffing: The initial imperative when it comes to social media marketing is to simply get there—to have a presence in the community of interest. But focusing on presence can result in brand assets that are underutilised and underperforming in terms of the objectives set for the campaign. Organisations in the trial and transition phases tend to focus on establishing Facebook profiles and Twitter accounts, or perhaps on planning a UGC contest. These companies take an "if you build it, they will come," Field of Dreams approach without addressing ways to build and maintain traffic and interest. Ultimately, though, social media marketing is built on the community, content, and technology inherent to social media. To make it successful, the brand must be active in the space, and that means committing staff time to posting, responding, and developing content.

■ Content: A related issue is the failure to introduce new, fresh, and relevant content. Developing interactivity, emphasising relevance, monitoring the asset for needed maintenance, responding to visitor feedback, and providing new content will keep the asset fresh and inspire a curiosity to return among the core audience. Importantly, these components of successful social media marketing require an ongoing commitment of human resources.

■ Time horizon: Social media works differently than traditional advertising and may require patience before results are delivered. Although a television campaign can utilise a heavy buy early in its media plan to incite near-immediate awareness and build momentum, social media is just the opposite. It can take months for a social media campaign to build awareness, and there are plenty of social media failures that never gain traction. Assuming the plan itself is sound, organisations must be patient while the community embraces the content and the relationship. Although the results may take longer to see, the overall effectiveness and efficiency of the social media model can be well worth the patience and resources required.

■ Focus on objectives: It's not uncommon for organisations to focus on action steps rather than desired outcomes from social media. In other words, they take a short-term tactical approach rather than a long-term strategic approach. An inappropriate objective might read: "Increase engagement by responding to comments on Twitter and Facebook within 24 hours of posting, posting three status updates per business day, and adding links to social media accounts on the corporate blog." Do you see the error? The emphasis is on the action steps the social media manager will complete (tactical), but there's no focus on what the social media activities should do for the brand. There is no value in doing social media marketing for the sake of social media—the value lies in accomplishing marketing objectives. Social media are more than the "flavour of the month"—they have the potential to provide lasting and measurable benefits when campaigns are done right.

- Benefits to users: Social media platforms live or die on the quality of the content they offer. That content must add value to the social community. A social media marketing plan answers the question: How will we distribute our content using social media channels? But it also must answer other questions: how can we engage our target audiences in social media communities? What kind of content do our audiences value? Do they want content that informs? Entertains? How can we develop an ongoing stream of relevant, fresh content?
- Measurement: Organisations fail to properly measure results. Marketing consultant Tom Peters famously observed, "What gets measured gets done." As social media marketing has developed, some evangelists have encouraged new disciples to keep the faith, emphasising the growth and popularity of the media as reason enough to develop a presence in the space. In the long term, that's just not good enough. For organisations to succeed in social media marketing, measurement is critical. Measuring outcomes ensures that the organisation is learning from what worked and what didn't. Importantly, as organisations begin to shift more marketing dollars from traditional advertising to social media marketing, managers will seek out comparisons on metrics such as ROI between social media and other media options.

Managing Social Media Marketing in the Organisation

So, there we have it—a framework to plan a social media marketing campaign. In Chapter 5, we'll take a closer look at the tactics social media marketers use and how social media teams plan for the daily, weekly, monthly, and annual activities. But social media teams aren't the only employees who play a role in social media. Other divisions may interact with the social media team to share brand assets, meet information technology needs, address customer concerns, design creative materials, evaluate risk and potential legal liabilities, identify prospects, coordinate sales and special offers, develop human resource recruitment materials, and so on. In other words, social media teams will likely interact with marketing, sales, customer support, information systems, web design, legal, human resources, and finance. In addition, employees can be valuable brand advocates on social media channels. But they can also cause problems. Stories abound of employees who tweeted an insult on impulse that reflected poorly on the employer brand and harmed customer relationships. To address the roles employees play across the organisation, companies rely on social media policies.

The Social Media Policy

Companies need to develop, adopt, and publicise a social media policy among employees. A social media policy is an organisational document that explains the rules and procedures for social media activity for the organisation and its employees. Just like you, many employees are already engaged in social media. They may be active on social networking sites and micro-sharing tools like Facebook and Twitter. While employees may use social media to communicate with friends and access entertainment opportunities (maybe even when they're supposed to be working!), there's a good chance they will mention their employers and maybe even vent about office politics or shoddy products. Managing that risk is a must for companies. And many companies will recognise that these employees can act as powerful brand ambassadors when they participate in social media. As we mentioned, Zappos takes advantage of the fact that many of its employees participate in social media, and these enthusiastic team members promote the company in the process.

Of course, there's no guarantee that an employee (at least on his or her own time) will necessarily say only glowing things about the company. Brands use formal documents to ensure that the company is protected in a legal sense and also to encourage employees to participate in ways that are consistent with the brand's overall strategy. Here are excerpts from three companies' policies:

- Microsoft: "If you plan to tweet about any professional matters (such as the business of Microsoft or other companies, products, or services in the same business space as Microsoft), in addition to referencing your alias@microsoft.com email address, whenever possible, use the service's profile or contact information to assert that you are a Microsoft employee and/or affiliated with a specific group or team at Microsoft."
- Sun Microsystems: "Whether in the actual or virtual world, your interactions and discourse should be respectful. For example, when you are in a virtual world as a Sun representative, your avatar should dress and speak professionally. We all appreciate actual respect."
- Intel: "Consider content that's open-ended and invites responses. Encourage comments. You can broaden the conversation by citing

others who are blogging about the same topic and allowing your content to be shared or syndicated. If you make a mistake, admit it. Be upfront and quick with your correction. If you're posting a blog, you may choose to modify an earlier post—just make it clear that you have done so."

Honda's Social Media Policy

Honda's basic guidelines are for Honda associates, suppliers, vendors, consultants, and individuals employed by a third party and assigned to Honda who are participating in social media activities related to Honda's brands and business activities. The full policy is available online. Five key points are highlighted in the policy:

> Honda recognises that our dedicated associates and business partners are often our best advocates and that your engagement in online conversations may help inform and positively influence the public's perception of the company. When engaging in social networks, industry blogs, forums, wikis, and other similar sites, your actions, writing, and content are not only a reflection of you but also of Honda. Remember that you are an ambassador for Honda and all of its brands, so think before you post, and consider that online comments may exist forever.

Extracts from this policy are as follows:

- Be transparent. If you have something to say, use your real name. When commenting about something related to our industry, state who you are and your role in the company or on the project. Be clear that you are not an authorised representative speaking on behalf of the company. (See full disclosure and disclaimer obligations.)
- Be deferential. Do not post or engage with comments and/or "likes" on any official Honda public communication channels unless you are an authorised spokesperson for the company. Only authorised associates or teams communicate on behalf of Honda through the company's sites and properties.
- Be credible. When electing to share your personal opinions about Honda on "non-Honda" sites, be thoughtful about your comments and how they reflect on Honda's position and your role in the company.

Keep your focus on the topic at hand and be credible in your area of expertise.

■ Be vigilant. It is your obligation to protect Honda's confidential or proprietary information, including policy, product details, financial records, trade secrets, and business plans. Do not share anything publicly that might be considered sensitive in nature.

■ Be considerate. Think before you publish a comment that could be perceived as disrespectful. Never disparage a competitor, customer, supplier, partner, our company, or your colleagues. Do not engage in a battle of words or make it personal. If in doubt, do not do it.

Source: Honda issues social media guidelines for its employees
(businessmanagementdaily.com)

The Word-of-Mouth Marketing Association (WOMMA) developed a quick guide to designing a digital social media policy, shown in Table 2.4 Its purpose is to guide how the organisation, its employees, and agents should share opinions, beliefs, and information with social communities. Not only is it good business, but it can also help prevent legal problems. The WOMMA guide encourages organisations to make several decisions and include those in an organisation-wide social media policy. Organisations must decide upon:

■ Standards of conduct: Standards of conduct in a social media policy refer to the basic expectations for employee behaviour in social communities. At a minimum, WOMMA recommends that the standards require that all online statements about the business be honest and transparent. Deceptive, misleading, or unsubstantiated claims about the organisation or its competitors must not be issued. Further, good manners must be used in social communities (no ethnic slurs, personal insults, rumours, lies, or other offensive statements).

■ Disclosure requirements: Transparency is key in online communities. Employees must disclose that they are affiliated with the organisation. If they are receiving material compensation or gifts in exchange for posting, this must be disclosed. Disclosing affiliations ensures that readers can still find the posts credible and trustworthy. WOMMA recommends that bloggers include a simple statement: "I received [insert product name] from [insert company name], and here is my opinion…" In addition, when using posts on social networks, WOMMA recommends that the poster use hashtags to disclose the nature of relationships reflected

Table 2.4   WOMMA Guidelines

Key Aspects of the WOMMA Disclosure Form
Personal and Editorial Blogs
• I received _____from_____sent me _____   • Product review blogs   • I received _____from _____to review.   • I was paid by _____ to review
Additionally for product review blogs, WOMMA strongly recommends creating and prominently posting a "Disclosure and Relationship Statement" section on the blog fully disclosing how a review blogger works with companies in accepting and reviewing products, and listing any conflicts of interest that may affect the credibility of his or her reviews.
Providing Comments in Online Discussions
• I received _____from _____   • I was paid by _____   • I am an employee (or representative) of _____
Microblogs
Include a hash tag notation, either: • #spon(sponsor)   • #paid (paid)   • #samp(sample)
Additionally, WOMMA strongly recommends posting a link on your profile page directing people to a full "Disclosure and Relationships Statement." This statement, much like the one WOMMA recommends for review blogs, should state how you work with companies in accepting and reviewing products, and list any conflicts of interest that may affect the credibility of your sponsored or paid reviews.
Status Updates on Social Networks
• I received _____from _____   • I was paid by _____
If status updates are limited by character restrictions, the best practice disclosure requirement is to include a hashtag notation of either #spon, #paid, or #samp. Additionally, WOMMA strongly recommends posting a full description or a link on your social network profile page directing people to a "Disclosure and Relationships Statement." Note that if an employee blogs about his or her company's products, citing the identity of the employer in the profile may not be sufficient disclosure. Bloggers' disclosures should appear close to the endorsement or testimonial statement they are posting.
Video and Photo Sharing Websites
Include as part of the video /photo content and part of the written description:
• I received _____from_____   • I was paid by _____
Additionally, WOMMA strongly recommends posting a full description or a link directing people to a "Disclosure and Relationships Statement."

Source: Authors (2024)

in the posts: #emp (employee/employer), #samp (free sample received), and #paid (paid endorsement).

■ Standards for posting intellectual property, financial information, and copyrighted information: Many of the potential legal problems within social media relate to the inappropriate sharing of information. WOMMA recommends that organisations keep all intellectual property and private financial information confidential. Prior to posting copyrighted information, appropriate permissions should be collected.

An Organisational Structure to Support Social Media

Who "owns" social media within an organisation? Some brands assign the responsibility to a disciplined "silo," such as the marketing department, whereas others rely upon a centre of excellence model that pulls people with different kinds of expertise from across the organisation to participate. This eliminates the internal political issues relating to who in the company has primary responsibility for social media, so it's easier to integrate social media applications with other marketing initiatives.

Aside from the organisational structure to support social media marketing efforts, businesses must make decisions on the level of resources to dedicate. Social media is an ongoing conversation across potentially several communication vehicles. Some businesses dedicate multiple employees to managing the conversation calendar, whereas others assign a single person. The organisational task is to assign the least number of resources needed internally and then supplement those resources with help from the organisation's social media agency resources.

There are five basic models for social media structure:

■ Centralised
■ Organic
■ Hub and spoke (coordinated)
■ Multiple hub and spoke (dandelion)
■ Holistic honeycomb

1. In the centralised structure, the social media department functions at a senior level and reports to the CMO (chief marketing officer) or CEO (chief executive officer) and is responsible for all the social media activations. The potential problem here is that all social media

activity may not be adequately represented. Is customer care going to be good if social media marketing is housed under marketing rather than customer service?

2. In an organic structure, no one person owns social media. Instead, all employees represent the brand and incorporate social media into their roles. This is implemented through training and used across the organisation. The danger here is that the content can end up off-message. Any employee can sign up to respond to customer queries on Twitter. That means the company cannot control what employees say. Therefore, the company must have a well-developed social media policy in place to guide employee behaviour in social communities.

3. In the hub and spoke (also called the *coordinated*) model, a team of people who are cross-functionally trained are ready to address various social media needs. This is currently the most popular structure for social media management.

4. The dandelion model is essentially a multi-layered hub and spoke model. It is appropriate for companies with strategic business units (SBUs) that still represent a core brand.

5. The holistic model is currently the least used. It truly refers to a structure within which all employees are empowered to use social media and do so according to the company's strategy.

Social Media Management Systems

Regardless of the structure a company uses or the policy it develops, it must also devise a day-to-day system for managing social media activities, tracking content from development to distribution, managing social ad campaigns, analysing effectiveness, monitoring and listening, and capturing and analysing social data for market research. Companies may also use vendors to aid in social customer relationship management (social CRM), host owned social sites, generate reviews and ratings, facilitate influencer marketing tactics, and provide content. In particular, companies benefit from incorporating cloud services for social media management, social monitoring and listening, social ad management, and social media analytics and modelling. Whether on a small or large scale, one of the most used systems is

Hootsuite. Notably, Hootsuite offers a special programme for university users that includes the option to become Hootsuite Certified.

A Framework for Strategic Social Media Marketing

The framework for social media marketing depicted in Figure 2.5 describes an organisation's use of social media marketing along four dimensions: 1) scope, 2) culture, 3) structure, and 4) governance.

■ Scope: Does the organisation use social media marketing internally and externally to collaborate with stakeholders, or is social media predominantly limited to use as an external communications channel? The answer categorises organisations as defenders, who use social media marketing primarily as a one-way communication tool to entertain consumers and inform stakeholders; or as explorers, who seek collaboration with many different stakeholders, such as clients, employees, and suppliers.

■ Culture: Is the organisation's culture conservative (traditional with a focus on mass communications) or modern (permeable, open, and flexible)?

■ Structure: Are the organisation and departmentalisation of the social media marketing assignments hierarchical or networked?

■ Governance: Does the organisation define social media regulations and employee practices (autocracy) or allow norms to develop organically (anarchy)?

Decisions on social media marketing should be guided by the firm's internal influencers (e.g., general vision, mission, corporate goals, corporate culture, available resources), which in turn should be in line with external influencers (e.g., communities, competition, government regulation). The framework doesn't suggest a right or wrong choice. Rather, depending on the organisation's overall strategic focus and stakeholders, social media marketing should be organised for fit and congruence with the organisation's design.

The model represents a key aspect of strategic social media marketing. Firm: At the centre, representing the organisation or business formulating the social media marketing strategy.

SMM Scope:

Defender: Firms that use social media primarily for one-way communication or dictating messages to the audience.

Explorer: Firms that embrace a two-way dialogue and collaboration, promoting a laissez-faire approach to interaction.

SMM Culture:

Conservatism: Represents a traditional approach where the culture is encapsulated and centralised, likely focusing on mass communication.

Modernism: Indicates a more open, permeable culture that is dissolved and decentralised, likely to embrace new and varied forms of communication.

SMM Structure:

Hierarchies: This suggests a more traditional organisational structure with defined levels and clear lines of authority.

Networks: This indicates a more modern, flat structure where teams and individuals might work in a more interconnected and less hierarchical manner.

SMM Governance:

Autocracy: This represents strict control over social media practices and messaging, where rules and policies are clearly defined and enforced.

Anarchy: Suggests an environment with minimal or no control over social media activities where practices develop organically. Stakeholders (outer ring): Reflects the external parties that the firm engages with, including customers, partners, suppliers, and the general public.

Vision, Mission, Corporate Goals, Corporate Culture, and Corporate Resources (left side vertical axis): These are the internal guiding principles and resources that inform the firm's approach to social media marketing. This framework is designed to help businesses analyse and understand their current approach to social media, identify potential areas for change, and ensure that their social media strategies are aligned with their broader corporate vision and goals. It prompts firms to consider whether they should

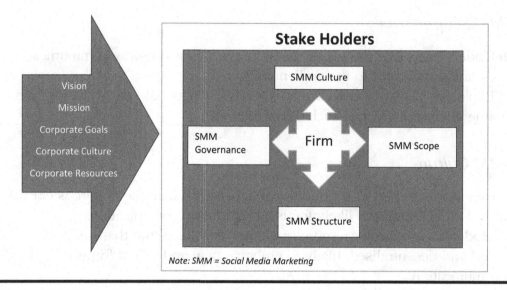

Figure 2.5 Strategic social media marketing framework. Source: Authors (2024)

be more open and explorative or more controlled and conservative in their social media marketing efforts.

Chapter Summary

Where does social media marketing planning fit into an organisation's overall planning framework? Social media marketing should be part of an organisation's marketing plan. Like integrated marketing communications plans, organisations may also develop standalone plans offering greater social media marketing. What are the phases of social media marketing maturity? How does social media marketing change for companies as they shift from the trial phase to the transition phase and eventually move into the strategic phase? The phases of social media marketing maturity are *trial*, *transition*, and *strategic*. In the trial phase, organisations are pursuing social media tactics in an ad hoc manner, with a focus on gaining experience in social media. The tactics are not well linked to the organisation's overall marketing plan and may be haphazardly executed. Organisations in the transition phase think more systematically about how to plan social media activities that support marketing objectives. When an organisation enters the final, strategic phase, it utilises a formal process to plan social media marketing activities with clear objectives and metrics. Social media is now integrated as a key component of the organisation's overall marketing plan.

What Are the Steps in Social Media Marketing Strategic Planning?

The social media marketing strategic planning process consists of the following steps:

- Conduct a situational analysis and identify key opportunities.
- State objectives. Gather insight into and target one or more segments of social consumers.
- Select the social media channels and vehicles.
- Create an experience strategy.

Establish an activation plan using other promotional tool (if needed). Manage and measure the campaign.

How Can Organisations Structure Themselves to Support Social Media Marketing?

Companies can structure themselves as centralised, decentralised, hub and spoke, dandelion, or holistic. Each option represents a trade-off between control and responsiveness. Organisations can also use social media management systems. What are the key components of an organisational social media policy, and why is it important to have such a policy in place? Policies may include several guidelines, such as standards of conduct, disclosure requirements, and standards for posting intellectual property, financial information, and copyrighted information. Companies need policies to ensure that social media activity is consistent with their overall brand.

Exercises

- Visit www.thecoca-colacompany.com/socialmedia, where you'll find Coca-Cola's social media policy, or find the policy for another company. Identify the key components WOMMA recommends be included in a corporate social media policy. How could the policy be improved?
- Identify a social media campaign for a favourite brand. In what ways does the campaign invite you to take part? In what zones does the strategy lie? Does the campaign include sharing technologies to ensure your activities are shared with your network?
- Explore Hootsuite Academy, a training service for Hootsuite, a social media management system.

Review Questions

1. Describe the different channels of social media and discuss how they add value to marketing strategies. What are the unique advantages of each channel in reaching target audiences?
2. Explain the process of strategic planning in social media marketing. How does a company like Honda use various social media channels and strategies to enhance its brand and market presence?
3. Discuss the three phases of social media marketing maturity: *trial*, *transition*, and *strategic*. Provide examples of activities or strategies that characterise each phase.
4. How should organisations integrate social media marketing into their overall marketing plans? What are the key considerations for measuring the effectiveness of social media campaigns?
5. Why do some organisations enter the trial phase without planning and research? Is there value in getting social media experience before social media marketing becomes part of the marcom plan?
6. Explain the phases in the social media marketing maturity life cycle.
7. What types of organisational structures are businesses using for social media marketing? What are the pros and cons of each?
8. Explain the steps in the social media marketing strategic planning process.
9. What approaches to budgeting can be used by organisations planning for social media marketing?

References

Baraniuk, C. (n.d.). *How online "chatbots" are already tricking you.* How Online "chatbots" Are Already Tricking You - BBC Future. https://www.bbc.com/future/article/20140609-how-online-bots-are-tricking-you

Barbaschow, A. (2019). Microsoft and the learnings from its failed Tay artificial intelligence bot. *ZDNet.*

Felix, R., Rauschnabel, P. A., & Hinsch, C. (2017). Elements of strategic social media marketing: A holistic framework. *Journal of Business Research, 70,* 118–126.

Irshad, M., & Ahmad, M. S. (2019). Investigating the determinants of consumers' attitude towards social media marketing: Moderating role of gender. *Online Journal of Communication and Media Technologies, 9,* 1–15

Lawrence, R. (2022, September 23). Phillip Schofield once unleashed rant after he had to queue. *Mail Online.* https://www.dailymail.co.uk/tvshowbiz/article-11243385/Phillip-Schofield-unleashed-rant-wait-two-hour-line-board-flight.html

Odoom, R., Anning-Dorson, T., & Acheampong, G. (2017). Antecedents of social media usage and performance benefits in small-and medium-sized enterprises (SMEs). *Journal of Enterprise Information Management, 30,* 383–399

Stelzner, M. A. (2012). *2012 social media marketing industry report: How marketers are using social media to grow their businesses.* Social Media Examiner

Zhang, Y., Song, W., Shao, J., Abbas, M., Zhang, J., Koura, Y. H., & Su, Y. (2023). Social bots' role in the COVID-19 pandemic discussion on Twitter. *International Journal of Environmental Research and Public Health, 20*(4), 3284

Chapter 3

Social Commerce

Chapter Outline

- Introduction
- Social commerce
- Social commerce and the shopping process
- Social commerce strategies
- Social promotions and partnerships
- Social commerce fraud
- Social commerce zone
- Psychology of influence
- Conclusions

Chapter Outcome

By the end of this chapter, the reader will be able to:

Analyse the interplay between social commerce and e-commerce:
- Illustrate the integration points where social commerce enhances and complements e-commerce strategies.

Evaluate the impact of mobile devices and applications on social commerce:
- Demonstrate the ability to identify and analyse specific features and functionalities of mobile platforms that contribute to social commerce development.

DOI: 10.4324/9781003307457-3

- Propose recommendations for optimising social commerce experiences through mobile platforms.

Examine social shoppers' role in consumer decision-making:
- Identify key touchpoints in the consumer journey where social media plays a pivotal role.

Identify social commerce elements to meet shopper needs:
- Create a framework for marketers to align their strategies with the preferences of social commerce users.
- Propose enhancements to existing social commerce strategies based on identified shopper needs.

Assess the value of ratings and reviews for consumers and marketers:
- Evaluate and develop strategies to leverage positive ratings and reviews while mitigating the impact of negative feedback.

Explore psychological factors influencing social shopping:
- Illustrate and apply psychological insights to develop marketing strategies that resonate with social shoppers' motivations and preferences.

Introduction

In the dynamic realm of e-commerce, the convergence of social media and online shopping has given rise to an innovative and transformative phenomenon known as "social commerce." Social commerce, a new sub-set of e-commerce, is characterised as the combination of both online commercial activities and social interactions mediated by social media platforms. Wang et al. (2019), as well as Algharabat and Rana (2021) referred to social commerce as an amalgamation of social media and the internet that aims to enrich people's engagements in the sale and marketing of various products within online communities. Generally, s-commerce is defined as "an extension of e-commerce sites, integrated with social media and Web 2.0 technology to encourage online purchases and interactions with customers before, during, and after the purchase" (Meilatinova, 2021, p. 1). Effectively, social commerce harnesses the power of social media platforms, seamlessly integrating shopping experiences into the fabric of users' online interactions. Nowadays, social commerce is an increasingly important part of e-commerce as it leverages social media to assist in e-commerce transactions and business activities (Wang et al., 2019). It is an integration of both commercial and social interactions.

The social commerce paradigm is considered a part of electronic commerce (e-commerce) and has emerged as an extensive growth of social networking sites (SNSs) (Algharabat & Rana, 2021). According to them, assumptions and understanding of people in social commerce move from a simple and general description of human social nature to a rich exploration with different angles from social psychology, social heuristics, national culture, and economic situations. Management and business strategies, as they noted, also evolved from short-term to long-term thinking, with the emergence of such concepts as branded social networks/communities, niche social networks/communities, niche brands, co-creating, team-buying, and multichannel social networks. IT platforms and capabilities for social commerce evolved from blogs to social networking sites (SNSs), media-sharing sites (MSSs), and smartphones. Information in social commerce also evolved from peer-generated, community-generated (crowdsourcing), consumer- and marketer-created, and global crowdsourced. Technological disruptions such as those mentioned in the article will play a fundamental role in the future of social commerce, and it is because of this technological sensitivity and dynamism that an attitude of curiosity and constant research must be maintained concerning the model since social commerce and technology can evolve faster than expected (Olivares et al., n.d.).

These evolutionary paths of social commerce require scholarly attention. Today, social commerce is approximately known both in terms of practical as well as theoretical areas, and little effort has been made to determine the current state of the studies in this new research area (Esmaeili & Hashemi, 2019). Despite the rapid development and adoption of social commerce, the current understanding of social commerce is still scattered and limited. Social commerce research is in the early stages of development since there is little theoretical work on how social commerce operates and little is known about the social commerce business cycle. Furthermore, the current understanding of the distinction between social commerce and e-commerce includes the use of social media as a tool to connect customers, considering social commerce as a new marketing mode of e-commerce. We believe that this understanding of social commerce could be further reconsidered by Wang et al. (2022). The wide adoption and application of social commerce by businesses in such areas as user behaviour, business models, e-commerce website design, adoption strategy, social process network analysis, and firm performance (Busalim, 2016) presents ample research opportunities that can have both theoretical and practical significance and implications. In this regard, this chapter is developed to trace the evolution of social commerce, differentiate social commerce from e-commerce, describe the tools for effective social commerce site creation, and explain managing the marketing mix in social commerce. The chapter also discusses creating effective interactions with social consumers, the role of ratings and reviews in providing value to customers and e-retailers, factors influencing social shopping, channels of social commerce, and social security and privacy issues in social commerce.

Social Commerce

It's a cold day in mid-December, and David is spending some time on Facebook reading about his friends' recent activities. A social ad for fresh flowers appears on the side of his news feed, which promotes flowers as a Christmas gift and provides an endorsement that thousands of people like this particular fresh flower. Remembering that he hasn't yet sent a Christmas gift to his grandmother in Texas, David gets a brainstorm—he doesn't have the time to spend hours at the mall looking for something for Grammy. He clicks the ad to reach Fresh Flowers' Facebook page. There he sees a promotion for 20% off his order if he "likes" the page and a "Shop Now" call to action. With a click of the "Shop Now" button on the "Shop" tab of the Fresh Flowers page, David can browse flower selections and price points.

Not sure whether fresh flowers are the best choice, David first visits Fresh Flowers' Facebook Wall. Comments from past customers fill the page, and David can read the posts from satisfied and dissatisfied customers along with the responses from company service representatives. He chooses three arrangements he likes, but then he uses Facebook Messenger to ask his two sisters to help him decide which is best. They both respond within 10 minutes (and as usual, they both pick the same one!). Now David is confident he's got a winner! He could use the "Buy" button on Facebook to complete his transaction, but he's running late for a class. He uses Fresh Flowers' chatbot on Facebook Messenger to place the order. The bot, named GWYN, makes a few additional gift suggestions and places the order. Share technologies post to David's Wall: "David bought a holiday arrangement at Fresh Flowers" and "David likes Fresh Flowers."

Once the flowers arrive and David knows how much Grammy liked them, he plans to return to the page to share a review on Fresh Flowers' Wall. From there, the cycle begins again as another individual sees shared posts about the brand and/or social ads.

Social Shopping

This refers to the active participation and impact of other people on the decision-making process of a consumer, which often takes the form of opinions, recommendations, and experiences that are communicated through channels such as social media. To put it another way, the phrase "social shopping" refers to the practices that customers engage in when they integrate social media into their decision-making process when making purchases. On the other hand, social commerce refers to the commercial application of social media platforms with the purpose of acquiring and retaining clients. The social media value chain and the characteristics of social communities are represented in the social commerce that exists today. Facebook, Instagram, and Pinterest are examples of social networking sites that act as channels via which users and brands can share information, experiences, and offers. These channels can be used for peer-to-peer or consumer–brand communication. Additionally, social shopping malls like Tonaton and social markets like Etsy and eBay are examples of channels that have the potential to facilitate social trade. It is also possible for e-commerce websites to participate in social commerce by socially enabling the website with features that allow customers to discuss, comment on, and evaluate products. Users are able to participate and engage in word-of-mouth communication across all channels, which has the potential to impact purchasing decisions and sales transactions. Along the same lines, influencers will be present on every channel. Personalisation of user experiences and functionality for participating in social commerce will be provided by social software, which will include algorithms, apps, and bots. This functionality will allow users to actively participate in social commerce by searching for product reviews, browsing recommended lists, or utilising voice commands to shop. The use of a connected device is required for individuals to engage in social commerce.

Social Commerce and the Shopping Process

At the end of the day, shopping online is still shopping. Sure, the way we locate and purchase products may not look the same, but the successful marketer understands that our basic shopping orientations (e.g., to obtain a needed product or service, to connect with others, to stimulate our senses) are the same as those our ancient ancestors possessed.

Furthermore, it's helpful to break down the process of shopping in terms of the stages of consumer decision-making. Though we may make some simple decisions in fewer steps, important decisions require five steps:

- Problem recognition;
- Information search;
- Alternative evaluation;
- Purchase;
- Post-purchase evaluation.

When we look at these stages, we realise that what seems at first to be an "obvious" and quick decision ("throw something in the cart") is a lot more complicated.

On the bright side, many current social media applications are out there to help consumers make it through each of these stages. Table 9.1 summarises the decision-making stages and illustrates some of these social media and social commerce tools that are already changing how we shop (but not why we shop!). So social commerce is a part of e-commerce, and it leverages social media to aid in the exchange process between buyers and sellers. That seems straightforward enough, but social media is sufficiently complex and broad to influence e-commerce in all five of the consumer decision-making stages. *Discovering information about a product on social media, whether through user comments, influencer content, or advertising, may cause problem recognition.* A recent study found that 81% of consumers have bought something they saw shared on social media, but less than 2% said their purchases were influenced by traditional advertising. It also found that 96% of Pinterest users gathered information and purchased research on the site. Marcus Miller (2016). Nearly half of the pinners surveyed were using Pinterest to plan for purchases related to a major life event—getting married, buying a home, or having a baby. Michael Yamartino, head of Commerce at

Pinterest, explained: "Pinterest is a discovery platform, in the same category as Google. For brands, it's about repurposing content from their site and publishing their entire product catalogue as you might a site map for Google to aid discovery." People in the problem recognition phase may also engage in *participatory commerce*, a sub-set of social commerce in which people participate in the design, selection, and/or funding of product innovation. Sites like Threadless and Kickstarter facilitate the collaboration between prospective customers and innovators.

Online clothing company Betabrand crowdsources the design and selection of all the products it manufactures and sells. Have an idea for apparel that meets an unmet need? Pitch it at Betabrand's website. Once your design is submitted, Betabrand's community will vote on the design and make suggestions for improving it. One of Betabrand's big success stories? Dress in yoga pants! That's right, pants that are stylish and formal enough for work, but with the comfort and stretch needed for a yoga class. They make taking advantage of that lunchtime yoga class feasible, and it all happened through social commerce.

The next stage, information search, is the primary driver of social commerce and social shopping behaviours. We noted earlier that even for offline purchases, wired consumers tend to search online for information before making an actual purchase. In a book sponsored by Google, Jim Lecinski explains the process of coining the term *ZMOT—Zero Moment of Truth*. Retailers, particularly those in the consumer packaged-goods sector, have long understood a related concept on which the concept is based. It draws from the notions of the *First Moment of Truth (FMOT)*, the moment a consumer chooses a product from the store shelf; and the *Second Moment of Truth (SMOT)*, the moment the consumer uses the product and feels satisfaction or dissatisfaction. ZMOT emphasises that consumers today may consider various factors online before making a purchase decision. Though the number of sources and types of sources vary by region and product category, on average, consumers will use more than ten sources of information before making a purchase. These sources may be owned media content vetted by the brands in question, paid media in the form of an ad, or word-of-mouth content posted by users on social media channels. There are several sources of information available via social media, but the most influential are reviews and ratings. Savvy brands will strive to be involved in this part of the purchase process, cultivating positive word-of-mouth and other forms of influence impressions, leveraging the content by encouraging its spread online, and facilitating the development of the content.

ZMOT information may or may not be social, but much of it is—whether a Pinterest board of favourites at Macys.com or a review of pizza places on Yelp. This information, particularly that provided by *reviews* and *ratings*, influences consumers at multiple stages in the buying process. Reviews are assessments with detailed comments about the object in question. Ratings are simply scores generated by users that reflect assessments of attributes like perceived quality, satisfaction, or popularity on a scale. Estimates vary from study to study, but research consistently shows that the vast majority of internet-connected shoppers globally search for product information online first. What makes a review or rating valuable? Ratings are a *heuristic*—a mental shortcut consumers use to help them with decision-making. For instance, if you want to choose a restaurant near the amphitheatre where you are attending a concert this weekend, you might pull up all the restaurants in the area and then choose the one with the highest average rating. Reviews provide more detailed information for those who want to evaluate the choice at a deeper level. Consequently, a good review should include product information such as features and specifications, an overall impression of the product with a positive or negative judgement, a list of pros and cons, experience with the product, and a final recommendation. With these components, the review will have sufficient information for the readers to judge relevance and credibility and apply the content to their purchase situation.

The way people search varies, but most start with a search engine and consequently can find all kinds of online content, including user-generated and brand-generated content on social channels. Search engines like Google are an obvious starting point for an online information search, but searches also occur on Facebook, YouTube, TripAdvisor, and elsewhere. Research suggests that Amazon—not Google—is the first source of online information search for more than 50% of internet users! Shoppers may not always complete their purchases online; instead, they carry out *web rooming*—the term for researching purchases online but going to a brick-and-mortar store to complete the purchase. Consider these statistics on the use of ratings and reviews:

- 95% of consumers report having read reviews before making a purchase decision.
- Two-thirds of consumers read between one and ten reviews before making a purchase.

■ 70% of mobile shoppers are more likely to purchase if the mobile site or app includes reviews. 82% seek out negative reviews as an indicator of authenticity.
■ 60% have viewed a review on their smartphone while shopping in-store.

In other words, this isn't casual behaviour. Shoppers are intensely studying reviews to improve their purchase decisions. Researching products online makes sense—it can save time, increase confidence, and reduce the risk that might be associated with the purchase. It also ensures better, more credible information. Besides using opinions early in the decision process, consumers may also use ratings and reviews as a form of validation just before a purchase. This is called *verification*. Buyers seek out information online early in the purchase process, and then many returns validate the decision. Many later also write reviews and rate products in the post-purchase stage (the Second Moment of Truth—SMOT). Because reviews are so influential, retailers are inviting customers to rate their experience and write a review soon after products are delivered. Recommendations from friends and family are all around us, and the prevalence of social media in the lives of wired consumers heightens our ability to share these opinions. The average consumer mentions specific brands in conversations with others more than 60 times a week. Just imagine how those influential impressions can travel when shared via social networks. This number could increase as people use social media to seek out recommendations. A study by researchers at Penn State found that 20% of Twitter posts were from people asking for or providing product information (Zhang, M. et al.2010).

Recommendations and referrals can be simple or integrated into their execution. Facebook's "like" button, now available on millions of external web pages, is a form of recommendation. When you click it, you publicly announce that you recommend the content on the page. While others can see the total number of "likes," anyone in your network can also see that you made a recommendation. This information also influences the consumer's alternative evaluation stage, with shoppers reporting that they read reviews to evaluate options both for products and retailers, compared prices and checked for deals, and considered the opinions of others. Whereas ratings and reviews are visible to everyone who wishes to see them, recommendations and referrals originate from the recipient's social graph. This makes them more influential than reviews and ratings because they leverage the social capital of the referrer. A Harris Interactive poll found that

71% of respondents said recommendations from family and friends have a substantial influence on their purchase decisions. And while we tend to trust reviews from strangers, we are more trusting of recommendations from people we know; 90% of the respondents to the survey said they trust an online recommendation from someone in their network.

Social Commerce Strategies

The first level of social commerce strategy is to utilise user-generated content, encourage it, and facilitate it with social sharing and shopping functionalities customers want, providing tools that make content creation and. sharing of word-of-mouth communication via social media easy and rewarding. At the simplest level, an online retailer can include sharing tools on its website. These tools may enable visitors to tweet an item, pin a picture to Pinterest, or save an item. More engaging tools include those that enable site visitors to create social video testimonials using their mobile phones (with social software apps like Video Genie) or to "share stories" in an onsite gallery. eMarketer estimates that 94% of major online retailers now include such social sharing tools on their websites. Online retailers can also enable other features that, while not user-generated, are based on user behaviour and still represent a kind of social recommendation. These social commerce tools can encourage sales, brand loyalty, and advocacy. Wish lists, gift lists, and similarity recommendations (e.g., "others who bought this also bought") are examples. Here's a summary of the opportunities marketers can provide to encourage social commerce sharing that may facilitate sales:

■ Share tools: These are social software plug-ins that enable easy sharing of products sold on a retailer's website on social networks. The most popular plug-in today for retailers is Pinterest. This sharing is a form of recommendation, in that others in the user's social graph can treat the pin as an endorsement.
■ Recommendation indicators: These are simple buttons that provide an onsite endorsement of a product. The most common options are Facebook's "like" and Google's +! buttons.
■ Reviews and ratings: These are onsite reviews and ratings with tools for writing and rating.

■ Testimonials: These are a form of recommendation that enables users to share a more personal story about their experience, possibly as a video endorsement.

■ User galleries: These are virtual galleries where users can share their creations, shopping lists, and wish lists. This approach is sometimes called user-curated shopping and may occur onsite or offsite in a community like Wanelo.

■ Pick lists: These are lists that help shoppers share what they want onsite, typically in the form of a wish list.

■ Popularity filters: These are filters that enable the shopper to show products by most popular, most viewed, most favourite, or most commented on.

■ User forums: These are groups of people who meet online to communicate about products and help each other solve related problems.

Social Promotions and Partnerships

In addition to leveraging user-generated content both through onsite tools and cross-platform partnerships, marketers can also facilitate sales using sales promotions offered through social deal partners and shopping carts on social vehicles like Facebook and Twitter. The most extensive format would be to truly socialise the shopping function on the retailer's website. A few adventurous retailers gave this a shot (most notably, Levi's), but thus far, full implementation has not gained momentum. Amazon is perhaps the world's most friendly retailer for social shopping, but synchronous, shared online shopping experiences are still not featured. Another form is to provide shopping from within the SNS. Facebook offers shopping from brand profile pages with its "Shop Now" button. Purchases are also enabled through Pinterest's "Rich Pins," Instagram's "Shoppable Stories," and Snapchat's "Deep Links." Facebook has experienced the greatest success, with 86% of retailers identifying it as their most important social network for promoting specific products. Shopify reported that Facebook drove two-thirds of the visits to Shopify-operated stores, with an average order value worldwide of $55.00. Pinterest had an average order value of $58.95 but drove fewer visits. The best vehicle with which to partner also depends on the type of retailer. Pinterest generated 74% of social orders in the antiques and collectibles industry at Shopify-operated stores.

Marketers can also partner with other sites, like social shopping portals. Some shopping portals enable users to share products they "want, need, or love," which are linked to the product's page on the retailer's website. This enables the conversion from browsing to truly buying. Some portals think of themselves as a digital mall where users can post favourite items and comment and share them with friends. Users link their favourites to specific retailer websites so that sales can be driven from Wanelo to the retailer's site. It can be described as a multi-retailer catalogue built as a social network. Products are listed with a "buy" button that connects to the retailer. To summarise, these more integrated approaches e-retailers can take for social commerce include offering sales promotions and social shopping opportunities, often with a partnering company. Marketers can use social commerce in several ways. The simplest approach is to encourage social sharing of the brand's offerings by providing sharing tools on the site. Some of these tools will result in recommendations and referrals. Creating a campaign that encourages fans to create user-curated shopping lists or enabling a space for reviews and ratings can encourage other content. Conversion can be enhanced with social deals and campaigns planned with partners and with in-network shopping functionalities.

Social Commerce Fraud

Social media has become a breeding ground for cybercrime-related activity, attracting fraudsters from around the world who take advantage of these platforms because they are free, are easy to use, and offer a global reach. One of the most frequent tactics is to pose as a legitimate brand on social media. The fraudsters then scam customers while undermining the brand's reputation and creating negative brand sentiment. A study to discover the extent of social media brand fraud analysed nearly 5,000 brand profiles on Twitter, Facebook, YouTube, and Instagram. It found that nearly 20% of social media brand profiles were fake accounts. The fraudulent accounts were used to offer counterfeit products and services, phish for personally identifiable information (PII), infect victims with malware, and maliciously attack brands. Some fraudulent pages are created solely to generate ad revenue. Enterprising fraudsters use brand identities to trick followers into visiting junk websites. These sites then spam customers with ads or download adware onto their computers. Advertising fraud accounted for more than two-thirds of the fraudulent accounts identified in the study. Some are motivated by a political agenda and create fraudulent accounts to attack a brand's image. Most often, they closely imitate the brand to make fun of the company or its customers. These protest accounts diminish the brand value and create a negative or even hostile experience for customers. Social media fraudsters target users with the same "bait" they use in other cyberattacks. This includes legitimate-looking content with offers that appear too good to pass up. Fake accounts so closely resemble the real corporate accounts that telling them apart can be difficult for novice users. They often retain the company's look and feel, including official logos. Why are social shoppers susceptible to social commerce fraud? There are several possible reasons. In social commerce, almost anyone can become an online seller because they do not have to invest in a website or pay for access to online marketplaces. Online social media's ability to provide anonymity can attract dishonest sellers or con artists who prey on unsuspecting consumers. People also tend to trust online reviews and recommendations, even though we don't know the people who provided them. Social commerce fraudsters use trust appeals to leverage this norm, even faking reviews and celebrity endorsements. Fraudulent accounts can also inflate the likes and followers of the account to suggest that the accounts are real and endorsed by others.

The Social Commerce Zone

No matter the number of times or the types of places you choose to shop, shopping remains an exciting activity. It is even better when it is done in groups—even when your shopping buddies don't agree with your choices. Our shopping companions, known among marketers as purchase pals, help us to think through our alternatives and make a decision. They validate the choices we make. When we don't have a purchasing pal with us, we might turn to surrogate pals like sales associates and other shoppers. Shopping together can be a shared activity that strengthens our relationships with others but also reduces the risks we associate with making purchase decisions. Perhaps this has been one reason for the prevalence of in-store shopping over online shopping. E-commerce may finally have a solution for those who hate to shop alone but who would still rather browse online while in their comfortable environments: *social commerce.*

Social commerce is a sub-set of e-commerce (i.e., the practice of buying and selling products and services via the internet). It uses social media applications to enable online shoppers to interact and collaborate during the shopping experience. It also assists buyers in completing the stages of the purchase decision process, as well as assisting marketers in selling to customers. Social commerce encompasses social shopping, social marketplaces, hybrid channels, and tools that enable shared participation in a buying decision. Thus, social commerce enables people, both networks of buyers and sellers, to participate actively in the marketing and selling of products and services in online marketplaces and communities. Social commerce lets consumers share product information electronically, easily post opinions and access the opinions of others, and communicate with friends, family, and associates about shopping decisions without regard to place or time. Whenever consumers navigate product information online using social commerce tools, such as bookmarking their favourite products, emailing product summaries, and subscribing to Really Simple Syndication (RSS) feeds of other users' favourite product lists, they are social shopping. Social shopping provides utility to our shopping experience because it lowers our perceived risk. We can feel more certain, by using social shopping tools, that we got the best price, made the best choice, and knew whether our friends would approve of our decision. It's the digital answer to our desire as consumers to shop with others—but with the added convenience and power of online technologies.

The *social commerce zone* is a part of e-commerce, where people buy and sell products on the internet. Social commerce provides a means for interactive shopping, including reviews, ratings, and social shopping. There are websites where you can chat with merchant personnel or with friends while you are shopping.

Types of Social Commerce Zones

- **Social communities** are channels that focus on activities and relationships and include social networking sites (online hosts such as Facebook and LinkedIn), forums, wikis, and message boards.
- **Social publishing** helps distribute information to different audiences and includes channels such as blogs (web log sites with content that is updated regularly) and media sharing sites with searchable content featuring videos (YouTube), photos (Flickr), and music and podcasts (iTunes).
- **Social commerce** is e-commerce territory where people buy and sell products on the internet. Social commerce provides a means for

interactive shopping, including reviews, ratings, and social shopping websites where you can chat with merchant personnel or with friends while you are shopping.

■ **Social entertainment is** an opportunity for games and entertainment. Social games like FarmVille, entertainment networks, action games, puzzle games, and reality games have increased revenues in the social gaming industry.

Psychology of Influence

Social media marketers who want to win customers find it helpful to understand what we know more generally about the psychology of influence—the factors that make it more or less likely that people will change their attitudes or behaviour based on a persuasive message. Some social shopping tools play to our cognitive biases, the "shortcuts" our brains take when we process information. Unlike computers that impassively process data and produce the same result each time (when they work!), humans aren't so rational. Two people can perceive the same event and interpret it quite differently based on their individual histories, genders, and cultural biases. For example, our reactions to colours are partially "coloured" by our society, so a North American might interpret a woman in a white dress as an "innocent bride," while an Asian might assume the same woman is going to a funeral since white is the colour of death in some Eastern cultures.

Cognitive biases are important when we look at purchase decisions, especially because they influence what we may pay attention to and how we interpret it. Even though consumers have access to more information than ever before when it comes to purchasing decisions, they are also faced with the limitations of bounded rationality. Bounded rationality captures the quandary we face as humans when we have choices to make but are limited by our cognitive capacity. As consumers, we typically start by conducting an information search and then evaluating potential alternatives. With thousands of online retailers carrying products, millions of product reviews to sort through, and hundreds of "friends" to ask for recommendations, online commerce is fraught with information overload; there's simply too much data for us to handle.

When consumers are confronted with more complexity than they can manage comfortably, bounded rationality kicks in. We adjust to the overload by finding ways to make decisions without considering all the information for an optimal choice. Instead, we are often satisfied—this means we expend just enough effort to decide what's acceptable but not necessarily the one that's "best." We call the shortcuts we use to simplify the process *heuristics.* This term describes "rules of thumb" such as "buy the familiar brand name" and "if it's more expensive, it must be better."

This process of using heuristics to simplify the decision-making process is sometimes referred to as thin slicing, where we peel off just enough information to make a choice. When we thin slice, we ignore most of the available information; instead, we "slice off" a few salient cues and use a mental rule of thumb to make intuitive decisions.

The psychology of influence identifies six major factors that help determine how we will decide.

Social Proof

We arrive at many decisions by observing what those around us do in similar situations. When a lot of people select one option (e.g., a clothing style or a restaurant), we interpret this popularity as social proof that the choice is the right one. There are several ways that marketers use social proof. For instance, identifying brands as the number one choice, the market leader, and so on all point to evidence of social proof. In social commerce applications, tools can enable shoppers to see the social proof related to the product. Although in every age there certainly are those who "march to their own drum," most people tend to follow society's expectations regarding how they should act and look (with a little improvisation here and there, of course). Conformity is a change in beliefs or actions as a reaction to real or imagined group pressure. For a society to function, its members must develop norms or informal rules that govern behaviour. Without these rules, we would have chaos. Imagine the confusion if a simple norm such as stopping at a red traffic light did not exist. We conform in many small ways every day, even though we don't always realise it. Unspoken rules govern many aspects of consumption. In addition to norms regarding the appropriate use of clothing and other personal items, we conform to rules that include gift-giving (we expect birthday presents from loved ones and get upset if they don't materialise), sex roles (men often pick up the check on a first date), and personal hygiene (our friends expect us to shower regularly). We don't mimic others' behaviours all the time, so what makes it more likely we'll conform? These are some common culprits:

- **Cultural pressures:** Different cultures encourage conformity to a greater or lesser degree. The American slogan "Do your own thing" in the 1960s reflected a movement away from conformity and towards individualism. In contrast, Japanese society emphasises collective well-being and group loyalty over individual needs.

- **Fear of deviance:** The individual may have reason to believe that the group will apply sanctions to punish nonconforming behaviours. It's not unusual to observe adolescents who shun a peer who is "different," or a corporation or university that passes over a person for promotion because she or he is not a "team player."

- **Commitment:** The more people are dedicated to a group and value their membership in it, the greater their motivation to conform to the group's wishes. Rock groupies and followers of TV evangelists may do anything their idols ask of them, and terrorists can be willing to die for their cause. According to the principle of least interest, the person who is least committed to staying in a relationship has the most power because that party doesn't care as much if the other person rejects him or her. Remember that on your next date.

- **Group unanimity, size, and expertise:** As groups gain in power, compliance increases. It is often harder to resist the demands of many people than only a few—especially when a "mob mentality" rules.

- **Susceptibility to interpersonal influence:** This trait refers to an individual's need to have others think highly of him or her. Consumers who don't possess this trait are role-relaxed; they tend to be older, affluent, and have high self-confidence.

Any content that we can share with others includes a social proof component. When you choose items for an online wish list and then share that list with your network of friends, you've given your friends social proof that the items listed are desirable. Testimonials have long been a source of social proof that a product is the right one to choose. Social tools such as TikTok make it possible for customers to share their stories with video clips they record with their mobile phones or webcams. At one time, testimonials were limited to those of typical person endorsers, celebrity endorsers, or word-of-mouth communication. Now, users can share testimonials with a written story, comments, or a video.

Authority

The second source of influence is authority. Authority persuades with the opinion or recommendation of an expert in the field. Whenever someone has expertise, whether that expertise comes from specialist knowledge and/ or personal experience with the product or problem, we will tend to follow that person's advice. We can save time and energy on the decision by simply following the expert's recommendation. In advertising, we see the use of authority in ads for pain relievers that state "9 out of 10 doctors recommend." A doctor should know which medicine is best for pain, and the copy in the advertisement delivers this advice. However, the use of authority is also in play when we see ads from someone who has experience with choosing a product for a specific functional need. For example, when a renowned athlete endorses a beverage, it's not based on credentials around nutrition but rather on their personal experience with needing a beverage that can rehydrate them efficiently. We listen to them because, as elite athletes, they ought to know which product is best. In the realm of social media, authority can be activated in several ways, including referral programmes, reviews (from experts as well as from existing customers who can speak with the voice of experience), branded services, and user forums. Although citizen endorsers are not paid agents representing a brand, they do hold a position of authority in the minds of other consumers. Professional experts and reviewers, whether book critics, movie critics, doctors, or lawyers, have authority in specific, relevant product categories, but so do citizen endorsers who have used the product. In other words, one's experience with the product serves as a source of authority.

Affinity

Affinity, sometimes called "liking," means that people tend to follow and emulate those people whom they find attractive or otherwise desirable. If we like someone, we are more likely to say yes to their requests or to internalise their beliefs and actions as our own. We talked about how advertising often uses endorsers as a source of authority. They can also be used as a source of affinity. While an athlete may be an expert when it comes to whether a beverage is the best choice for hydration during times of physical exertion, he is simply a likeable celebrity when he endorses Timex watches. With social media, affinity is almost always present because social shopping is tied to your social graph—to your friendships. Some tools that leverage affinity as a source of influence are "ask your network" tools that enable shoppers to request real-time recommendations from their friends, deal feeds (where friends share deals), shopping opportunities posted in friends' news feeds, pick lists, referral programmes, sharing tools, and shop together tools.

Scarcity

We tend to instinctively want things more if we think we can't have them. That's the principle of scarcity at work. Whenever we perceive something as scarce, we increase our efforts to acquire it, even if that means we must pay a premium for the item and buy it before we would otherwise have wanted it. Marketing promotions that use scarcity as an influence tool might focus on time-sensitive deals, limited-edition products, or products (Source: Authors, 2023). that are limited in supply. In social commerce, scarcity applications include deal feeds, news feeds with special offers, group buy tools, referral programmes, and deal directories.

Reciprocity

The rule of reciprocity says that we have an embedded urge to repay debts and favours, whether we request help or not. Reciprocity is a common norm of behaviour across cultures. We reciprocate kindnesses in part because we feel it is the fair and right thing to do (a social contract we have with others) and in part because reciprocation is important to well-functioning relationships. Reciprocity influences daily interactions all around us. It may be as simple as choosing a birthday present for someone for whom you wouldn't normally buy a present, but you do because they gave you a gift on your birthday. Marketers activate the rule of reciprocity to encourage consumers to choose a specific brand and to show loyalty to the brand over time. The key is to initiate an offer of some kindness, gift, or favour to the target audience. The targeted consumers will then feel compelled to respond in kind.

This is the basic principle behind the sales promotion technique of sampling, where a marketer offers a free trial of a product to consumers. The free trial illustrates the relative advantage of the product, but it also creates the perception of having received a gift in the minds of consumers. Consequently, sales of sampled products are higher than those of products that are not sampled. Some retailers send birthday and holiday cards to their top clients. Even something as simple as a greeting card can be perceived as kindness that should be reciprocated. In social commerce, several tools can be perceived as a favour or kindness offered by the brand. These include deal feeds, group buys, referral programmes, and user forums.

Consistency

People strive to be consistent with their beliefs and attitudes and with past behaviours. When we fail to behave in ways that are consistent with our attitudes and past behaviours, we feel cognitive dissonance, a state of psychological discomfort caused when things we know and do contradict one another. For example, a person may believe it's wrong or wasteful to gamble, yet be drawn to an online gambling site. To avoid this discomfort, we strive for consistency by changing one or more elements in the situation. Thus, our gambler may decide that he or she is betting on the house only due to "intellectual curiosity" rather than the thrill of betting. The need for consistency is a broad source of influence because it can be activated around any attitude or behaviour. Marketers may instigate the need for consistency with image ads, free trial periods, automated renewals, and membership offers.

Some of the social shopping tools that include a consistency component include asking your network, social games, pick lists, sharing tools, shopping together tools, reviews, forums, and galleries.

CASE STUDY 4

MANTRA BAND LEVERAGES USER-GENERATED REVIEWS TO DRIVE SALES

When Aysel Gunar was a student in business school, she created her first bracelet. Jewellery-making is a popular hobby for creative adults, and many have launched profitable businesses featuring original and handmade jewellery. That's not what Aysel had in mind. The founder and CEO of Mantra Band said she was simply "looking for a way to be more present and mindful in my day-to-day life." With that in mind, she created her first bracelet with the words "Live in the Moment." Fast forward a few years, and that simple concept is the foundation of a successful online company. Mantra Band uses Shopify to commercialise its Facebook page. With Shopify, customers can shop directly from Facebook. The social commerce functionality is further enhanced with Yapto, a social commerce app that optimises user-generated content (UGC) across multiple

SNSs. Yapto automates requests for customer reviews post-purchase and incentivises users to submit photos too. The content can then be shared on Mantra Band's Facebook page as well as on Instagram Stories and Rich Pins on Pinterest, all such that the UGC itself is in essence a shoppable ad for Mantra Band. The app also curates organic UGC about Mantra Band from Instagram, Facebook, and Twitter so the company can analyse customer feedback and repurpose the UGC across its social media channels. Aysel attributes the open dialogue Mantra Band has with customers on the social commerce app, emphasising the trust and social proof reviews provide.

RESULTS AND OUTCOMES

The results? Mantra Band earned 36,000 5-star reviews. Customer retention was driven by coupons delivered through the app to stimulate another purchase. The proof is in the conversion rate: a 550% lift in conversions! Check out Mantra Band's engagement on its Facebook page, where, in addition to thousands of reviews, fans have contributed hundreds of photos and comments: www.facebook.com/mantrabands.

Benefits of Social Commerce

So far, we've talked about the ways that marketers can approach social commerce. But what benefits does social commerce offer to marketers?

1. It enables the marketer to monetise the social media investment by boosting site and store traffic, converting browsers to buyers and increasing average order value.
2. It solves the dilemma of social media return on investment (ROI). ROI is a metric for determining how much value an investment generated. Some criticise social media for its lack of accountability, but linking sales to social media eliminates this criticism.
3. Social commerce applications result in more data about customer behaviour as it relates to the brand.
4. Social shopping applications enhance the customer experience. They make online shopping fun and functional, which should mean higher levels of customer loyalty and better long-term customer lifetime value.

5. Social shopping makes sharing brand impressions easy. The brands earn referral value with these easy-to-use word-of-mouth tools.
6. Brands can keep up with the competition and maybe differentiate themselves from others in the e-commerce space.

The Influence of Social Media and Customer Ratings on Social Shopping

Social media users rely on social commerce at every stage of the decision-making process. Social commerce is a part of e-commerce, and it leverages social media to aid in the exchange process between buyers and sellers. Social media is sufficiently complex and broad to influence e-commerce in all five of the consumer decision-making stages. Social media users rely on social commerce the least in the purchase stage. This may change as marketers improve their social shopping experience and use new technologies like conversational commerce using chatbots in social messaging apps.

Ratings are simply scored by people, acting in the role of the critic, and assigned to something as an indicator. The rating may reflect perceived quality, satisfaction with the purchase, popularity, or some other variable. Reviews are assessments with detailed comments about the object in question. They explain and justify the critic's assigned rating and provide added

Figure 3.1   Workplace wellbeing. Source: Authors (2024)

Table 3.1   Social Commerce Tools for Purchase Decision Stages

Decision Stage	Social Commerce Tools
Problem Recognition	Social ads on social networking sites Shared endorsements from friends posted in activity streams Curated images and lists on sites like Pintrest Local ion-based promotions (e g.. Yelp) Participatory commerce (e.g.. Kicks tarter)
Information Search	Comments (influence impressions) throughout social channels (opinions posted on a brand's Wall, tweets about an experience, etc.) Queries end responses within social networks (e.g.. Linked -Inn and Facebook) Ratings and reviews posted on sites (eg.. Yelp. Zagat.) Product and pricing information tagged to image posts Social search queries on SNS Wish lists, gift registries
Evaluation of Alternatives	Barcode scanning/price comparisons Recommendations, testimonials, recommendation agents, and popularity titters (ask your network- apps, video testimonials such as Video Genie. and top lists from retailers such as Amazon) Ratings and reviews Referrals
Purchase	Shop within network options (e.g.. Fac e-book Buy. Insta-Shop) Social shopping malls (e g., Wanolo) Peer-to-peer marketplaces (e.g., Etsy) Group buys (e g., LivingSocial. Groupon) Conversational commerce (chatbot services)
Post-Purchase	Comments posted on SNS Requesl lor help or com ment to brand on SNS Participation m loyalty program with social benefits Ratings and reviews on review sites and retailer website Reviews end product experiences posted on blogs

Source: Authors (2024)

content to those viewing the content. Both serve as a source of research during the information search and evaluation of alternatives stages of the buying process and as a tool for verifying a decision before the purchase. For retailers, positive reviews generate increased sales by bringing in new customers. Further, people who write reviews tend to shop more frequently and spend more online than those who do not write reviews. Consumers are willing to pay a price premium for products with higher ratings, too. Ratings and reviews also enhance organic search traffic to the website. It also helps to describe the psychological factors that influence social shopping. Research on the psychology of influence identifies six major factors that help to determine how we will decide; these can be applied to social commerce. These sources of influence are social proof, authority, affinity, scarcity, consistency, and reciprocity. Social proof occurs when we can see what others would choose or have chosen. Authority persuades with the opinion or recommendation of an expert in the field. Professional experts and reviewers, whether book critics, movie critics, doctors, or lawyers, have authority in specific, relevant product categories, but so do citizen endorsers who have acted on the product. Affinity, sometimes called "liking," means that people tend to

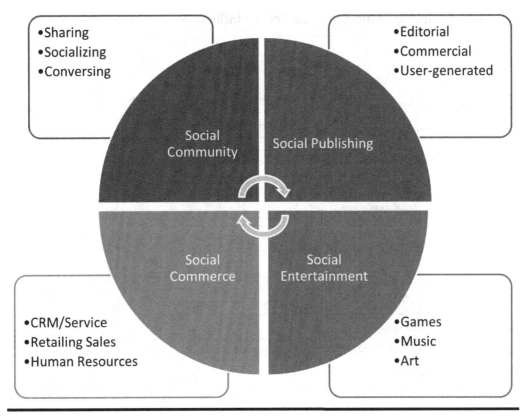

- Sharing
- Socializing
- Conversing

- Editorial
- Commercial
- User-generated

Social Community

Social Publishing

Social Commerce

Social Entertainment

- CRM/Service
- Retailing Sales
- Human Resources

- Games
- Music
- Art

Figure 3.2   The social commerce zone. Source: Tuten (2023)

follow and emulate those people for whom they have an affinity. With social media, affinity is almost always present because social shopping is tied to your social graph—to your friendships.

We tend to instinctively want things more if we think we can't have them—that's the principle of scarcity at work. In social commerce, scarcity applications include deal feeds, news feeds with special offers, group buy tools, referral programmes, and deal directories. Under the rule of reciprocity, we have an embedded urge to repay debts and favours, whether or not we request help. In social commerce, several tools can be perceived as a favour or kindness offered by the brand. These include deal feeds, group buys, referral programmes, and user forums. The final source of influence is our tendency to be consistent. People strive to be consistent with their beliefs and attitudes and with past behaviours. Some of the social shopping tools that include a consistency component include asking your network, social games, pick lists, sharing tools, shopping together tools, reviews, forums, and galleries.

Table 3.2   Social Shopping Tools and Source Influence

Social Shopping Tool	Social Proof	Authority	Scarcity	Affinity	Consistency	Reciprocity
"Ask your network"			•	•		
Brand butler services					*	*
Deal directories			*			
Deal feeds			*	•		*
Filters	*					
Group buy			*			
Lists			•	•		
Recommendations	*	*		*	*	
Referral programs		*		*	*	*
Reviews		*			*	
Share tools	*			•		
Shop together				*		
Storefronts			•			
Tes-timonia ls	*	*				
User forums	*	*				•
User galleries				*		*
Geo-location promotions			*	*		

Source: Authors (2024)

Figure 3.3   Review patterns. Source: Authors (2024)

What Influences the Credibility and Authenticity of the Reviews and Ratings Shoppers View?

Several factors are at play. People consider the source of the review (a user or product expert), the volume of ratings, and the valence (positive or negative). When a high volume of reviews and ratings are available, people tend to favour reviews from other typical people. The volume of reviews has a stronger impact on sales than the presence of negative reviews! When the review volume is low, opinions from experts such as bloggers or professional critics are preferred. People look for cues to judge their similarity to the reviewer and the reviewer's purchase context. Similarity increases trust in the review. Even the congruence between the shopper's opinion and that reflected in the reviews plays a role. In other words, even when users are searching for information to guide a decision, they are prone to confirmation bias. Reviews that focus on benefits to the consumer are more influential than those that focus on product attributes.

Even with 25% of online shoppers noting that they don't always consider online reviews to be fair or trustworthy, shoppers read the content and judge for themselves whether they feel a review is useful or not. Consumers trust the information provided by other consumers via social media more than television, magazine, radio, or internet advertising; more than sponsorships; and more than recommendations from salespeople or paid endorsers. The only source more trusted is recommendations from friends or family. The opinions of other typical users have far more influence on purchase decisions and brand attitudes than the content shared by the brand itself. What about microcelebrity influencers? A third of consumers say they are more likely to purchase a product endorsed by a non-celebrity blogger than by a celebrity.

By the time the shopper reaches the purchase point, he or she has used an average of ten sources of information, with about half being a source delivered via social media. These social media users rely on social commerce at every stage of the decision-making process, but not least at the purchase stage. This may change as marketers improve their social shopping experience and use new technologies like conversational commerce using chatbots in social messaging apps.

The Second Moment of Truth (SMOT), the experience of using the product, is just as relevant as it always was. The product has to be delivered according to the brand promise. This marks the beginning of the post-purchase evaluation phase in the decision-making process, where the consumer evaluates the purchase and experiences satisfaction or dissatisfaction. The customer may write reviews and post comments for others to use. This is a point in the customer journey during which social media users may post questions and comments directly to brands on the SNS. Social media is the most preferred communication channel for reaching company customer service representatives. It's preferred by more people than live chat on the company website, email, telephone, or in-store assistance. Brands using social media for customer care will be alerted to these posts and respond. Marcus Miller of Search Engine Land (Marcus Miller, 2016) calls this the Third Moment of Truth (TMOT), the moment of advocacy. Why? It's the critical juncture between a customer becoming a brand ambassador (if the communication was positive) or a customer becoming a hater. Most social media users expect a response from a business in under 4 hours, and 42% expect a response within 1 hour. Brands that respond quickly and effectively can turn complaints into positive experiences and compliments into delight. Sadly, most brands don't. 79% of customers expect a response to their social media posts within 24 hours. But even though 63% of social media complaints are responded to within 24 hours, only 32% of people are happy with their response time. And, while 39% of social media users expect a response within 60 minutes, the average response time for businesses is about 5 hours: https://blog.hubspot.com/service/social-media-response-time. Being ignored is an insult in the conversational realm of social media. And customers respond to this behaviour in kind: 36% of ignored customers say they will try to shame the company online, 29% say they intend to switch to a competitor for future purchases, and 14% say they write negative reviews. While the customer being ignored may be happy and show brand love, future use and brand loyalty are both damaged (Robertson et al., 2022).

The marketing value of social commerce marketers will be influenced by social commerce activities, whether they choose to engage in them or not. That's because the reputation economy in which we live ensures that there is a publishing platform for individuals. We see content creation increase with access to social channels and communities, social software, and digital devices. Regardless of whether a brand is active, this content will be generated and will be accessible through a search online. For instance, one study of Yelp reviews looked at over 4,000 small businesses with reviews on its site. None of the businesses were also engaging in advertising on Yelp. Fortunately for them, they still benefited.

The study revealed that unsolicited, organic Yelp reviews were associated with increases in revenue of $8,000 annually on average. What's more, brands that facilitated a presence on Yelp saw an average uptick of $23,000.35. Another study found that for independent restaurants, a one-star rating increase on Yelp was associated with an annual increase in revenues of 5%–9%.

Product opinions affect shoppers, but that isn't the only way they impact the marketing process. Online reviews generate increased sales by bringing in new customers. Further, people who write reviews tend to shop more frequently and spend more online than those who do not write reviews. Those who review products make up just a quarter of online shoppers, but they account for a third of online sales. And consumers are willing to pay a price premium for products with higher ratings. For e-retailers, this means that it makes good business sense to host ratings and reviews of features. Ratings and reviews also enhance organic search traffic to the website. Organic search results improve because reviewers tend to use the same keywords (tags) in their product descriptions that searchers will use. Petco, a pet supplies retailer, found that having customer reviews on its website generated five times as many site visits as any previous advertising campaign. Those who browsed Petco's top-rated products had a 49% higher conversion rate than the site average and an average order amount that was 63% higher than the site average.

Best Practices for Leveraging Social Reviews and Ratings

Ultimately, it's important to remember that users are reading online reviews because they want to know what people like themselves think of a product. They must be able to trust those reviews; if they can't, the reviews won't be effective. In general, people trust reviews shared on social media, but brands must be stewards of that trust. Estimates suggest that as much as 30% of online reviews are fraudulent. Reviews likely to be deceptive tend to include information that is not related to product use and lack verified purchase information. Customers who have not purchased the product in question or marketers (on their products or for rival brands) may provide these reviews. Researchers estimate that legitimate reviews may come from as few as 1.5% of reviewers.

Amazon has taken steps to maintain the integrity of its customer review system, which millions of consumers rely on to make smart purchase decisions and avoid faulty or substandard products. In some cases, Amazon has even sued individuals who offered incentivised reviews, which are reviews of a product that were received for free or at a discount in exchange for the review. A study of 65 million reviews across 32,000 product categories on Amazon by Review Meta found that incentivised reviewers were significantly less likely than non-incentivised reviewers to give a one-star rating and four times less likely to be critical in the review.

Incentivised reviewers also review hundreds of products on average, potentially inflating sales performance for otherwise mediocre-quality products. In response, Amazon updated its community guidelines to prohibit incentivised reviews (Jamshidi, S. et al., 2019).

What other steps should marketers take? To make the most of the opportunity, marketers should develop a social commerce approach with these characteristics:

■ Authenticity: Accept organic word-of-mouth, whether positive or negative.
■ Transparency: Acknowledge opinions that the brand invited, encouraged, or facilitated.
■ Advocacy: Enable consumers to rate the value of opinions offered on the site.
■ Participation: Encourage consumers to contribute posts.
■ Reciprocity: Acknowledge the value of the opinions that customers offer.
■ Infectiousness: Make it easy for users to share reviews on blogs and social networking platforms.
■ Sustainability: Online opinions are so influential because they live on in perpetuity. If a consumer tells a friend about a satisfying brand experience on the phone, the story once told is no longer retrievable or trackable.

What does this mean for marketers? First, marketers must ensure high standards when it comes to product quality and service if they wish to survive in the world of social reviews. It is so easy for anyone to tell everyone about his or her brand experiences, whether good or bad. That means those experiences had better be good. Those that fail will have their sordid story broadcast to the social world as customers submit reviews and those reviews are shared via social networks. Second, brands should embrace, not hide—because, really, online, there is no place to hide—consumer opinions. Instead, organisations can engage in word-of-mouth marketing by actively giving people reasons to talk about the brand while facilitating the conversations. There are five actions that brands can take to build valuable online reviews:

- Educating people about your products and services.
- Identifying people most likely to share their opinions.
- Providing tools that make it easier to share information.
- Studying how, where, and when opinions are being shared.
- Listening and responding to supporters, detractors, and neutrals.

In other words, marketers should encourage the conversation by informing consumers about the brand, offering consumers a forum for expressing opinions about the brand, and responding (making the communication two-way) to comments consumers make on the forum and elsewhere. Customers can be invited to offer reviews, resulting in more engagement and the propagation of positive word-of-mouth communication about the brand.

Perhaps most important is the final component of word-of-mouth marketing—listening. There is valuable information about the need for product improvements, like product features and service quality, embedded in ratings and reviews.

Why Don't All E-Retailers Offer Reviews and Ratings on Their Sites?

Aside from the problem that marketers and advertisers have overlooked their value and influence, the most cited reason given for not allowing online reviews on sites is the fear that dissatisfied customers will use the review feature as a venue to flame a brand. Given the adage that negative word-of-mouth communication is more damaging than positive word-of-mouth communication is beneficial, some retailers have erred on the side of caution when it comes to offering a review feature. The ratio of negative to positive reviews found on various sites suggests that this fear is unfounded.

Retailers can benefit from negative reviews and should welcome them. Consumers want to see negative reviews to be able to accurately assess the degree of product risk they face when purchasing. They seek to minimise perceived performance and financial risk associated with purchases. Negative reviews give them the information they need to assess risk. The negative reviews also enhance credibility. Consumers often assume that if the reviews seem too good to be true, they probably are. Lastly, negative reviews give valuable information to the retailer on products that should be improved, augmented, or discontinued.

Chapter Summary

Social commerce is a subset of e-commerce (i.e., the practice of buying and selling products and services via the internet). It uses social media and social media applications to enable online shoppers to interact and collaborate during the shopping experience and to assist retailers and customers during the process. Encompassing online ratings and reviews, applications, numerous shopping-related apps, deal sites and deal aggregators, and social shopping malls and storefronts, social commerce is the last zone of social media. Though most online shopping is performed using a desktop or laptop computer, mobile devices are driving much of the growth of social commerce. Consumers are increasingly completing their purchases online, with a comScore study suggesting that 44% of smartphone users had made purchases using their device rather than completing a transaction offline.

Review Questions

1. Explain the concept of purchase pals. Do you pull your offline and online purchase pals from the same pool of friends and family, or are they different somehow?
2. How is social commerce related to e-commerce? In the future, will e-commerce be able to exist without social applications? Why or why not?
3. What are the benefits that accrue to businesses implementing social shopping applications?
4. What is the distinction between social shopping and social commerce?
5. How are reviews different from recommendations? Why are ratings an important cue to include with a review site?
6. Explain the concept of bounded rationality as it relates to social shopping.
7. Which stage of the decision-making process is most affected by the dimensions of social commerce? Explain.
8. What is thin slicing?
9. Explain the six sources of influence prevalent in social commerce applications.
10. Search Instagram for brands you like. Can you buy the products you find? Is a recommendation tool included on the page? Can you add products to your shopping cart and check out from within the page? In your opinion, what could make the site more effective?

11. Which are more influential, reviews from experts or reviews from customers? Explain.
12. Review the list of social shopping applications presented in the chapter and visit some of the sites that use these applications. Social shopping applications provide functionality for customers, such as enhanced organisation, price comparisons, risk reduction, and access to product information, but they also make the shopping experience more fun. Tag the list of applications based on the benefit the application provides—utility or fun. Which aspect of social shopping is most important to shoppers?
13. How do you feel about reviews that are incentivised? Do you still trust them? How do you decide?
14. Of the tools of influence that can affect social commerce behaviour, are some more influential than others? Explain. How can marketers leverage each influence tool in social media marketing?

References

Algharabat, R. S., & Rana, N. P. (2021). Social commerce in emerging markets and its impact on online community engagement. *Information Systems Frontiers*, *23*, 1499–1520.

Busalim, A. H. (2016). Understanding social commerce: A systematic literature review and directions for further research. *International Journal of Information Management*, *36*, 1075–1088.

Esmaeili, L., & Hashemi, G. S. A. (2019). A systematic review on social commerce. *Journal of Strategic Marketing*, *27*(4), 317–355.

Jamshidi, S., Rejaie, R., & Li, J. (2019). Characterizing the dynamics and evolution of incentivized online reviews on Amazon. *Social Network Analysis and Mining*, *9*, 1–15.

Marcus, M. (2016, February 29). SEO & the zero moment of truth. *Search Engine Land*. Retrieved June 21, 2017, from http://searchengineland.com/seo-zero -moment-truth-242692

Meilatinova, N. (2021). Social commerce: Factors affecting customer repurchase and word-of-mouth intentions. *International Journal of Information Management*, *57*, 102300.

Olivares, L. I. F., Cheneffusse, F. A. C., & Grados, E. M. C. G. (2022). The origins and evolution of social commerce: Enhancing E-commerce platforms with social features. In *Proceedings of the 5th European International Conference on Industrial Engineering and Operations Management* Rome, Italy, July 26–28, 2022.

Robertson, J., Botha, E., Ferreira, C., & Pitt, L. (2022). How deep is your love? The brand love-loyalty matrix in consumer-brand relationships. *Journal of Business Research, 149*, 651–662.

Tuten, T. L. (2023). Social media marketing. Sage Publications Limited.

Wang, W., Chen, R. R., Ou, C. X., & Ren, S. J. (2019). Media or message, which is the king in social commerce? An empirical study of participants' intention to repost marketing messages on social media. *Computers in Human Behavior, 93*, 176–191.

Wang, X., Wang, H., & Zhang, C. (2022). A literature review of social commerce research from systems thinking perspective. *Systems, 10*(3), 56.

Zhang, Z., Ye, Q., Law, R., & Li, Y. (2010). The impact of e-word-of-mouth on the online popularity of restaurants: A comparison of consumer reviews and editor reviews. *International Journal of Hospitality Management, 29*(4), 694–700.

Chapter 4

Mobile Ecosystems and Apps in Social Media Marketing

Chapter Outline

- Mobile network technologies
- Generations in mobile network technologies
- Wireless and mobile devices
- Mobile financial services and payment applications
- Mobile apps and social media
- Case studies on mobile platforms and applications
- Mobile network technologies

Chapter Outcome

By the end of this chapter, the reader will be able to:

Explain mobile network technologies:
- Demonstrate a comprehensive understanding of mobile network technologies through clear and concise explanations.

Identify types of mobile network technologies:
- Demonstrate the ability to recognise and apply knowledge of specific mobile network technologies in real-world scenarios.

DOI: 10.4324/9781003307457-4

Explain mobile financial services and payment systems:
■ Analyse the components and functionalities of mobile financial services and payment systems and the role of mobile technologies within this landscape.

Identify key challenges associated with mobile payment applications:
■ Evaluate and identify key challenges related to the implementation and usage of mobile payment applications.

Introduction

This chapter explores the complex landscape of mobile network technologies, which serve as the fundamental infrastructure for contemporary communication, particularly within the context of corporate operations. As we traverse this terrain, we shall examine the complex network of connectivity alternatives accessible on portable devices, each fulfilling certain functions and presenting distinctive advantages. The initiation of our expedition will entail a comprehensive comprehension of fundamental technologies, namely Bluetooth, an essential component in the realm of short-range wireless communication; and Wireless Application Protocol (WAP), which established the fundamental framework for mobile internet browsing. Subsequently, we shall delve into the domain of location-based services and navigation, elucidated by the Global Positioning System (GPS), a technological innovation that has significantly transformed the fields of travel and logistics. Moreover, this chapter will provide an introduction to two significant technologies, namely Worldwide Interoperability for Microwave Access (WiMax) and General Packet Radio Service (GPRS). It will emphasise their respective contributions in the realm of enhancing internet accessibility and facilitating data communication capabilities.

Throughout this discourse, readers will acquire a comprehensive understanding of Enhanced Data for Global Evolution (EDGE) and Wireless Fidelity (WiFi), technological advancements that have substantially enhanced the velocity and dependability of mobile internet connectivity. The discourse will conclude with an analysis of High-Speed Downlink Packet Access (HSDPA), a technological innovation that represents the progress made in the field of high-speed mobile data transfer. In this chapter, we will examine the progression of mobile network technologies, starting from their modest origins characterised by basic data interchange between pagers and mobile phones and leading up to the contemporary environment where they facilitate a wide range of functionalities. These functionalities encompass a wide range of activities, including the seamless sharing of information, engaging in online gaming, and accessing multimedia content across several devices.

The focal point of our discourse will revolve around the use of modern technologies in corporate settings. This study aims to analyse the impact of technological advancements such as Bluetooth, WiFi, and GSM on the operational strategies of enterprises. As discussed by Shi et al. (2019), these innovations have significantly altered the corporate landscape by facilitating enhanced customer engagement, optimising operational processes, and creating innovative marketing avenues. By comprehending these technologies and their respective applications, individuals will possess the necessary knowledge to effectively utilise the complete capabilities of mobile connectivity in both their professional and personal spheres.

Definition of Terms

Standards and Protocols

Understanding the diverse landscape of mobile devices and their interoperability is crucial in today's technology-driven world. Various manufacturers produce a wide array of devices, each running on distinct software platforms. This diversity is evident in everyday scenarios, such as when a user with a Nokia phone successfully communicates with someone using a Motorola device, even if they are on different mobile networks. Seamless interaction across these varied devices and networks is made possible by adherence to universal standards. Standards in the mobile industry are akin to a common language that manufacturers agree to use, ensuring that their products can effectively communicate and operate with those from other companies. These standards are essential for the compatibility and functionality of different devices when connected. They play a pivotal role in enabling a Nokia handset to connect with, for instance, a Motorola phone, transcending the barriers of differing technologies and network infrastructures.

In addition to standards, the concept of a communications protocol is fundamental to the interaction of mobile devices. Protocols are sets of rules that govern the transmission and reception of data between connected devices. They define critical aspects of communication, such as the authentication process for users to gain access to information and the manner in which this information is presented on a device. These protocols ensure that, regardless of the device or manufacturer, there is a consistent and secure method for exchanging information. Expanding our understanding of standards and protocols not only provides insight into how different devices interact but also highlights the intricacy and sophistication of the technology that enables our interconnected world. By adhering to these established guidelines, manufacturers and mobile networks create an ecosystem where diverse technologies coexist and collaborate, paving the way for innovations and advancements in mobile communication.

Bandwidth

Bandwidth is a vital and pivotal concept within the realms of telecommunications and computers. It serves as a measure of a network's ability to facilitate the movement of data between various devices. Bandwidth is a metric frequently associated with concepts such as bit rate or "throughput," as it quantifies the capacity of a network connection to send data within a specific time frame. This metric is commonly expressed in bits per second (bps). According to research by Shastri et al. (2022), a thorough understanding of bandwidth is essential for evaluating the effectiveness and performance of communication systems. Building upon this given definition, it is important to note that bandwidth encompasses more than just the measurement of speed, as it serves as an indicator of the overall capacity of a network. From a practical standpoint, an increased bandwidth capacity enables a network to accommodate a greater volume of data, resulting in enhanced transmission speeds and improved efficiency in data management. This becomes particularly crucial in situations where there is a significant amount of data being transmitted, such as the streaming of high-definition videos, the execution of massive file transfers, or the management of several concurrent online activities.

The notion of bandwidth is subject to variability, contingent upon the specific network connection employed (e.g., fibre optic, wireless, or copper cable), the calibre of the network infrastructure, and the protocols employed for data transfer. Additionally, outside factors like network congestion, the distance between communication points, and weather conditions can affect the effective bandwidth. In the realm of mobile communications, notable progressions in cellular technologies, such as the transition from 3G to 4G and subsequently to 5G, have yielded substantial enhancements in bandwidth capacity. Consequently, these breakthroughs have resulted in notable improvements in data transfer speeds and the provision of more resilient internet experiences for end-users. The augmentation of bandwidth has played a crucial role in enabling the proliferation of data-intensive apps and services, thereby fundamentally transforming our modes of engagement with digital material and communication. Furthermore, the notion of bandwidth holds significant importance in the realm of network architecture and management. Network managers use bandwidth allocation as a crucial tool to enhance data transmission and ensure that critical applications have access to the resources they need for optimal performance. The comprehension of bandwidth by consumers facilitates the making of well-informed choices in the selection of internet service providers or mobile plans, or the configuration of networks to cater to specific requirements. The advancement of technology has led to a persistent focus on achieving greater bandwidth, which serves as a significant catalyst for advancements in network architecture and internet technologies. The technology assumes a crucial role in influencing the trajectory of digital communication and facilitating novel prospects in connectivity, entertainment, and business operations.

Types of Mobile Network Technologies

A network is a connection that allows multiple devices to communicate and share information and other resources. In a telephone network, for instance, multiple desk phones are connected via cables so that voice can be transmitted across an office, country, or continent. Even though desk phones are fixed, there are currently mobile devices that can be moved from one location to another. Additionally, these devices can connect to establish a mobile network. These mobile devices are connected through mobile network technologies. Some of these technologies are outlined in Figure 4.1 below and further discussed in the sections that follow.

Figure 4.1 shows the types of mobile network technologies.

Bluetooth

Bluetooth is a mobile or wireless technology standard for exchanging data over distances of up to 100 metres. This standard is open, indicating that anyone is free to incorporate it into their devices for a variety of purposes. For instance, while some mobile phones can use Bluetooth to transmit information to another phone, another mobile phone can be used as a remote

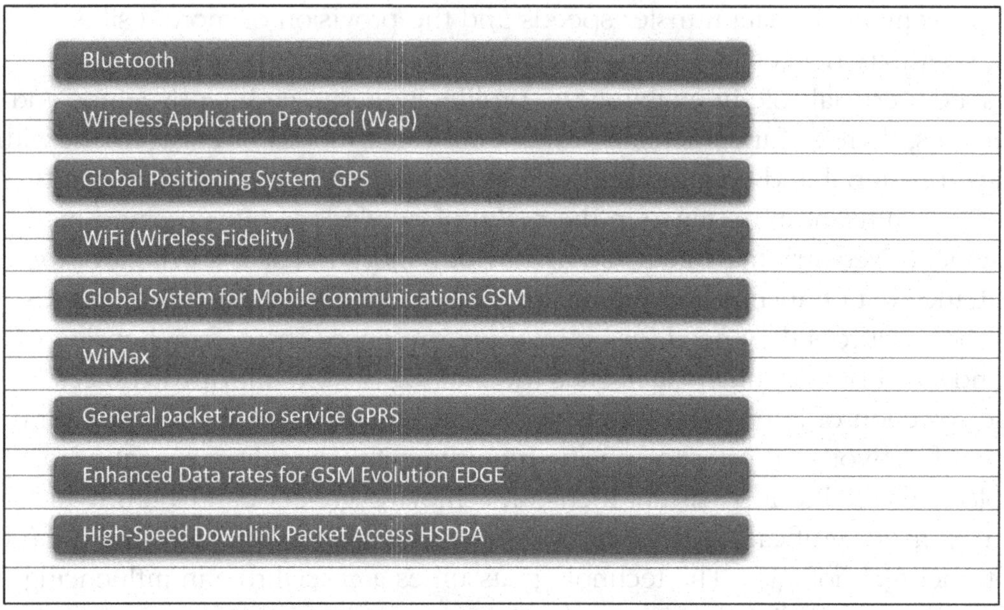

Bluetooth

Wireless Application Protocol (Wap)

Global Positioning System GPS

WiFi (Wireless Fidelity)

Global System for Mobile communications GSM

WiMax

General packet radio service GPRS

Enhanced Data rates for GSM Evolution EDGE

High-Speed Downlink Packet Access HSDPA

Figure 4.1   Types of mobile network technologies

control for a Bluetooth-enabled television. By connecting Bluetooth-enabled devices, a personal area network (PAN) is created (Sevier & Tekeoglu, 2019).

WAP

WAP means Wireless Application Protocol. It is a set of protocols for connecting cellular phones and other radio devices to the internet. Sometimes used to refer to the mobile web, WAP is a means through which mobile phones access information on the internet. There is no need to download special applications to access the information because, most often, the mobile device has its own software called the WAP browser. However, WAP has limited usage abilities; one cannot download some kinds of information, like videos.

GPS

The Global Positioning System (GPS) is a technology mainly for the provision of information about geographical location. There is a purpose-built satellite navigation system based in space to provide such information no matter the weather conditions, so long as the location is anywhere on or near the Earth. Such a service is available to anyone with a device that has a GPS receiver embedded in it. The information provided by the system is important for military, civil, and commercial users around the world. When the GPS-enabled device receives the information from the satellites, it can calculate and display its position either as a moving object on a map or latitude and longitude. GPS can be used in business to monitor an organisation's assets, like vehicles and workers (Milner, 2016).

WiFi (Wireless Fidelity)

WiFi is a local area network (LAN), a network within a small area, such as a building, that employs high-frequency radio signals to transmit and receive data over a few hundred feet. It enables an electronic device to exchange data over a computer network without using network cables. Typically, it is used to connect mobile devices, such as portable computers and smart-phones, to the internet (Naraine et al., 2020). Currently, some businesses charge a fee for wireless internet access. A voucher comprising a login ID and password is purchased by interested users in order to connect to the network. Organisations such as universities offer authorised members or students with their own devices free wireless internet connectivity. Airports, hotels, and restaurants can also offer wireless internet access to attract consumers and promote their businesses. The region where wireless signals can be received is typically referred to as a "hotspot" (Galkin et al., 2019). WiFi is used because it is a cost-effective way to create a local area network. It is also advantageous for outdoor areas and tourist destinations where cables cannot be installed. Current computers and mobile phones include wireless network adapters for this purpose. Regardless, WiFi networks have a limited range (Jaffar et al., 2019). Depending on the sort of transmitter employed, their range is typically 32 metres (120 feet) indoors and 95 metres (300 feet) outdoors. WiFi's practical range limits mobile use to inventory-taking machinery in warehouses or retail spaces, as well as barcode-reading devices at checkout stands. Mobile use of WiFi over greater distances is restricted, for example, to automobiles travelling between hotspots. Other wireless technologies are more suitable for communicating with vehicles in motion. Also, because it has a higher power utilisation than other technologies such as Bluetooth, WiFi transmitters must be constantly powered. WiFi's excessive power consumption threatens the battery life of mobile devices, particularly mobile phones (Guo et al., 2019).

GSM

The Global System for Mobile Communications (GSM) is the most prevalent form of communication between mobile devices, particularly phones. On more than 210 networks worldwide, approximately 2.2 billion people use it. The system suggests a network to which mobile phones can connect by scanning nearby cells. A cell is essentially an area where a network provider, such as Vodafone or Verizon, transmits signals. This technology has also progressed beyond audio communication to include video calling and conferencing (Mir et al., 2019).

SIM (Subscriber Identity Modules) cards allow users to transfer from one network to another, which is an advantage of the GSM system. Ghana has enabled the Mobile Number Portability System, which enables users to retain the same number even if they transfer from Vodafone to Airtel or vice versa. In contrast, GSM has a maximum range of 120 kilometres for cell sites. Concerns have also been raised regarding the potential carcinogenic effects of using GSM phones and even residing near a cell site.

WiMax

This abbreviation, which stands for Worldwide Interoperability for Microwave Access, refers to a standard for wireless communications intended to provide high data transmission for fixed stations. It is part of a "fourth generation," or 4G, of wireless communication technology that extends the range of a standard WiFi network. In practice, however, WiMax provides data transfer rates that must be shared among multiple users, resulting in slower speeds. It is still a viable option for providing mobile broadband connectivity to a variety of devices across cities and countries (Kansal et al., 2021).

GPRS

General Packet Radio Service (GPRS) is a data (non-voice) transmission service for GSM networks of the second and third generations. GPRS fees are typically proportional to data volume. Voice data transmission, which is ordinarily billed per minute, is now billed per second of connection time, regardless of whether the user transfers data during that time. Users can pay per use or purchase a data bundle from their mobile network, which offers this service (1GB for 30 days on MTN Ghana costs $20). Use that exceeds the limit is either charged per megabyte or prohibited. Pay-as-you-go pricing is typically per megabyte of traffic. GPRS speed is proportional to the number of simultaneous users (Acácio et al., 2022). Despite this difficulty, GPRS supports the sending, receiving, and broadcasting of short messages, "always on" internet access, and multimedia messaging service (MMS; the ability to send a message that incorporates text, images, video, and sound).

EDGE

Enhanced Data Rates for GSM Evolution (EDGE), also known as Enhanced GPRS (EGPRS) or Enhanced Data Rates for Global Evolution, is an extension of the digital mobile network technology Enhanced Data Rates for GSM Evolution (EDGE), which permits faster data transmission rates. EDGE, which is considered superior to GPRS, was initially installed as an enhancement for GSM networks with GPRS to make it simpler for existing GSM carriers to perform a complete upgrade to EDGE (Hassan et al., 2019). It does not require any hardware or software modifications to the GSM network. Transceiver units compatible with EDGE must be installed, and the base station subsystem must be upgraded to support EDGE. In practice, the difference in performance between GPRS and EDGE is minimal.

HSDPA

HSDPA is an acronym for High-Speed Downlink Packet Access. It is an advanced variant of the 3G (third generation) protocol that governs mobile device communications. Occasionally, it is referred to as 3.5G, 3G+, or enhanced 3G. It enables networks to have increased data transfer velocities and storage capacity. Current HSDPA systems support download speeds of up to 42 megabits per second. HSPA+, which provides speeds of up to 337 Mbit/s, allows for additional performance increases (Minopoulos et al., 2019).

Generations of Mobile Network Technologies

Generations refer to the periods within which mobile network technologies were developed. The mobile network technologies were developed and introduced sequentially, with some being introduced subsequent to others. Generations refer to certain historical periods characterised by significant technical progress. The term *generation* is sometimes shortened as "G" and accompanied by a numerical value to denote the specific technological generation. For example, the term "3G" denotes the third generation. Presented below is a comprehensive depiction of the many generations. Each generation of mobile network technology signifies a specific stage of technological progress in mobile communications. Every generation, usually represented as "G" followed by a number, represents a substantial advancement in abilities, altering the methods by which we interact and obtain information. These generations exemplify the progression of mobile networks from simple voice transmission to advanced multimedia services.

First Generation (1G)

The emergence of 1G signified the commencement of mobile wireless technology. 1G networks mostly relied on analogue equipment and were restricted to transmitting voice calls using radio signals. The first Blackberry 850 served as a prime example of analogue phone technology during that time period. In countries like Ghana, telecom networks such as Celltel were the first to introduce the utilisation of radio frequencies for mobile communication. Nevertheless, the first generation (1G) of mobile communication technology had notable constraints, particularly in its inadequate capacity to efficiently transmit non-voice data, thereby restricting its application to basic voice services. During the initial phase of mobile technology, the predominant type of mobile device was an analogue cell phone. The utilisation of radio signals for the transmission and reception of data is a fundamental attribute of such devices. The Blackberry 850, as stated by Camaj et al. (2019), is a prime illustration of an analogue phone. In Ghana, several telecommunications networks, such as Celltel, commenced utilising radio frequencies. The transfer of non-verbal information (data) is greatly limited.

Second Generation (2G)

2G revolutionised mobile communication by replacing analogue technology with digital technology. This transition facilitated the transfer of both speech- and text-based data, thus broadening the range of mobile communication. The Global System for Mobile Communications (GSM) and Code Division Multiple Access (CDMA) emerged as the fundamental technologies for 2G networks. An important improvement in this era was the introduction of 2.5G, which refers to intermediate technologies such as General Packet Radio Service (GPRS), Enhanced Data Rates for GSM Evolution (EDGE), and an upgraded version of CDMA called CDMA2000. These developments resulted in a slight enhancement in data transmission speeds in comparison to the initial generation. The instruments of this era were characterised by their digital nature. Digital transmission enables the transfer of information, including both audio and data, in a text format (Hinderer & Pousa, 2021). The technology of this generation encompasses GSM and CDMA (Hinderer & Pousa, 2021). 2.5G is a marketing designation used to refer to several technologies, including GPRS, EDGE, and an enhanced version of CDMA called CDMA2000 (Kolluru & Reddy; 2021). Evidently, there has been a modest rise in the transmission frequencies for 2G data.

Third Generation (3G)

3G networks revolutionised mobile technology by enabling not only voice and text communication but also data services and additional functionalities such as video transmission. The data transfer rates of 3G networks peaked at 400 kbps, with some carriers achieving speeds of up to 7.5 Mbps under specific circumstances, commonly known as 3.5G. This technological progress facilitated the development of more intricate mobile applications, such as rudimentary web browsing and video streaming, converting mobile phones into versatile gadgets. Network-enabled devices facilitate the transfer of speech, data, and other advanced services, including video. The maximum speed of 3G networks is approximately 400 kbps. Certain mobile network carriers give a maximum speed of 7.5 Mbps on 3G networks, also known as 3.5G.

Fourth Generation (4G)

The advent of the fourth generation of mobile networks revolutionised the industry by providing fast broadband capabilities capable of efficiently managing large amounts of data-intensive material, such as high-definition video and intricate online applications. Although 4G has been extensively deployed worldwide, the connection speeds generally do not surpass 10 Mbps. The advent of 4G brought about a significant transformation in mobile internet services, rendering them on par with conventional broadband internet services in terms of speed and dependability. This development laid the foundation for a globally interconnected and digitally advanced society. The networks of this generation are commonly referred to as the future. High-speed broadband is capable of supporting a larger amount of visual information, such as videos and photographs, which was beyond the capacity of 3G networks. The majority of countries have adopted 4G technology; however, the connection speeds remain below 10 Mbps. Every iteration of mobile network technology has introduced significant improvements, fundamentally altering our interactions with mobile devices and our ability to retrieve information. The progression from simple phone calls in 1G to fast internet and multimedia services in 4G exemplifies the dynamic and continuously changing character of the telecommunications sector.

Wireless and Mobile Devices

Mobile or wireless devices are devices that are easily carried along and connected to each other through wireless means without wires or cables (Campi et al., 2020). Such devices, especially phones, are also described as cellular. The connection between these devices enables the users or owners to make and receive voice calls, send and receive text messages, and execute other tasks. The tasks include saving contact information or setting an alarm or reminder.

Examples of mobile or wireless devices include:

■ Laptop and netbook computers;
■ Palmtop computers or personal digital assistants;
■ Mobile phones and smartphones;
■ Global Positioning System (GPS) devices; and
■ Wireless debit/credit card payment terminals.

Characteristics of Mobile and Wireless Devices

Mobile devices generally have the following characteristics:

■ **One-handed use:** Mobile devices are normally operated with one hand. However, this varies between devices. For instance, a mobile phone with a full keyboard may be operated with both hands for more convenience.
■ **Limited:** Mobile devices are limited in terms of processing abilities. Generally, the smaller the device, the lower the processing capabilities it has. For instance, smartphones may not be able to do the graphic manipulations that a desktop or notebook computer could do. Also,

Table 4.1 Generations of Mobile Technologies Comparison

1G	1970s–1980s	Wireless phones (cellular) are introduced, primarily for voice only.
2G	1990s–2000	Increased performance achieved by allowing multiple users on a single channel. More and more cellular phones are used for data as well as voice.
2.5G	2001–2004	The internet turns the focus towards data transmission. Enhanced multimedia and streaming video are now possible. Phones support limited web browsing.
3G	2004–2005	Enhanced multimedia and streaming video capabilities are increased. Standards are created to allow universal access and portability across different device types (telephones, PDAs, etc.)
4G	2006+	Speeds reach up to 40 Mbps. Enhanced multimedia, streaming video, access, and portability are increased still further. Devices are equipped for world-wide roaming.

Source: Radio Shack Guide to Wireless Telecommunications, http://goo.gl/bOkE6

because mobile devices are portable, their uptime depends on their battery life, which tends to shorten over long periods of use.

- **Small:** Mobile devices visibly have sizes that are not up to their stationary counterparts. It is this feature that makes them portable.
- **Identifiable:** Mobile devices have some features embedded that make it possible to differentiate one device from another, just as humans can be identified by name. One of such features is the use of SIM cards in mobile phones and some tablet computers.
- **Ubiquitous:** Users of mobile devices can have access to information anywhere, no matter where they are, provided there is some connectivity in that area. For instance, employees can access their work email on their mobile phone no matter the country they are in, as long as they have internet access.
- **Context-aware:** The geographical location of mobile devices can be obtained using a feature like the Global Positioning System (GPS). Based on the location of the device (and the user), some services could be recommended to the user. For instance, a user could be notified of the proximity of a restaurant to a user who has set out for lunch.

Benefits of Mobile Devices

Using mobile devices could assist enterprises in providing better customer service. During a meeting with customers, for instance, their information and details could be readily accessed and updated via the internet without the need to be physically present in the office. Alternatively, a bank could allow consumers to order services such as chequebooks for later pickup without having to physically visit the bank. In some restaurants, wireless payment terminals allow customers to pay for their meals without departing from their seats. Such systems result in a great deal of working flexibility, allowing people to work from home and/or while travelling, for instance.

Disadvantages of Mobile Devices

The cost of acquiring such wireless devices, especially the more sophisticated ones, is very high. There is also some cost involved in setting up the equipment and training personnel to use it effectively for their work.

Further, such mobile devices can expose confidential and valuable information to people who are not supposed to have it.

Mobile Financial Services

The use of mobile and wireless devices is increasing, particularly on the GSM network. Mobile banking is regarded as one of the most valuable mobile services in the United Kingdom. Africa is not excluded from this latest phenomenon that crowns the push for more mobile services. GSM customers in Ghana, for example, have access to banking, airtime top-up, and insurance (Smith, 2012). In other regions of the globe, these services encompass international money transfers. M-Pesa (in Kenya), MTN Mobile Money, and Airtel Money (throughout Africa, including Ghana) are the most prominent financial services in Africa (Asravor et al., 2022). Most organisations provide mobile financial services, with all telecommunications companies offering this service. Banks and other service providers, such as stores, are now collaborating with telecom operators to offer mobile financial services (Abdul-Rahaman & Abdulai, 2022).

Mobile Payment Applications

The use of mobile devices distinguishes mobile payments from other payment methods. The utilisation of mobile payment methods is a crucial success factor for mobile commerce. Due to the increasing prevalence of mobile devices and the number of networks, the opportunity to use such devices for payment purposes has arisen. This has resulted in the emergence of mobile payment applications or systems. The term refers to all payments for products, services, and bills that are authorised, initiated, or completed using a mobile device (Schierz et al., 2010). It is believed that there must be a transmission of value using a mobile device.

Characteristics of Mobile Payment Methods

Even though mobile payment systems have existed for some time, their adoption and use are still considered to be in their infancy. The level of acceptance and consequent use of mobile payment procedures is primarily contingent on customer costs, security, and ease of use (Kreyer et al., 2002). Costs refer to the amount required to gain access to the platform. The provider and the user may incur expenses. Users may be charged to subscribe to the service or platform, to transmit value, or even to acquire the device and connectivity to the payment platform.

Types of Mobile Payment Applications

There are four types of mobile payment methods or applications (Valcourt et al., 2005). The types include:

- Internet payment methods;
- Point-of-sale mobile payment method;
- Payments for mobile commerce applications;
- Person-to-person mobile payment.

Internet payment methods refer to ways by which one can send and receive money and, especially, make an online payment. One popular website that enables these is Paypal.com. Even though it is a traditional website, PayPal Mobile has been developed for members to manage their accounts no matter where they are. To do this, customers must download the PayPal mobile app (available for iPhone, Android, and BlackBerry) from their website. The service can also be accessed through text messaging.

The traditional point-of-sale (POS) terminals that we normally see in supermarkets and restaurant counters are currently a target for the mobile revolution. Systems have been developed so that credit card payments can be made and received using a mobile device. This is achieved through a combination of specialised devices and apps. This system is targeted and could be very useful for mobile salespeople to process checks, credit cards, and gift cards. It automatically sends a receipt to the payer.

Payments for mobile commerce applications are normally embedded on the SIM cards of mobile phone networks. It seems that this service is currently restricted to the top-up of airtime and the subscription of other value-added services. Currently, there are partnerships between the banks and telecom companies that allow subscribers to access their bank accounts on their mobile devices.

Person-to-person mobile payment seems to be the most common payment system available, especially in Africa. In Ghana, one can send money to another person via MTN Mobile Money. The value can be used as payment for a product or service or redeemed at an authorised Mobile Money point.

Mobile Apps and Social Media

A mobile application (or mobile app) is a software programme designed to execute a particular task on smartphones, tablets, and other mobile devices (Putranto & Rochmawati, 2020). Mobile applications were initially designed to increase user productivity. The synchronisation of email, tasks, and contacts are examples of such applications. Nonetheless, demand over the years has led to a rapid expansion into other areas, including games, banking, and even online purchasing (Arif & Ali, 2019). Apps are accessible via platforms designed specifically for their distribution or installation. Typically, the creator and owner of the mobile operating system is responsible for designing and managing these platforms. Apple's App Store, Google's Play, Microsoft's Windows Marketplace, and RIM's BlackBerry App World are some of these platforms. On these platforms, users can download paid and free applications to their mobile devices (smartphones and tablets).

Mobile App Platforms

Google Play

This Google service comprises an online store for music, movies, books, and applications for the Android operating system. The service is accessible via the internet. Any Android-powered phone should include the Play Store application, which provides access to Google Play (formerly Android Market). Although the Play Store is not the only location for Android applications, it is the most prominent for the Android platform.

Apple Store

The App Store is Apple Computer's official online application distribution platform. These devices consist of an iPad (a tablet computer), an iPhone (a mobile phone), and an iPod touch (a portable audio player). The platform has reported over 10 billion downloads as of January 2011. These figures may be attributable to the over 200 million Apple device users.

Nokia Store

Nokia's platform for programme downloads is known as the Nokia Store. The Nokia Store continues to serve as the distribution platform for its initial mobile software lines. In addition, Nokia has decided to implement Microsoft's Windows 7 on its new phone models.

Windows Phone Marketplace

Microsoft has created the Windows Marketplace for mobile and wireless devices operating on the Windows Phone 7 platform. This is a service that allows users of phones with the company's phone operating system to obtain specialised applications for free or for a fee.

Social Media

Social media typically refers to technologies that facilitate two-way communication between individuals, organisations, and communities (Winarso, 2020). It describes a collection of applications that enable internet or web users to share, contribute, interact, and engage with content (information) and other online users. This phenomenon has evolved to accommodate the growing number of mobile and wireless devices. Thus, the terms *mobile social media* and *mobile social networking* have emerged. Mobile social media and networking have become significant as a means for businesses to get closer to their consumers (Baird & Paradnis, 2011). This creates an opportunity to increase revenue while decreasing expenses and inefficiencies.

The design of social media is predicated on the human propensity to share, whether it be photos, interests, or ideas. Others use it for gaming purposes. Currently, mobile devices are manufactured with cameras and GPS sensors that enable the user to create complex and engaging content, thereby enhancing sharing. Mobile social networking and media are considered "communities of the future" (Peters, 2012). Even though 47% of European smartphone users access the internet daily, 66% of such users enter their social media profile(s) daily (Jacobson et al. 2020). To this end, there are sites and applications that have been or are being designed specifically for mobile devices. Such websites and applications include itsmy.com, frengo.com, and twango.com. Examples of social media networking include Facebook, WhatsApp, Twitter, and LinkedIn.

Anthropology's (ANT) Approach to Social Media

ANT is the scientific study of humankind's origins, physical and cultural evolution, biological traits, and social conventions and beliefs. Focus is placed on how humans interact, act, communicate, and share their social and common interests on a technology-enabled platform in social media (Toren, 2020). By comprehending how these social actions evolve, it is possible to determine which technologies, applications, and tools can be used to empower them. Consequently, we should use social media to accomplish specific, measurable outcomes that are connected to specific organisational objectives.

In essence, social media should acknowledge that people are the pivot. Businesses evolve for the benefit of their customers, not for the survival of the business and its proprietors. Thus, in the ANT approach, one shifts from tactics to "knowing the customer." If you comprehend why the customer is with you, you will know what to do. Google was created with users in mind, not enterprises. Amazon also delved into social behaviour to facilitate book purchases.

The question you should ask is how you can improve their performance. Utilise mobile devices and social media to:

■ Establish feedback communities for your business, product, or brand;
■ Share brand-related content and information with interested members;
■ Distribute the brand "virally" via social media applications.

Activities

Section 1: Mobile Network Technologies

Activity
Which of the following mobile network technologies—Bluetooth, WAP, GPS, WiMax, GPRS, EDGE, and HSDPA have you used before? For which purpose did you use it? Did the technology enable you to achieve your goal of using it? Describe your experience.

Section 2: Generations of Mobile Network Technologies

What is your understanding of the mobile network generations? Describe the principal differences between the generations discussed.

Section 3: Wireless and Mobile Devices

1. What is your understanding of mobile and wireless devices?
2. Which of the characteristics of mobile devices do you find most useful, most convenient, or most beneficial?
3. If you have any such mobile or wireless devices, what are some of the benefits you derive from their use? Is there any disadvantage to using such devices?

Section 4: Mobile Financial Services and Payment Systems

1. Does your current mobile network offer mobile financial services?
2. Could you describe it briefly? What is your experience with such a service?
3. In your own words, define mobile payment applications.
4. Which of the above-mentioned characteristics matters most to you?
5. Why?
6. Which of the above payment methods have you experienced? Describe your experience in 100 words.

Section 5: Mobile Apps and Social Media

1. How can you describe a mobile app in your own words? Is there any specific mobile app you have used before?
2. Which operating system does your phone run on? Describe your experience with downloading any app from the associated application download platform. If you have not experienced it yet, which app on any of these platforms do you think could be very useful?
3. Which is your favourite social networking website? Is it accessible through your mobile phone? Is there a dedicated "app" to access it?
4. Visit the platforms mentioned in the text and draw a comparison between their main features.

Section 6: Case Studies on Mobile Platforms and Applications

1. What do you think are the most essential mobile apps?
2. What can a company in Ghana learn from the cases above?

Assignment

Discuss how Ghanaian businesses can adopt mobile platforms and applications in their business activities.

Case Studies on Mobile Platforms and Applications

This section presents two case studies on mobile platforms and applications. It also presents questions that will guide readers in reviewing their understanding of the lessons provided in this chapter.

Case Study 5

Could You Survive Without Mobile Apps?

A third of small businesses say they couldn't get by without mobile apps. (11% say they use them only because they're "cool"). More than a third of small businesses say they couldn't survive—or that it would be a challenge to survive—without mobile apps, according to a new survey by AT&T, a mobile network operator in the United States. The AT&T study found that 72% of small businesses used mobile apps in their operations. AT&T surveyed 2,246 small business owners, with small being defined as between 2 and 50 employees, both part-time and full-time. Top on the list of app users were GPS and mapping, with nearly half (49%) of companies using them. A distant second: a tie between social media marketing and document management, with 26% of firms apiece. Other popular apps are location-based services (24%), time management (23%), travel and expense tracking (22%), and mobile credit card payments (20%). The biggest reason for using mobile apps: saving time, said 62% of those polled. Of those polled, 59% cited increased productivity, and 29% said cost-saving. (11% admitted to using mobile apps "to be cool and hip."). Other survey findings: small businesses with Facebook pages jumped to 41% from 27% in 2009. More than a third of those polled said social media was good for business, with 37% saying Facebook increased traffic to their company websites (Source: Robin, 2016).

Case Study 6

A Year of 3G in Vietnam: Attracting the Young Can Accelerate Growth

According to the Nielsen Company (a research institution), 6 months after 3G launched, just under half (48%) of Vietnamese mobile users were aware of it, and only 3% were subscribed. The latter number has risen to 11% one year later, a result on par with other markets. Given the strong overall penetration of mobile phones in Vietnam, however, one might have expected a faster rate of adoption. It's not that consumers don't know what 3G can be used for; the vast majority of those surveyed knew that 3G phones were capable of mobile TV viewing, video calling, and browsing the internet. But a glance at what consumers are currently using their mobile phones for might provide some insight as to why functions like those are not yet more popular.

The user of the mobile internet in Vietnam still falls into the category of "early adopter," and to get beyond this initial group, service providers can focus on several key areas to expand usage of their networks: promote smartphones, price data packages creatively, and cultivate the youth market.

Marketing a 3G Lifestyle: Cultivating the Young Generation

The real key to boosting 3G service in Vietnam is nurturing the young generation, who typically adopt new technology more quickly than their elders. In Vietnam, people under the age of 24 represent more than half (54%) of the population. Narrowing the scope of our investigation to people aged 15–24 (who comprise 20% of the Vietnamese population), half (48%) are subscribed to mobile services. Initially given phones by their parents to keep in touch, youth gain more control over usage and handset selection as they mature. They occasionally use their devices to make calls but prefer to use them for texts and SMS. They are much higher than average data users, which would seem to make 3G networks and smartphones natural fits for them. But to date, most young Vietnamese know very little about 3G and/or don't see a need for it. By the time they are young adults, they have very definite preferences when it comes to how they use services and select devices.

Seizing the Opportunity

By taking a few relatively simple actions, mobile service providers and handset manufacturers can attract a greater number of young consumers to 3G:

- **Get them:** Start by focusing on parents, who will buy kids their first mobile phones and develop and promote parent–child calling plans. Incentivise current customers to recruit friends to sign up for service.
- **Educate them:** Advertise on channels popular with youth, such as VTV3, HTV (HCM), and subscription channels including Disney, HBO, and Star Movies, as well as on local websites like HiHi, HeHe, ZingMe, and so on. Offer discount coupons with 3G information.
- **Keep them:** Younger mobile users will change handsets often—sometimes as much as once a year. Make sure they are buying your brand by staying ahead of trends and pricing devices at the right time. If

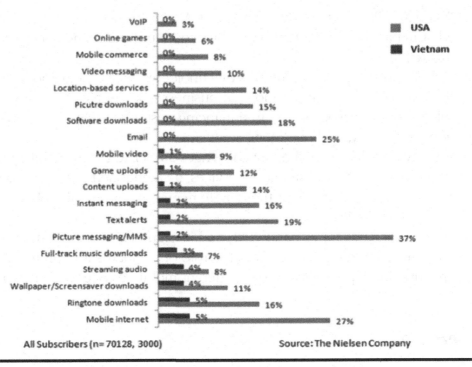

Figure 4.2   Mobile applications used in the last 30 days

smartphones are too expensive for most, try marketing media phones, which feature many of the same kinds of functions. Service providers should promote network quality.

It's not a key concern for teens, but young adults tend to stick with those networks they view as having good coverage and quality. Offer services of interest such as English tutorials via video (sure to appeal to parents!), Disney programming, or the latest Korean soap operas, but make sure revenue comes from advertising, not subscribers.

■ **Sell to them:** The young use multimedia, but budget is a concern; try using advertising-driven models, such as sponsored text messages for service discounts. Be creative in pricing data plans; apart from standard monthly top-ups, try daily or weekly pricing plans, or offer one-time credits when they run out of minutes.

Review Questions

1. Describe the evolution of mobile network technologies from the early stages to the current state. How have technologies like Bluetooth, GPS,

WiMAX, GPRS, EDGE, WiFi, and HSDPA transformed over time, and what impact have they had on mobile communication and social media marketing?

2. How do different mobile network technologies such as Bluetooth, WAP, WiFi, and GSM find applications in business operations? Discuss the role these technologies play in enhancing customer engagement, operational efficiency, and marketing strategies.

3. Identify and discuss some key challenges associated with mobile payment applications and financial services, as mentioned in the chapter. What are the limitations of these systems in the context of mobile network technologies?

4. Explain the concept of bandwidth and its significance in mobile communication. Additionally, discuss the role of standards and protocols in ensuring interoperability among different mobile devices and networks.

References

Abdul-Rahaman, A., & Abdulai, A. (2022). Mobile money adoption, input use, and farm output among smallholder rice farmers in Ghana. *Agribusiness*, *38*(1), 236–255.

Acácio, M., Atkinson, P. W., Silva, J. P., & Franco, A. M. (2022). Performance of GPS/GPRS tracking devices improves with increased fix interval and is not affected by animal deployment. *Plos one*, *17*(3), e0265541.

Arif, K. S., & Ali, U. (2019, January). Mobile Application testing tools and their challenges: A comparative study. In *2019 2nd International conference on computing, mathematics and engineering technologies (iCoMET)* (pp. 16). IEEE.

Asravor, R. K., Boakye, A. N., & Essuman, J. (2022). Adoption and intensity of use of mobile money among smallholder farmers in rural Ghana. *Information Development*, *38*(2), 204–217.

Baird, C. H., & Parasnis, G. (2011). From social media to social customer relationship management. *Strategy & Leadership*, *39*(5), 30–37.

Camaj, J., Kendra, M., Šperka, A., & Mašek, J. (2019). Development and current trends in the use of mobile devices. *Transport Technic and Technology*, *15*(2), 28–35.

Campi, T., Cruciani, S., Maradei, F., Montalto, A., Musumeci, F., & Feliziani, M. (2020). Wireless powering of next-generation left ventricular assist devices (LVADs) without percutaneous cable driveline. *IEEE Transactions on Microwave Theory and Techniques*, *68*(9), 3969–3977.

Galkin, B., Kibiłda, J., & DaSilva, L. A. (2019). A stochastic model for UAV networks positioned above demand hotspots in urban environments. *IEEE Transactions on Vehicular Technology*, *68*(7), 6985–6996.

Guo, L., Wang, L., Lin, C., Liu, J., Lu, B., Fang, J., ... Guo, S. (2019). Wiar: A public dataset for wifi-based activity recognition. *IEEE Access*, *7*, 154935–154945.

Hassan, N., Yau, K. L. A., & Wu, C. (2019). Edge computing in 5G: A review. *IEEE Access*, *7*, 127276–127289.

Hinderer, H., & Pousa, C. (2021). Digital Communication in B-To-B Sales. In *International business development: A concise textbook focusing on international B-to-B contexts*, Ludwig Martin, (ed.), (pp. 197–222). Springer Fachmedien Wiesbaden.

Jacobson, J., Gruzd, A., & Hernández-García, Á. (2020). Social media marketing: Who is watching the watchers?. *Journal of Retailing and Consumer Services*, *53*, 101774.

Jaffar, F. H. F., Osman, K., Ismail, N. H., Chin, K. Y., & Ibrahim, S. F. (2019). Adverse effects of Wi-Fi radiation on male reproductive system: A systematic review. *The Tohoku Journal of Experimental Medicine*, *248*(3), 169–179.

Kansal, L., Gaba, G. S., Sharma, A., Dhiman, G., Baz, M., & Masud, M. (2021). Performance analysis of WOFDM-WiMAX integrating diverse wavelets for 5G applications. *Wireless Communications and Mobile Computing*, *2021*, 1–14.

Kolluru, D. S., & Reddy, P. B. (2021, December). Review on communication technologies in telecommunications from conventional telephones to smart phones. In *AIP conference proceedings* (Vol. 2407, No. 1, p. 020003). AIP Publishing LLC.

Kreyer, N., Pousttchi, K., & Turowski, K. (2002). Characteristics of mobile payment procedures. In: *The Thirteenth International Symposium on Methodologies for Intelligent Systems*, 10–22.

Milner, G. (2016). What is GPS?. *Journal of Technology in Human Services*, *34*(1), 9–12.

Minopoulos, G., Kokkonis, G., Psannis, K., & Ishibashi, Y. (2019). A survey on haptic data over 5g networks. *International Journal of Future Generation Communication and Networking*, *12*, 37–54. 10.33832/ijfgcn.2019.12.2.04

Mir, N. A., Riar, C. S., & Singh, S. (2019). Physicochemical, molecular and thermal properties of high-intensity ultrasound (HIUS) treated protein isolates from album (Chenopodium album) seed. *Food Hydrocolloids*, *96*, 433–441.

Mir, S. H., Ashruf, S., Bhat, Y., & Beigh, N. (2019). Review on smart electric metering system based on GSM/IOT. *Asian Journal of Electrical Sciences*, *8*(1), 1–6.

Naraine, M. L., O'Reilly, N., Levallet, N., & Wanless, L. (2020). If you build it, will they log on? Wi–Fi usage and behavior while attending national basketball association games. *Sport, Business and Management: An International Journal*, *10*(2), 207–226.

Peters, J. D. (2012). *Speaking into the air: A history of the idea of communication*. University of chicago Press.

Putranto, D., & Rochmawati, E. (2020). Mobile applications for managing symptoms of patients with cancer at home: A scoping review. *International Journal of Nursing Practice*, *26*(4), e12842.

Robin, B. R. (2016). The power of digital storytelling to support teaching and learning. *Digital Education Review*, *30*, 17–29.

Schierz, P. G., Schilke, O., & Wirtz, B. W. (2010). Understanding consumer acceptance of mobile payment services: An empirical analysis. *Electronic Commerce Research and Applications, 9*(3), 209–216.

Sevier, S., & Tekeoglu, A. (2019, January). Analyzing the security of Bluetooth low energy. In *2019 International conference on electronics, information, and communication (ICEIC)* (pp. 1–5). Institute of electricals and electronic engineers (IEEE).

Shastri, K., Reshef, O., Boyd, R. W., Lundeen, J. S., & Monticone, F. (2022). To what extent can space be compressed? Bandwidth limits of spaceplates. *Optica, 9*(7), 738–745.

Shi, Y., Han, Q., Shen, W., & Zhang, H. (2019). Potential applications of 5G communication technologies in collaborative intelligent manufacturing. *IET Collaborative Intelligent Manufacturing, 1*(4), 109–116.

Smith, P. K. (2012). Cyberbullying: Challenges and opportunities for a research program—A response to Olweus (2012). *European journal of developmental psychology, 9*(5), 553–558.

Toren, C. (2020). Anthropology as the whole science of what it is to be human. In *Anthropology beyond culture*, Richard G. Fox and Barbara J. King (eds.), (pp. 105–124). Routledge.

Valcourt, E., Robert, J. M., & Beaulieu, F. (2005, August). Investigating mobile payment: Supporting technologies, methods, and use. In *WiMob'2005, IEEE international conference on wireless and mobile computing, networking and communications, 2005*, Jenq-Shiou Leu, Yuan-Po Chi, Shou-Chuan Chang and Wei-Kuan Shih (eds.), (Vol. 4, pp. 29–36). IEEE.

Winarso, W. (2020). Technology, social media and behaviour of young generation in Indonesia; a conceptual paper. *International Journal of Scientific & Technology Research, 9*(4), 986–989.

Chapter 5

Social Networking Sites: A Focus on Mobile Marketing Strategies

Chapter Outline

- Introduction
- Growth of mobile connectivity and device use in developing economies
- Mobile connectivity and social media
- Mobilising your brands
- Designing mobile apps for mobile shopping
- Buy buttons and location identification on social networking sites
- Marketing strategies: mobile first, audience first, and omnichannel
- Satisfying customer experience on mobile devices
- Conclusions

Chapter Outcome

By the end of this chapter, the reader will be able to:

Explore the link between marketing and social media:
- Illustrate how marketing objectives align with and leverage the capabilities of various social media channels.

DOI: 10.4324/9781003307457-5

Analyse how social networking sites facilitate marketing:
- Evaluate the specific features and functionalities of social networking sites that support and enhance marketing efforts.

Emphasise the importance of integrating social media into marketing:
- Articulate the significance of seamlessly integrating social media into overall marketing strategies.

Examine appropriate marketing strategies for social networking sites:
- Identify and analyse effective marketing strategies tailored specifically for social networking sites.

Optimise customer experience on social networking sites:
- Develop strategies to maximise the customer experience on social networking sites.
- Implement best practices for engaging with customers, fostering community, and enhancing overall satisfaction on social media platforms.

Introduction

Mobile phone penetration continues to increase in emerging and developing countries. In several of these countries, half or more of the population now uses smartphones, and smartphone use is especially common among younger and more educated groups (Silver et al., 2019). According to the Global System for Mobile Communications (GSMA), as of March 19, 2019, 5.17 billion people in the world's population had mobile devices (BankMyCell, 2020). This is an indication that about 66.77% of the world's population has access to a mobile device. According to Salehan and Negahban (2013), this trend is followed by fast growth in the use of mobile phones for accessing online social networking sites (SNS). Social networking is ranked among the top five activities by mobile users (Salehan & Negahban, 2013). As of January 2019, the global mobile social network penetration rate was 42%; this number has increased to 49% as of January 2020, representing 3.75 million active global mobile social media users worldwide (Clement, 2019). Hence, as a communication service, mobile SNS has been widely adopted among users (Zhou, 2019). Compared to traditional SNS that are based on desktop computers, a main feature of mobile SNS is ubiquity, which reflects the fact that users can interact with others at any time and from anywhere with the help of mobile networks and terminals (Wang et al., 2016; Zhou, 2019). This, therefore, presents an opportunity for marketers to leverage social media for mobile marketing. It is argued that people often check social media on their phones since our lives are increasingly intertwined with social networks.

Therefore, the purpose of this chapter is to provide a deeper understanding of marketers regarding mobile marketing via social networking. This chapter also seeks to provide insights as to how marketers can benefit from mobile marketing through social networking. The chapter discusses the digital landscape; the growth of mobile connectivity and device use in developing economies; the challenges of mobile connectivity and device use in developing economies, mobile connectivity and social media; mobilising your brands; designing mobile apps for mobile shopping; buy buttons and location identification on social networking sites; marketing strategies (mobile first, audience first, and omnichannel); augmented reality marketing; and satisfying customer experience on mobile devices.

Growth of Mobile Connectivity and Device Use in Developing Economies

Mobile network technologies refer to the means through which various types of portable devices are connected to share information or communicate. It began with the ability to send information via a simple pager to a mobile phone, but currently, mobile networks allow users to send and receive information simultaneously, play games with each other online, and access images and videos from other devices (Rohini et al., 2022). Some examples of mobile network technologies are Bluetooth, WiFi, and GSM. Mobile network technologies have gone through different phases over the years. The periods within which the technologies were developed are known as generations. The word generation is usually shortened as "G" and preceded by a number depicting which generation that technology falls into. For example, "3G" means third generation. A description of the generations is given below.

First Generation (1G)

In the initial generation of mobile technologies, mobile devices were mostly cell phones, which were analogue devices. One important feature of such devices is the use of radio signals for transmitting and receiving data. An example of an analogue phone is the first Blackberry 850 phone. In Ghana, some telecom networks, like Celltell, began with radio waves. Transmission of non-voice information (data) is quite limited.

Second Generation (2G)

In this generation, devices were digital. Digital transmission allows for the transmission of both voice-based and data-based information in the form of text messages. Technologies in this generation include GSM and CDMA. 2G has been described as a marketing term that describes technologies like GPRS, EDGE, and an advanced form of CDMA called CDMA2000. Apparently, the data transmission speeds for 2G technologies were enhanced slightly.

Third Generation (3G)

Network technology devices allow for voice, data, and other advanced services like video streaming. Mobile network operators in Ghana have deployed 2G, 2.5G, and 3G networks but are yet to deploy 4G network technologies. 3G network speeds go up from 400 kbps. Some mobile network operators provide up to 7.5 mbps on the 3G networks (some call this 3.5G).

Fourth Generation (4G)

The networks in this generation are described as the future. 4G uses high-speed broadband to accommodate information that is laden with visuals (video and images), far more than 3G networks could accommodate. The United States (by Sprint), Norway, India, and Sweden have all got 4G up and running, although connectivity speeds do not exceed 10 Mbps. The united Kingdom will have it up and running by the end of 2012.

The proliferation of mobile connectivity and device utilisation in emerging economies has exhibited a truly astonishing trajectory. The proliferation of cost-effective smartphones and the growth of mobile network infrastructure have facilitated increased internet accessibility and the consequent enjoyment of connectivity among individuals residing in these areas. In numerous emerging nations, mobile devices have emerged as the predominant medium for internet access, displacing conventional modalities such as desktop computers or laptops. This transition has created a plethora of possibilities for these communities, granting them the ability to obtain knowledge, engage in communication with others, and partake in the worldwide digital economy. The proliferation of mobile connectivity has additionally enabled the dissemination of digital services across diverse industries, including healthcare, finance, education, and agriculture. Farmers are now able to utilise their mobile devices to obtain real-time weather information, market prices, and agricultural best practices, enabling them to make well-informed decisions and enhance their production. In addition, the proliferation of mobile payment methods has had a transformative impact on the accessibility of financial services in emerging economies. The advent of mobile technology has facilitated financial inclusion for individuals who were previously excluded from formal banking services. These people can now engage in various financial activities, such as money transfers, savings, and even obtaining microloans, using their mobile devices. This increased accessibility to financial services has the potential to empower individuals economically and contribute to poverty reduction. The observation of the transformative impact of mobile connectivity and gadget utilisation on individuals residing in emerging economies is a subject of great fascination. The potentialities are boundless, and I am enthusiastic to witness the ongoing constructive effects of these breakthroughs on global societies.

Mobile Connectivity and Social Media

A mobile application (or mobile app) is a software programme designed to execute a particular task on smartphones, tablets, and other mobile devices (Putranto & Rochmawati, 2020). Mobile applications were initially designed to increase user productivity. The synchronisation of email, tasks, and contacts are examples of such applications. Nonetheless, demand over the years has led to a rapid expansion into other areas, including games, banking, and even online purchasing (Arif & Ali, 2019).

Apps are accessible via platforms designed specifically for their distribution or installation. Typically, the creator and owner of the mobile operating system is responsible for designing and managing these platforms. Apple's App Store, Google's Play, Microsoft's Windows Marketplace, and RIM's

BlackBerry App World are some of these platforms. On these platforms, users can download paid and free applications to their mobile devices (smartphones and tablets).

Mobile App Platforms

Google Play

This Google service comprises an online store for music, movies, books, and applications for the Android operating system. The service was accessible via the internet. Any Android-powered phone should include the Play Store application, which provides access to Google Play (formerly Android Market). Although the Play Store is not the only location for Android applications, it is the most prominent for the Android platform.

Apple Store

The App Store is Apple Computer's official online application distribution platform. These devices consist of an iPad (a tablet computer), an iPhone (a mobile phone), and an iPod touch (a portable audio player). The platform has reported over 10 billion downloads as of January 2011. These figures may be attributable to the over 200 million Apple device users.

Nokia Store

Nokia's platform for programme downloads is known as the Nokia Store. The Nokia Store continues to serve as the distribution platform for its initial mobile software lines. In addition, Nokia has decided to implement Microsoft's Windows 7 on its new phone models.

Windows Phone Marketplace

Microsoft has created the Windows Marketplace for mobile and wireless devices operating on the Windows Phone 7 platform. This is a service that allows users of phones with the company's phone operating system to obtain specialised applications for free or for a fee.

Social Media

According to Untari et al. (2020), social media can be described as a technological environment that enables two-way communication between individuals, organisations, and larger groups. It comprises a diverse range of apps that enable internet or online users to not only share and create content but also to participate in meaningful conversations with other users. This dynamic occurrence has adjusted itself to accommodate the growing prevalence of mobile and wireless devices, resulting in the emergence of mobile social media and mobile social networking concepts. According to Baird (2014), these platforms have become crucial tools for organisations to foster a more intimate relationship with their customers. The relationship serves not only as a mechanism for improving consumer interaction but also as a strategic avenue for increasing revenue while concurrently mitigating expenses and inefficiencies.

The fundamental nature of social media is rooted in its design, which effectively leverages the inherent human inclination to engage in sharing various forms of content, such as photographs, personal hobbies, intellectual concepts, or personal encounters. Moreover, a significant number of individuals utilise these platforms for recreational purposes, such as engaging in online gaming activities. Contemporary mobile devices, possessing sophisticated attributes like high-resolution cameras and GPS sensors, enable the production of detailed and immersive content. This technological innovation greatly enhances the user's experience, promoting more profound and dynamic modes of sharing.

Peters (2012) provides a comprehensive analysis of the emerging phenomenon of mobile social networking and media, characterising them as "communities of the future" due to their increasing relevance in the realm of digital communication. The usage statistics provided by Veris (2020), which show that 47% of European smartphone users regularly use the internet and that a significant 66% actively interact with their social media accounts each day, support the aforementioned viewpoint. Considering this prevailing pattern, a multitude of websites and applications have been created with a distinct emphasis on optimising mobile functionality. Platforms such as itsmy.com, frengo.com, and twango.com have been specifically designed to optimise the mobile social networking experience. In addition, prominent social networking platforms like Facebook, WhatsApp, Twitter, and LinkedIn have modified their user interfaces and features to offer smooth mobile experiences, solidifying the influence of mobile devices in moulding our interactions on social media. The ongoing development of social media is evident, indicating that its incorporation with mobile technology is not merely a transitory phenomenon but rather a fundamental transformation in the way we establish connections, communicate, and engage with content. The convergence of mobile technology and social media is revolutionising the digital environment, presenting unparalleled prospects for individual self-expression, fostering communities, and facilitating corporate interactions.

Anthropology (ANT) Approach to Social Media

The Anthropology (ANT) Approach to Social Media provides a profound perspective on the interaction between human behaviour and technology. As Toren (2020) points out, anthropology is the scientific study of humanity, encompassing the exploration of our origins, cultural evolution, biological characteristics, and the myriad of social practices and beliefs that define us. In the context of social media, this approach focuses on understanding how people interact, behave, communicate, and share their interests and social activities within a technology-enabled environment. By delving into the anthropological aspects of social media, we can gain a deeper understanding of how social behaviours and interactions evolve in the digital realm. This understanding is critical in identifying the technologies, applications, and tools best suited to enhance and empower these social actions. The ultimate goal is to harness social media not just as a platform for engagement but as a tool for achieving specific, measurable outcomes aligned with organisational objectives. At the heart of this approach is the recognition that social media is fundamentally about people and their interactions.

In adopting the ANT approach, the focus shifts from merely deploying tactics to deeply understanding the customer. It involves comprehending the reasons behind a customer's engagement with a brand, which in turn informs effective strategies. Companies like Google and Amazon have exemplified this customer-centric philosophy. Google's inception was based on creating a user-oriented experience rather than a business-centric one. Similarly, Amazon tapped into the social behaviours of its users to revolutionise the way books are purchased online.

Applying this anthropological lens to social media in a business context involves several practical strategies. Businesses can use mobile devices and social media platforms to create feedback communities around their products, brands, or services. This allows for direct interaction with customers, gathering valuable insights and fostering a sense of community. Sharing brand-related content becomes more than just broadcasting information; it's about engaging with interested members in a meaningful way. Moreover, leveraging the viral nature of social media applications can effectively spread brand awareness and influence. The ANT approach to social media underscores the importance of understanding and catering to the human element in digital interactions. It suggests that the success of social media strategies hinges on a deep appreciation of human behaviour, cultural nuances, and the evolving dynamics of digital communication. By embracing this approach, businesses and organisations can create more impactful, human-centric social media strategies that resonate with their audiences and drive meaningful engagement.

Mobilising Your Brands

The use of a name, phrase, design, symbol, or a combination thereof to identify and differentiate its products and services from those of competitors is a fundamental marketing decision (Maurya & Mishra, 2012). Customers are able to purchase more efficiently when they can recognise competing products by their unique trademarks. In addition, it helps consumers avoid products with which they are dissatisfied and develop brand loyalty for more gratifying products. Brand loyalty facilitates consumer decision-making in that it eliminates the need for external or extensive inquiries.

To understand mobile brand engagement, we must first comprehend brands. In 1960, the American Marketing Association defined a brand as a name, term, sign, symbol, or design, or a combination thereof intended to identify and differentiate the products or services of one seller or group of sellers from those of competitors. A brand evokes a certain personality, presence, and product or service performance in the consumer's consciousness (Branding, n.d.). The transition of organisations from a goods-centric to a customer-centric perspective acknowledges brands as entities with functional and affective values. Ah (2019). A brand emerges as a result of the concept of designating a particular product (Naydenov 2019). Marketers use branding to set their product and service offerings apart from those of their rivals.

Mobile Brand Engagement

Brand engagement entails three key activities:

1. **Understanding the customer:** A brand is dependent on customer reception.
2. **Marketing communications:** Once created, brands need to be communicated and positioned for the relevant audience in the marketplace.
3. **Ongoing interactions with customers:** Organisational processes should revolve around the creation, development, and protection of brand identity in an ongoing interaction with target customers with the aim of achieving lasting competitive advantages in the form of brands.

The responsibility of the brand builder is to identify and communicate brand values that propel the organisation in the desired direction while recognising and enhancing any existing values, attributes, or personality characteristics that existing users associate with the brand. Mobile brand engagement entails the use of mobile or wireless devices in the creation, development, and protection of brand identity in an ongoing interaction with target customers, with the goal of obtaining sustainable competitive advantages through brands. Mobile brand engagement can also be viewed as a subset of the new forms of branding that leverage the capabilities of emergent technologies. This new branding technique is also referred to as branding 2.0 or web 2.0 branding. Branding 2.0 is a form of branding that typically engages an online brand community that is not merely formed around the brand but is the brand itself (Atulkar, 2020). Several local and international brands, for instance, have a presence on social networking websites such as Facebook. Coca-Cola, Prada, and BMW all have Facebook and Twitter community profiles. In Ghana, news organisations such as Joy FM Radio and Citi FM maintain Facebook profiles.

Designing a Mobile Brand Engagement Campaign

Mobile brand engagement necessitates a firm's understanding of the customer in order to develop and communicate the brand via mobile. It requires the company to comprehend the customer, develop an appropriate marketing communication strategy for target consumers, and establish continuous interactive engagement or interactive communication with the customer (McLean & Wilson, 2019). Social networking websites and platforms are examples of such interactive platforms. Some businesses use these platforms to communicate or reinforce their brand online, as well as to offer consumers additional services. For instance, Fidelity Bank in Ghana extends its consumer service via Facebook. All of these social networking websites are mobile and wirelessly accessible. Thus, the brand's communication is consistent and seamless. Others promote the brand on mobile websites and at the conclusion of text messages sent to mobile users.

With mobile brand engagement, the company or brand builder can also know where consumers are at all times and send messages that are not only consistent with the customer's profile but also with their location. For instance, if a customer requests information on a specific car via SMS or mobile internet, the response could include the branding elements (logo, name, slogan, and graphics) of the various car models of the car companies in the customer's locality.

When mobile brand engagement is incorporated with other forms of branding, such as websites, television, and outdoor branding, the results are enhanced.

Designing Mobile Apps for Mobile Shopping

The use of mobile and wireless devices is increasing, particularly on the GSM network. Mobile banking is regarded as one of the most valuable mobile services in the United Kingdom. Africa is not excluded from this latest phenomenon, which crowns the push for more mobile services. GSM customers in Ghana, for example, have access to banking, airtime top-up, and insurance (Smith et al. 2012). In other regions of the globe, these services encompass international money transfers. M-Pesa (in Kenya), MTN Mobile Money, and Airtel Money (throughout Africa, including Ghana) are the most prominent financial services in Africa (Asravor et al., 2022). Most organisations provide mobile financial services, with all telecommunications companies offering this service. Banks and other service providers, such as stores, are now collaborating with telecom operators to offer mobile financial services (Abdul-Rahaman & Abdulai, 2022).

Mobile Payment Applications

The use of mobile devices distinguishes mobile payments from other payment methods. The utilisation of mobile payment methods is a crucial success factor for mobile commerce. Due to the increasing prevalence of mobile devices and the number of networks, the opportunity to use such devices for payment purposes has arisen. This has resulted in the emergence of mobile payment applications or systems. The term refers to all payments for products, services, and bills that are authorised, initiated, or completed using a mobile device (Schierz et al., 2010). It is believed that there must be a transmission of value using a mobile device.

Characteristics of Mobile Payment Methods

Despite the fact that mobile payment systems have existed for some time, their adoption and use are still considered to be in their infancy. The level of acceptance and consequent use of mobile payment procedures is primarily contingent on customer costs, security, and ease of use. Costs refer to the amount required to gain access to the platform. The provider and the user may incur expenses. Users may be charged to subscribe to the service or platform, to transmit value, or even to acquire the device and connectivity to the payment platform.

Types of Mobile Payment Applications

There are four types of mobile payment methods or applications:

Internet payment methods;
Point-of-sale mobile payment methods;
Payments for mobile commerce applications;
Person-to-person mobile payments.

Internet payment methods refer to ways by which one can send and receive money and, especially, make an online payment. One popular website that enables these is PayPal.com. Even though it is a traditional website, PayPal Mobile has been developed for members to manage their accounts no matter where they are. To do this, customers must download the PayPal mobile app (available for iPhone, Android, and BlackBerry) from their website. The service can also be accessed through text messaging.

The traditional point-of-sale (POS) terminals that we normally see in supermarkets and restaurant counters are currently a target for the mobile revolution. Systems have been developed so that credit card payments can be made and received using a mobile device. This is achieved through a combination of specialised devices and apps. This system is targeted and could be very useful for mobile salespeople to process cheques, credit cards and gift cards. It automatically sends a receipt to the payer.

Payments for mobile commerce applications are normally embedded on the SIM cards of mobile phone networks. It seems that this service is currently restricted to the top-up of airtime and the subscription of other value-added services. Currently, there are partnerships between the banks and telecom companies that allow subscribers to access their bank accounts on their mobile devices.

Person-to-person mobile payment seems to be the most common payment system available, especially in Africa. In Ghana, one can send money to another person via MTN Mobile Money. The value could be used as payment for a product or service or redeemed at an authorised Mobile Money point.

Buy Buttons and Location Identification on Social Networking Sites

According to statistics, the number of smartphone users has increased from about 3.7 billion in 2016 to about 7 billion in 2023. With the use of smartphones, people can access various social media platforms for several purposes, almost becoming the main means of communication within and across borders (BankMyCell, 2020). Social media network sites are used for conversations, content creation, and the dissemination of news and information. Businesses are leveraging the increasing utilisation of these social media platforms to expand their audience and reach through "buy buttons."

Buy buttons and location identification are elements on social media sites that facilitate affinity between users and businesses on social media platforms. They are features that can improve the quality of the purchasing experience and offer users of social networking sites information that is helpful to them. Buy buttons, for example, are time-saving technologies that enable users to make purchases without leaving the social media platform on which they are working. They simplify the process by removing the requirement for users to visit external websites, which makes it simpler for consumers to make purchases of products or services that they find while perusing their social feeds (Martinez-Lopez et al., 2020).

The past decade has seen a proliferation of buy buttons because of the results they present to users. Social media sites like Facebook, Twitter, WeChat, and YouTube allow users to transition from interactions to social surfing, thereby increasing direct sales and improving the effectiveness of branding (Lindsey-Mullikin & Borin, 2017). Buy buttons also help users identify their location on social networking sites, which can be helpful not only for individual users but also for businesses. The use of social media platforms creates opportunities for businesses to interact with the audiences they are trying to reach by permitting users to post their locations or check in at specific locations. Users will be able to find local businesses, events, and deals, while businesses will be able to use this information to deliver personalised suggestions and sales.

Buy buttons provide new opportunities for customer engagement, increased visibility, and the possibility of increased sales because of their presence and easy navigation on social media sites. This notwithstanding, it is important to keep in mind the need to protect users' privacy and maintain a secure environment (Mehraj et al., 2021). Social networking sites must prioritise user privacy and protection by ensuring that personal information, such as location data, is handled in a secure and open manner.

Marketing Strategies: Mobile First, Audience First, and Omnichannel

Marketing strategies are always evolving, and three prominent approaches that have garnered considerable attention in recent times are the "Mobile First," "Audience First," and "Omnichannel" strategies. The Mobile First strategy emphasises the prioritisation of mobile experiences throughout the design of marketing campaigns and the optimisation of websites and applications. With the increasing access to and utilisation of smartphones, businesses recognise the importance of delivering seamless and user-friendly mobile experiences to engage and retain customers. By implementing a Mobile First strategy, organisations can guarantee that their content and marketing endeavours are customised to cater specifically to mobile consumers, enhancing user happiness and increasing conversion rates (Ahene Djan, 2021). Particularly in this fourth industrial era, increased competition and changing customer orientations have required the adoption of digital strategies in the marketing spectrum. Business owners are adopting innovative digital approaches to increase and deepen their market share.

The Audience First strategy is centred on comprehending and directing efforts towards specific customer segments. The approach prioritises the development of tailored and pertinent marketing initiatives through the examination of client data and insights. By understanding customer behaviour, preferences, and needs, organisations can effectively deliver customised messages and experiences that deeply engage with their target audience. This approach promotes client loyalty, improves consumer involvement, and increases the probability of successful conversions. By prioritising the audience in marketing endeavours, organisations may establish more robust connections and achieve superior outcomes.

The Omnichannel approach allows a cohesive and uniform customer experience across all channels and touchpoints. It acknowledges that consumers engage with companies across multiple channels, including websites, social media platforms, mobile applications, brick-and-mortar establishments, and other mediums. By incorporating these many channels and creating a unified experience, organisations can enhance their brand visibility and augment client pleasure. The Omnichannel approach enables clients to transition effortlessly between various channels, thereby guaranteeing the delivery of coherent messages and a cohesive brand encounter throughout their entire customer journey. These tactics are not mutually exclusive, and it is common for organisations to integrate them in order to develop impactful marketing campaigns (Nguyen et al., 2022). As an illustration, an organisation may choose to embrace a Mobile First methodology while integrating an Omnichannel approach in order to provide a cohesive mobile experience across several channels.

According to Oslon et al. (2021), achieving effective marketing strategies that yield results requires a deep understanding of the target customer base. This will facilitate the provision of tailored experiences through various interaction channels. By adopting the Mobile First, Audience First, and Omnichannel approaches, organisations can boost their marketing endeavours and establish more robust relationships with their clientele.

Satisfying Customer Experience on Mobile Devices

Recently, customer relationship management (CRM) has acquired widespread popularity across numerous disciplines and industries. The essence of CRM for a business is the ability to provide differentiated relationship value and communicate continuously with each consumer. CRM improves a company's ability to coordinate its marketing and service strategies to establish and maintain long-term partnerships (Gil-Gomez et al., 2020). Technologies such as mobiles are presently bringing about fundamental changes in the way businesses conduct CRM activities. Mobile customer relationship management (mCRM) refers to the use of mobile or wireless devices and applications by businesses to get to know their clients and provide personalised services to increase customer satisfaction and client loyalty over time (Rodriguez & Boyer, 2020). There are two issues with traditional CRM channels. First, there is the possibility that the message will be missed because it was sent on the incorrect medium at the incorrect time; and second, there is the constant risk of information inundation (Juanamasta et al., 2019). Because communication via the mobile medium is based on customer preferences and the customer has granted permission to receive messages, it is presumed that the use of the mobile medium will solve these issues. mCRM can be explained from three angles: technological, process, and conceptual approaches (Rodriguez & Boyer, 2020).

Technological approach: This considers CRM to be a data-processing instrument to support marketing activities. Hence, mCRM consists of activities and technologies that help the company create and maintain a relationship with the client. For example, a list of mobile numbers of a company's customers becomes a data repository that can be used to contact the customers.

Process approach: CRM is the process of gathering and using information about customers to personalise the corporate business and strategies to satisfy every client's individual needs. For example, a firm may use mobile devices to frequently contact customers and provide personalised customer service remotely.

Conceptual approach: CRM is a customer-oriented business strategy that seeks to create and actively manage personalised relationships with customers. This strategy is based on relationship marketing, or one-to-one marketing. For example, the University of Ghana (UG) is among the universities to have adopted a mobile service for communicating application status to potential students. The service enables freshmen and women to track their application status via message service (SMS). Students who apply to the institution can find out their admission status in advance. The advantage for the student, in addition to time savings and ease of use, is that they can print their admission letters from the university website, pay for their fees, and know their accommodation status before the academic year begins. In this respect, one can argue that the application process has a customer-driven focus.

Despite the opportunities, the inclusion of the mobile medium as a channel through which to manage customer relationships poses challenges as well. For instance, companies need to build the technological infrastructure that facilitates the management of customer relationships through the mobile medium. In addition, the technological infrastructure enabling the utilisation of the mobile medium needs to be integrated into the existing CRM system or customer databases. Further challenges stem from the fact that customers need to opt in for the mCRM programme and provide the company with the information necessary for initiating communication with them.

Conclusions

The high rates of young people using one or multiple mobile network accounts offer a large potential for all kinds of marketing-related applications and services. They also present the opportunity for marketers to approach marketing management through a new lens. Gyenge et al. (2021) define marketing management as the process of planning and executing the conception, pricing, promotion, and distribution of goods, services, and ideas to create exchanges that satisfy individual and organisational goals. From this definition, marketing management implies sequential stages of temporal and spatial separation between buyers and sellers. Mobile marketing tends to blur these boundaries and distinctions in the traditional view of managing marketing activities.

Mobile marketing incorporates interactivity and transcends traditional communication, allowing for different communication models—business-to-business, business-to-consumer, consumer-to-consumer, and consumer-to-business—to take place concurrently and sometimes in real time (Xiao et al., 2020). Interactive communication is developed when organisations create a medium for the exchange of information between themselves and channel partners. Most companies, for instance, are now posting FAQs (frequently asked questions) on their websites, which answer most of the common problems of customers and channel partners. These FAQs can also be made accessible via mobile, either through a mobile version of the company's website, through text messaging, or through social networking websites accessible on mobile. Interactive communication tends to build customer trust, which can also enhance brand loyalty.

As internet access becomes cheaper and offers faster speed, the opportunities for enhancing marketing communications increase. Mobile internet is now accessible on mobiles, laptops, tablet computers, or wireless devices. The advantage is the mobility and portability of these devices, and hence, the opportunity to integrate them with other marketing communication channels. Several companies are integrating the offline experience of their brands with the virtual, online, and mobile experiences. For example, Reebok, the athletic wear manufacturer, aired a commercial during the 2003 Super Bowl with the objective of driving viewers to their website (Super Bowl Ad Centre, 2003). Soon after the Super Bowl, traffic on the Reebok website, including the mobile version, rose significantly to over 2 million unique visitors. The company also captured over 250,000 online registrations and then became the target for additional online promotions.

The scenario has since become more phenomenal since consumers now attend the Super Bowl with smartphones like iPhones and can access the websites of advertisers while the game is ongoing. Hence, the integration of new technologies into traditional marketing channels opens better opportunities for effective interactive marketing and brand engagement.

Social media currently dominates the internet. The internet is increasingly becoming concentrated on how technology connects and empowers people (Tong et al., 2020). Through social media, Internet users can connect with friends, share opinions, music, and videos, and even purchase products online. To leverage social media platforms alongside other mobile marketing channels, marketing managers must have a deeper comprehension of how and why individuals utilise social media.

Companies' capacity to integrate mobile marketing channels into a potent customer-centric strategy will determine future trends in mobile marketing. An SMS campaign could be the first step in a company's mobile marketing campaign, which might then include a mobile website and/or mobile social media platform, mobile advertising, and mobile couponing. To protect the brands in this scenario, the challenge of mobile brand engagement is to establish the same credibility but a different presentation. Effective branding through various mobile channels or services necessitates the recognition of customer needs and preferences in various communication channels and the development of a multi-channel strategy that reinforces the brand through unique experiences while maintaining its credibility.

Review Questions

1. Discuss the growth of mobile connectivity and device use in developing economies, as outlined in this chapter. How has this growth impacted the use of social networking sites and mobile marketing strategies in these regions?
2. Examine the significance of mobile applications in the context of social networking and marketing. How do platforms like Google Play and Apple's App Store contribute to the distribution and success of these applications for mobile marketing?
3. Analyse the role of "buy buttons" and location identification features on social networking sites in mobile marketing. How do these features enhance the user experience and benefit businesses?
4. Evaluate the marketing strategies discussed in this chapter, such as the Mobile First, Audience First, and Omnichannel approaches. How do these strategies help in creating effective marketing campaigns on social networking sites for mobile users?

References

Abdul Rahaman, A., & Abdulai, A. (2022). Mobile money adoption, input use, and farm output among smallholder rice farmers in Ghana. *Agribusiness, 38*(1), 236–255.

Ah, S. (2019). Dimensions of internal branding–a conceptual study. *Journal of Management, 6*(1), 177–185.

Ahene Djan, V. (2021). *The effect of digital marketing on consumer buying behaviour: A case study of fan milk Ghana limited*. Ghana Institute of Journalism.

Arif, K. S., & Ali, U. (2019, January). Mobile application testing tools and their challenges: A comparative study. In *2nd International conference on computing, mathematics and engineering technologies (iCoMET)* (pp. 1–6). IEEE.

Asravor, R. K., Boakye, A. N., & Essuman, J. (2022). Adoption and intensity of use of mobile money among smallholder farmers in rural Ghana. *Information Development, 38*(2), 204–217.

Atulkar, S. (2020). Brand trust and brand loyalty in mall shoppers. *Marketing Intelligence & Planning, 38*(5), 559–572.

BankMyCell. (2020). *How many people have smartphones worldwide*. Retrieved September 28, 2023, from https://www.bankmycell.com/blog/how-many-phones-are-in-the-world

Baird, I. (Ed.). (2014). *Social networks in the long eighteenth century: Clubs, literary salons, textual coteries*. Cambridge Scholars Publishing.

Branding. (n.d.). *American marketing association*. Retrieved June 27, 2023, from https://www.ama.org/topics/branding/

Clement, J. (2019). Daily time spent on social networking by internet users worldwide from 2012 – 2018 (in minutes). New York: Statista. https://www.statista.com/statistics/433871/daily-social-media-usageworldwide/

Gil-Gomez, H., Guerola-Navarro, V., Oltra-Badenes, R., & Lozano-Quilis, J. A.(2020). Customer relationship management: digital transformation and sustainable business model innovation. *Economic research-Ekonomska istraživanja, 33*(1), 2733–2750.

Gyenge, B., Máté, Z., Vida, I., Bilan, Y., & Vasa, L. (2021). A new strategic marketing management model for the specificities of E-commerce in the supply chain. *Journal of Theoretical and Applied Electronic Commerce Research, 16*(4), 1136–1149.

Juanamasta, I. G., Wati, N. M. N., Hendrawati, E., Wahyuni, W., Pramudianti, M., Wisnujati, N. S., …. & Umanailo, M. C. B. (2019). The role of customer service through customer relationship management (Crm) to increase customer loyalty and good image. *International Journal of Scientific and Technology Research, 8*(10), 2004–2007.

Lindsey-Mullikin, J., & Borin, N. (2017). Why strategy is key for successful social media sales. *Business Horizons, 60*(4), 473–482.

Martinez-Lopez, F. J., Li, Y., Liu, H., & Feng, C. (2020). Do safe buy buttons and integrated path-to-purchase on social platforms improve users' shopping-related responses?. *Electronic Commerce Research and Applications, 39*, 100913.

Maurya, U. K., & Mishra, P. (2012). What is a brand? A Perspective on Brand Meaning. *European Journal of Business and Management, 4*(3), 122–133.

McLean, G., & Wilson, A. (2019). Shopping in the digital world: Examining customer engagement through augmented reality mobile applications. *Computers in Human Behavior, 101*, 210–224.

Mehraj, H., Jayadevappa, D., Haleem, S. L. A., Parveen, R., Madduri, A., Ayyagari, M. R., & Dhabliya, D. (2021). Protection motivation theory using multi-factor authentication for providing security over social networking sites. *Pattern Recognition Letters, 152*, 218–224.

Naydenov, K. (2019). Theoretical bases of tourism branding. *KNOWLEDGE-International Journal, 30*(6), 1761–1766.

Nguyen, A., McClelland, R., Hoang Thuan, N., & Hoang, T. G. (2022). Omnichannel marketing: Structured review, synthesis, and future directions. *The International Review of Retail, Distribution and Consumer Research, 32*(3), 221–265.

Olson, E. M., Olson, K. M., Czaplewski, A. J., & Key, T. M. (2021). Business strategy and the management of digital marketing. *Business horizons, 64*(2), 285–293.

Peters, L. A. (2012). *Utilizing social media to further the nationwide suspicious activity reporting initiative.* (Doctoral dissertation, Monterey, California. Naval Postgraduate School).

Putranto, D., & Rochmawati, E. (2020). Mobile applications for managing symptoms of patients with cancer at home: A scoping review. *International Journal of Nursing Practice, 26*(4), e12842.

Rodriguez, M., & Boyer, S. (2020). The impact of mobile customer relationship management (mCRM) on sales collaboration and sales performance. *Journal of Marketing Analytics, 8*(3), 137–148.

Rohini, P., Tripathi, S., Preeti, C. M., Renuka, A., Gonzales, J. L. A., & Gangodkar, D. (2022, April). A study on the adoption of wireless communication in big data analytics using neural networks and deep learning. In *2nd International conference on advance computing and innovative technologies in engineering (ICACITE)* (pp. 1071–1076). IEEE.

Salehan, M., & Negahban, A. (2013). Social networking on smartphones: When mobile phones become addictive. *Computers in Human Behavior, 29*(6), 2632–2639.

Schierz, P. G., Schilke, O., & Wirtz, B. W. (2010). Understanding consumer acceptance of mobile payment services: An empirical analysis. *Electronic Commerce Research and Applications, 9*(3), 209–216.

Silver, L., Smith, A., Johnson, C., Taylor, K., Jiang, J., Anderson, M., & Rainie, L. (2019). Mobile connectivity in emerging economies. *Pew Research Center, 7*, 1–92.

Smith, M., Szongott, C., Henne, B., & Von Voigt, G. (2012) June. Big data privacy issues in public social media. In *2012 6th IEEE international conference on digital ecosystems and technologies (DEST)*, 1–6. IEEE.

Tong, S., Luo, X., & Xu, B. (2020). Personalized mobile marketing strategies. *Journal of the Academy of Marketing Science, 48*, 64–78.

Toren, C. (2020). Anthropology as the whole science of what it is to be human. In *Anthropology beyond culture*, Richard G. Foxand Barbara J. King. (eds.), (pp. 105–124). Routledge.

Untari, D. T., Satria, B., Fikri, A. W. N., Nursal, M. F., & Winarso, W. (2020). Technology, social media and behaviour of young generation in Indonesia; a conceptual paper. *International Journal of Scientific and Technology Research, 9*(4), 986–989.

Wang, Y., Hsiao, S. H., Yang, Z., & Hajli, N. (2016). The impact of sellers' social influence on the co-creation of innovation with customers and brand awareness in online communities. *Industrial Marketing Management, 54*, 56–70.

Xiao, L., Mao, H., & Wang, S. (2020). Research on mobile marketing recommendation method incorporating layout aesthetic preference for sustainable m-commerce. *Sustainability, 12*(6), 2496.

Zhou, T. (2019). Understanding social influence on mobile social networking sites: A social support perspective. *Information Development, 35*, 220–229.

Chapter 6

Foundations of Mobile Commerce: A Gateway to Engaging in Emerging Markets

Chapter Outline

- Mobile commerce (m-commerce) defined
- Features and benefits of mobile commerce
- M-commerce services
- Factors which influence m-commerce adoption
- Global trends in m-commerce
- Case studies on using mobiles in micro-trading

Chapter Outcome

By the end of this chapter, the reader will be able to:

Define and identify features of mobile commerce:
- Identify specific functionalities and characteristics that distinguish mobile commerce from other forms of commerce.

Explore mobile commerce services:
- Analyse and categorise mobile commerce services based on their functionalities and applications.

DOI: 10.4324/9781003307457-6

Analyse factors influencing the adoption of mobile commerce:
- Formulate insights into the challenges and drivers influencing the acceptance and utilisation of mobile commerce.

Examine global trends in mobile commerce:
- Identify key market dynamics, emerging technologies, and evolving consumer behaviours shaping the landscape of mobile commerce.

Identify contemporary payment options in mobile commerce:
- Demonstrate the ability to evaluate and select appropriate payment methods based on user preferences and industry standards.

Introduction to Mobile Commerce

Mobile phones hold a lot of promise for the conduct of business in contemporary times. However, the starting point to achieving this promise is to understand the concepts behind the application of mobile phones and their link to business. There are a variety of definitions of mobile commerce in academic literature and among marketing and technology professionals. Within these definitions, m-commerce has been categorised as either a technology, a product, a service, or a combination of the three. It is believed that m-commerce encompasses technology, services, and products as components based on apparatus or devices, mode of operation, and use.

The most closely aligned definition to our discussion is the one by Jonker (2003), and the broader definition adopted is:

> all the activities related to a potential commercial transaction conducted through telecommunications networks for the exchange of information, goods, and services that interface with wireless or mobile devices, thereby establishing and maintaining relationships between suppliers, dealers, customers, strategic partners, regulators, other agents, and all the necessary parties in support of traditional delivery channels.

Table 6.1 M-commerce as a Technology, Product and/or Service

M-commerce as:
Technology M-commerce refers to any transaction of monetary value occurring over a wireless communication network through the use of wireless handheld devices. (Shrivastava et al., (2019) Mobile commerce, also referred to as m-commerce, is the use of wireless handheld devices such as cellular phones and laptops to conduct commercial transactions online. (Jayanthi, 2020).
Product M-commerce applications is used widely including in applications such as mobile banking, mobile purchasing, location-based services, mobile ticketing, and information services. (Shrivastava et. al., 2019)
Service Mobile commerce, being an extension to electronic commerce, refers to the commerce that is carried out by using wireless devices such as mobile phones, personal digital assistants, or other handheld devices. It is an innovative way to attract customers and provides greater convenience to its subscribers. (Shrivastava et. al., 2019)
Interaction of technology, product, and service The buying and selling of goods, services, and information, without any locational restriction by mobile devices that use a wireless connection to establish communication between all the necessary parties to complete the transaction (Jonker, 2003).

Source: Authors (2024)

Hence, m-commerce is not just a transaction; it extends to providing services and information. For example, m-commerce is seen to have some mobile applications that are used to provide a number of services.

These services include mobile banking, payments, information, and marketing services. M-commerce is also used by customer service providers seeking to offer a host of products and services to customers, thereby expanding the definition of m-commerce to include a range of mobile data services such as short message service (SMS), multimedia message service (MMS), mobile video streaming, mobile games, and location-based service (Lucas et al., 2023). These services also generate added value and a number of benefits for mobile users and/or adopters.

Mobile Commerce and Mobile Business

Regarding the use of mobile devices to create business value, m-commerce and mobile business (m-business) are considered synonymous. As we've already said, m-commerce includes all the things that could happen in a business deal that happen over telecommunications networks to exchange information, goods, and services that work with wireless or mobile devices. It also includes building and keeping relationships between suppliers, dealers, customers, strategic partners, regulators, other agents, and everyone else who is needed to support traditional delivery channels. It also refers to business transactions that mobile or wireless devices either directly or indirectly facilitate. This includes the exchange of business information, the maintenance of business relationships, and the conduct of business transactions using mobile or wireless devices.

M-business, however, is the use of mobile or wireless devices to conduct the business activities of a company, either internally or externally, in relation to its clients, suppliers, partners, and other stakeholders (Putri et al., 2020). M-business is therefore the direct or indirect use of mobiles or wireless devices to perform or facilitate the performance of organisational functions such as financial management, marketing management, strategy leverage, production management, information systems, logistic management, customer relationship management, and human resource management. M-commerce tends to be a subset of m-business, given that m-business involves the use of mobiles for all business-related activities (Puiu et al., 2022).

Features and Benefits of Mobile Commerce

Mobile phones provide a variety of functionalities, applications, and services through their various characteristics, which provide customers with additional value and advantages. Examining the characteristics of m-commerce reveals that it is a unique combination of time, location, and customisation. Other characteristics include correctness, promptness, instant connectivity, and identification (Boateng, 2011; Michael & David, 2003). These are also associated with time, place, and customisation.

Regarding immediacy, time, and accessibility, mobile phones improve the mobility of consumers by allowing them to access, share, and exchange information in remote and time-sensitive transactions. These features contribute to a reduction in travel or commuting expenses. Mobiles can also be integrated with global positioning systems, allowing businesses to track users' locations and provide location-specific products and services (Bounie et al., 2019). As services can be conveniently matched, "localised," or personalised to user or customer locations, convenience and cost savings can be derived from these functionalities. Personalisation is the degree to which communication between consumers and sellers is tailored to the consumers' preferences, requirements, and shopping preferences. It guarantees that consumers receive the most pertinent message (Kim et al., 2001).

Table 6.2 Features of M-commerce

Basic Features	*Turban et al., 2004*	*Michael and David (2003)*	*Stanoevska-Slabev (2003)*
Ubiquity Easier information access in real time Communication independent of the user's location	Ubiquity	Ubiquity	Ubiquity
Accessibility Contactable anywhere, anytime The choice to limit their accessibility to particular persons or times	Instant Connectivity	Accessibility	Immediacy /Time
Personalisation Preparation of information Creating services that customise the end-user experience	Personalisation	Personalisation	Personalisation
Localisation Knowing where the user is located at any particular moment Match services to their location	Localisation	Localisation	Localisation

Source: Authors (2024)

Personalisation not only improves their perception of the seller, but it also reduces their searching costs – the time and effort required to look for products and compare prices among various suppliers and competitors (Boadi et al., 2007; Boateng, 2011). Buyers and vendors are now comparatively accessible and can be reached from anywhere. It also gives them the option to restrict access to specific individuals or times. This characteristic of m-commerce facilitates both convenience and communication.

This combination of mobile features and attributes has the potential to generate strategic, relational, and operational benefits for users (buyers and merchants) (Boateng, 2011). Reducing coordination costs in the delivery of products, commodities, and services in the marketplace has operational benefits for the business. As sellers or suppliers, businesses will be able to communicate directly with prospective clients and trading partners regarding the availability of products and services. It is possible to exchange information regarding the quality, quantity, and delivery times of products. This may contribute to a decrease in the costs associated with searching for goods, services, buyers, and sellers; a decrease in delivery and inventory costs, particularly for perishable products; a decrease in the risk associated with frequent long journeys for goods; and an increase in the timeliness of decision-making, negotiating, and fulfilling transactional terms. Obtaining operational benefits can lead to relational advantages.

Relational benefits are associated with enhanced communication and relationships between parties (buyers, customers, sellers, and suppliers) involved in a mobile-facilitated transaction. The pervasiveness, localisation, and customisation capabilities of mobile phones can result in disintermediation, in which merchants bypass or avoid "middlemen" and shorten distribution channels to transact directly with potential customers and trading partners (Shankar et al., 2021). This enhanced and direct communication may increase the actors' motivation, confidence, and mutual comprehension. These relational advantages may lead to strategic advantages.

Strategic benefits are associated with those that increase market "reach" (access to new markets) as well as the commitment and performance of actors involved in a mobile transaction. The operational and relational benefits of a transaction can inspire actors to engage in long-term relationships for the benefit of all. These benefits include the strengthening of

Figure 6.1   Mobile commerce benefits. Source: Authors (2024)

relationships, loyalty, and retention between businesses and their customers and business partners; the differentiation and personalisation of products and services; and the expansion of a company's market reach as a result of an enhanced reputation, recommendations, and referrals. In effect, strategic advantages may stimulate growth and performance for the parties concerned in the transaction.

Cost refers to the cost savings and operational efficiencies that a consumer or business can achieve by employing mobile devices for business or commercial purposes. *Convenience* refers to having access to information whenever and wherever it is required. *Communication* refers to enhancing the content of information and relationships. In a transaction, information is exchanged in a timely manner and possibly more frequently. Improving marketplace information has the potential to reduce the costs associated with seeking out products and services and the timeliness of decisions associated with negotiating transactional terms and completing transactions. Through personalisation, immediacy, and accessibility, m-commerce improves communication, which contributes to the strengthening of participants' relationships and trust.

M-commerce Services

This section will discuss the various categories of m-commerce services and briefly describe their characteristics. These concepts will allow you to recognise and comprehend the various m-commerce services. Using mobile devices for commerce provides consumers with pervasive access to essential and supplemental services. Mobiles offer consumers essential services, including voice services for voice calls or mobile telephony and data services for text messaging, multimedia messaging, and Internet access. These fundamental services frequently support the delivery of products and services with added value. These value-added services, primarily in the information, entertainment, marketing and advertising, banking, ticketing, and retail sectors, are likely to promote consumer adoption of mobile commerce services (Ay et al., 2008; Verisign, 2007; Boadi et al., 2007).

Information services: Mobile information includes content services such as a subscription to news on various topics, including sports, politics, entertainment, and technology; weather updates; stock price information; travel information; and the provision of mobile search services. In Ghana and

Table 6.3   List of M-commerce Services

1. Mobile banking (m-banking) Mobile accounting Mobile brokerage Mobile financial information	2. Mobile entertainment (m-entertainment) Mobile gaming Downloads (music and ring tones) Downloads (video digital images and streaming)	3. Mobile information services News and current affairs Travel information Weather updates and stock prices Mobile Search Engines
4. Mobile marketing (m-marketing) Mobile couponing Direct marketing Mobile Newsletters	5. Mobile ticketing (m-ticketing) Public transport Sport and cultural events Air and rail ticketing	6. Mobile payment (m-payment) m-Purse m-wallet Mobile money transfer
7. Mobile retail/ shopping (m-shopping) Mobile purchasing of goods Product search Product and price comparisons		

Source: Authors (2024)

Nigeria, mobile network operators provide the most recent statistics for sporting events such as the English Premier League and the Spanish Primera Division. Through a partnership between a teleconference service provider (Forum Networks Limited), a mobile network operator (MTN), and the Public Affairs Directorate of Parliament, Ghana's parliamentary proceedings are now globally accessible. CitiFMonline (2012) states that anyone can listen to live parliamentary debates via any mobile telecommunication network by dialling an assigned number at standard call rates and long-distance charges. Mobile entertainment consists of content services like music downloads, videos, gaming, and ringtones, as well as text-based messaging services like audience voting. In Ghana and Nigeria, mobile network operators provide consumers with local melodies as downloadable ringtones. MTN Ghana, for instance, offers a song service, which allows users to transmit a song to other MTN subscribers by dialling a short code and following voice prompts.

The recipient will receive a phone call from the sender's number with a voice prompt instructing them to download the song (MTN Ghana, 2012). Mobile Content, a local content provider in Ghana, also sends text messages to mobile users with the movie schedule for Silverbird Cinemas (Mobile Content, 2012).

Marketing and advertising: Mobile operators and other businesses are connecting advertisers with specific demographics through targeted mobile advertising and mobile coupons. In Ghana, Google partners with local mobile network providers like Airtel and Tigo to offer the marketing service on Google Trader, which enables consumers to act as merchants who advertise and promote products to other consumers via mobile phones (Google Trader, 2012). Mobile Content, a local content provider in Ghana, also offers clients simple-to-use tools and well-established connections with mobile network operators, enabling merchants to easily aggregate and distribute messages, coupons, and content across multiple operator networks without incurring the time and expense of establishing a relationship with each individual mobile network operator (Mobile Content, 2012).

Banking and bill payment: Mobile banking enables customers to receive alerts, administer their accounts, pay bills, and transfer funds using their mobile devices. While at sea, mobile banking in Ghana enables fishermen to conduct business with fishmongers and receive payment for the sale of fish. Consumers can also receive text message alerts for any transaction made on their accounts (Boadi et al., 2007).

Ticketing: Mobile ticketing enables consumers on mobile devices to purchase event and transport tickets. In Kenya, Safaricom allows subscribers to purchase tickets from local airlines like East African, Air Kenya, and Aircraft Leasing Services; the Rift Valley Railways; and bus companies like Akamba, Crown Bus, and Busways. Subscribers access www.safaricom.com from their mobile devices, select their preferred flight or travel, and input their names and mobile numbers to receive a booking reference and payment instructions via M-Pesa (a local mobile payment system) (Kagwe, 2009).

In-store and peer-to-peer transactions Consumers are increasingly attracted to the convenience of paying for goods and services and transferring funds via mobile devices. Two mobile network operators in Ghana, MTN and Airtel, offer mobile payment systems that facilitate the purchase of mobile airtime and the transfer of funds between consumers. These mobile network operators enable consumers to link their mobile devices to their bank accounts so that they can conduct financial transactions. Despite the fact that many of these services are relatively new in Africa, they are reshaping mobile culture, and their emergence and growing prevalence are evidence of the accelerating growth of mobile commerce. To enable firms to generate value from these services, it is necessary to comprehend the factors that influence the adoption of these services by mobile consumers.

Factors that Influence M-Commerce Adoption

Adoption of m-commerce refers to the selection of mobile technologies and services for use by a user or business. Adoption is the choice to embrace and utilise a specific mobile device or service. As with other technologies, consumers adopt m-commerce by first becoming aware of an m-commerce service, then forming attitudes towards the service, and finally deciding whether to adopt or reject the service.

Adopters will utilise the commerce service after the adoption decision has been made and will confirm the adoption decision if the service functions as expected (Rogers, 1995). The adoption process is arguably a process beginning with the collection of information and ending with the actual implementation of the m-commerce service. Therefore, the user is the primary determinant of the adoption process's success.

M-commerce Adopters and Adoption Factors

M-commerce adopters or users play a threefold role: as technology users, as network members, and as consumers (Pedersen et al., 2002; AlHinai et al., 2007). Hence, to fully understand individuals' adoption of mobile commerce, these three integrated roles have to be explained.

M-commerce Adopters as Technology Users

Users are typically attracted to the technological features of the technologies they employ. The technology characteristics of m-commerce services or products tend to influence m-commerce adopters as technology consumers.

The characteristics of the technology can influence m-commerce adoption in seven dimensions: perceived usefulness/functional performance, perceived ease of use, acquisition cost, operating cost, ease-of-use, reliability, compatibility, and serviceability (Davis et al., 1989; Rogers, 1995; Suebsin & Gersri, 2009).

1. *Perceived usefulness* or *functional performance* refers to the extent to which an adopter of m-commerce believes that m-commerce will enhance job performance, provide anticipated benefits, or achieve functional performance.
2. *Perceived ease-of-use* refers to the adopter's perception of the minimal effort necessary to utilise the m-commerce service.
3. *Acquisition cost* is the amount that consumers must pay for an m-commerce service or product in order to possess or own it. For instance, consider the cost of a mobile phone or mobile banking application.
4. *Operating expenses* are incurred when a user utilises the m-commerce service—for instance, the cost of airtime to utilise mobile voice services.
5. *Reliability* refers to the independence of an m-commerce service or product's functionality as well as its useful lifetime.
6. *Compatibility* is the degree to which the new technology is compatible with other existing devices or business needs.
7. *Serviceability* refers to the time and cost required to restore or replace an m-commerce product or service if it malfunctions.
8. *Security* refers to the condition in which an m-commerce service or product is free from unauthorised use, exploitation, and disruption during use by an m-commerce adopter.

M-Commerce Adopters as Network Users

M-commerce adopters are more than just technology users. These users are usually part of a social–business network, such as friends, family, co-workers, and trading partners. This network usually influences an individual's perceptions, opinions, experiences, and actions in regard to the selection and use of m-commerce services and products (Sey, 2009; Boateng, 2011). Within the network, users recommend products and services to each other and also equally discourage unfavourable services from each other (AlHinai et al., 2007).

Therefore, social-business networks create a room for interaction, which affects an m-commerce adopter's decision to adopt or reject a particular service or product. This influence can be conceptualised as the perceived social pressure to perform or not perform the behaviour of selecting and using a particular m-commerce service or product.

M-commerce Adopters as Consumers

M-commerce adopters are more than just technology users and network users. They are also consumers. The consumer role takes place as soon as a user subscribes to a mobile or telephone service with a service provider or network provider (Gitau & Nzuki, 2014). This is a prerequisite for the use of an m-commerce service or product. After becoming a mobile phone user, the user gets the opportunity to decide whether or not to become an m-commerce adopter. The user subscribes to mobile commerce services at a fee, which is a continuous transaction for as long as the user seeks to be an adopter. Consequently, two sets of factors can influence the adoption of m-commerce from a consumer perspective: the characteristics of the mobile commerce service provider or mobile network operator, and the characteristics of the consumer (Bhatt, 2021).

First, the characteristics of the m-commerce service provider can influence the decision to become a customer of a particular mobile provider or network provider, which can affect subsequent intentions and decisions to accept services or products from that mobile service provider or network provider. These factors include the perceived reputation, image, or social capital of the service provider; the marketing and pricing strategies of the service provider; and the network coverage and infrastructure of the service provider (Boadi et al., 2007; Sey, 2009; Suebsin & Gerdsri, 2009). These characteristics of the service provider may also be influenced by other firm-level factors such as firm size, human resources, and financial resources, as well as environmental factors like market competition, legal issues, and industry push (Rana et al., 2019).

Second, the characteristics of the consumer also play a key role in the type of mobile services adopted and the extent of usage. Two key characteristics are the knowledge of the adopter and the income level of the adopter, or the availability of slack resources for use on mobile services. For example, in research on mobile commerce adoption by market traders, Boateng (2011) found that the knowledge of the market trader influenced the extent of usage and benefits obtained from using the mobile phone in trading activities. The knowledge of the market trader was found to be a function of both formal and informal education. Less educated market traders were less likely to adopt data services like text messages and more likely to adopt voice services. The knowledge of the adopter can also influence the assessment of the perceived usefulness and perceived ease-of-use of m-commerce services. Thus, the knowledge of the adopter can influence the extent of adoption as a technology user.

On the other hand, in telecommunication, affordability is linked to the cost of providing the service. Milne (2006) distinguishes two levels of lack of affordability based on two effects:

1. The barrier effect, which prevents people from owning a phone or from using shared access phones other than in emergencies;
2. The inhibitor effect, which discourages people from making as many calls as they need to, even when they own or have access to a phone.

Plainly, the barrier effect is more serious, and it is on the wane or absent in many contexts (Sey, 2009). Affordability is only fully achieved once the inhibitor effect is reduced to a level where people can make all the calls that they feel are necessary without cutting back on other essentials. Therefore, the income level of the adopter plays a key role in determining the mobile expenditure of the adopter. For example, Nigerian poor households spend up to 8% of their income on telephone services (Intelecon, 2005). Another study shows levels in the range of 10%–14% on telephone expenditure among poor households in Tanzania (Souter, 2005). Since mobiles tend to be considered an important social and business communication device, it is more likely that users will adopt the path of least cost of adoption when selecting m-commerce services and products. Thus, services priced beyond their perceived affordability may be less patronised. In effect, a customer's evaluation of the factors discussed above can result in either positive or negative outcomes for the adoption of m-commerce services and products. Therefore, there are three roles that have to be considered when investigating the adoption of m-commerce services. The interrelationships between the three roles are illustrated in Figure 6.2.

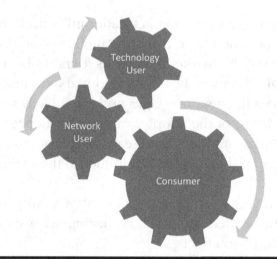

Figure 6.2   Roles played by mobile commerce users. Source: Authors (2024)

Global Trends in M-commerce

This section will discuss the global trends in m-commerce. These concepts will enable you to understand the global trends in m-commerce and develop a broader understanding of the potential of mobile commerce services and products.

Trends are defined by the new functionalities of mobile technology, or the features and characteristics of a new class of mobile commerce applications, from which the trend typically takes its name and its impetus. Firms that understand new mobile commerce trends will be able to leverage the new mobile technologies or m-commerce applications to deliver a richer user experience. Several research institutions and news agencies in the mobile industry have carried out evaluations on the top trends in mobile commerce in 2011 (Portio Research, 2012; Eler, 2011). These evaluation studies have also presented future predictions based on the behaviour of mobile users. The key findings from these studies are discussed as follows:

The Promise of Mobiles

The last 5 years have seen a tremendous growth in telephone ownership and use in developing countries (ITU, 2010). Until the mid-1990s, telephones in poor countries were mostly in cities. Some African countries had only a single telephone for every 1,000 people (Panos Brief, 2005). However, statistics from the International Telecommunication Union tend to suggest that mobile phone subscribers constituted over 75% of the world's population as of 2010 (ITU, 2010). The report also suggests that there are now more mobile cellular subscriptions in the developing world than in the developed world.

Arguably, people in both developing and developed countries have multiple mobile subscriptions for various reasons, including lowering traffic costs. It is, however, important to observe the rapid diffusion of mobiles in both developing and developed regions.

In countries like Ghana, mobile phones realised a penetration rate of 138.88% of the population as of December 2018 (NCA, 2019), with over 25 million registered mobile money accounts (Bank Of Ghana,-BOG, 2018, www.bog.gov.gh/payment-systems/payment-systems-statistics, Accessed on 3rd April 2019). The rapid diffusion of this relatively low-cost technology has spurred a development agenda questioning how mobile phones can be harnessed more effectively for business and for socioeconomic development in developing economies (Doe, 2020).

Tablet commerce on the rise: Depending on the type of mobile device, there are now two types of users: mobile phone users and tablet users. Tablets are forms of mobile devices that have recently become popular with the advent of the Apple iPad and the Samsung Galaxy Tab. These forms of mobile devices did previously exist in the form of palmtop computers and personal digital assistants (PDAs), but they were relatively obscure and were mainly adopted by corporate classes (Reid, 2012). Tablets are designed with a full touchscreen and a processor to carry out both entertainment and basic business activities, including email, internet browsing, taking and sharing pictures, and playing music and movies. However, as users' demands change or increase, tablets have become empowered by new operating systems such as iOs from Apple, Android from Google, and Windows Phone from Microsoft. These operating systems feature mobile application markets (iTunes App Store and Android Market/Google Play), which enable users to either purchase or freely download a diversity of applications.

A study by Adobe Research over the 2011 US holiday period found that tablet visitors spent more per purchase than visitors using smartphones or traditional desktops and laptops; tablet users spend 54% longer on sites than mobile users and purchase over 20% more than desktop visitors. The findings suggest that tablet visitors were the most valuable online customers in 2011. The high sale value is partly due to the ease of use of the devices.

Adobe analysed 16.2 billion anonymous visits to the websites of more than 150 top US retailers (Adobe, 2012).

Implications: Future mobile commerce applications must be designed to be user-friendly for use on a tablet. Online retail websites must develop applications to enable users to browse and purchase their products through smart mobile phones and tablets.

Top mobile markets: As of March 2012, 30% of the world's mobile users live in India and China. China is still leading with more than a billion subscribers, with India not far behind. Both China and India have more than twice the number of subscribers as the United States (Laricchia, 2023). According to the GSMA Africa Mobile Observatory 2011 report, Africa is the fastest-growing mobile market in the world and is the biggest after Asia. The top three markets in the continent by subscriptions are Nigeria, Egypt, and South Africa. Over the past 5 years, the number of subscribers across Africa has grown by almost 20% each year, and it is estimated to reach more than 735 million by the end of 2012 (GSMA, 2011).

Implications: The market for mobile commerce is widely increasing and likely to become more competitive as mobile network operators seek to protect their market share. Mobile network operators who can deploy innovative m-commerce applications at an affordable price that are relevant to both urban and rural dwellers are more likely to gain a competitive edge.

New Payment Options

Mobile wallets are digital versions of traditional wallets with some variations, notably storing information about credit and debit cards, coupons, loyalty points, and so on. Marketers can tap into two types of communication that can be sent to their subscribers. These are offers, coupons, and loyalty cards (Ibrahim et al., 2022). Mobile wallets require collaboration between mobile network operators, a banking or financial institution, and a service provider that intends to allow consumers to make purchases via mobile wallet. Portio's research notes that, globally, the contribution of mobile data services to the revenue of mobile network operators is increasing. Mobile data services contributed to 48%, 41%, and 33% of the revenues of mobile network operators in the United Kingdom, China, and India, respectively (Portio Research Mobile Factbook, 2012).

Thus, m-commerce applications like mobile wallets, which underpin other m-commerce services like mobile shopping and mobile payments, are critical to increasing revenue potential. Some wallets store data on the phone itself, while others store it in the cloud (remotely in the repository of the service provider). The latter allows users to use the mobile wallet on any computing device that connects to the internet. The former, storing the data on the mobile phone, always requires the mobile phone to be present in every transaction.

NFC opportunities: NFC (near-field communication) enables the exchange of data between devices (typically mobile devices) that are near each other. NFC devices are used in mobile payments as contactless cards that communicate with other devices to facilitate payments. Currently, only a few smart mobile phones, like the Samsung Galaxy SIII, have NFC enabled. There are also a few retailers that have integrated NFC devices for the payment of products and services. Thus, despite the advent of m-commerce technology, adoption may take some time on the part of users. However, NFC can be used for other functions beyond payments. NFC-enabled mobile devices may be able to exchange data—files, pictures, and information—and interact with each other when they are in proximity.

Carrier milling: Carrier billing allows subscribers to pay for services and purchase applications (from app stores) on their mobile phone bill instead of using a credit card or a third-party mobile payments service to pay at the time of purchase (Lopez, 2020). In this regard, mobile network operators collaborate with application markets like the Android market. For example, a number of mobile network operators in the United States, including Spring, T-Mobile, and AT&T, support carrier billing in the Android Market. This service works for post-paid mobile subscribers. PayPal, another online payment platform, also began to offer carrier billing after its parent company, eBay, purchased a mobile payment company.

Implications: These new forms of payment presuppose that consumers are more likely to spend more time and money in m-commerce if the payment systems are made more user-friendly and easily accessible across multiple platforms and devices.

Review Questions

1. Define mobile commerce (m-commerce) and discuss its various manifestations as a technology, a product, and a service. Refer to the definitions and categorisations provided in the chapter to explain how m-commerce integrates these three elements.
2. What are the key features of mobile commerce that distinguish it from traditional commerce? Discuss the benefits of these features for both businesses and consumers.
3. Explain how mobile commerce and mobile business are intertwined. How do these concepts contribute to the various organisational functions such as financial management, marketing management, and customer relationship management?
4. Discuss the global trends in mobile commerce and the factors influencing its adoption. According to various cited researchers and studies in the chapter, how do these trends and factors influence the use and development of m-commerce services in emerging markets?

References

Adobe Acrobat, X. I. (2012). *Convert an existing form into a fillable PDF form with Adobe Acrobat XI*. Quick Start Guide.

AlHinai, Y. S., Kurnia, S., & Johnston, R. B. (2007, July 9–11). *Adoption of mobile commerce services by individuals: A meta-analysis of the literature, management of mobile business*. ICMB 2007. International Conference.

Ayo, C. K., Adebiyi, A. A., Fatudimu, I. T., & Ekong, U. O. (2008). A framework for e-commerce implementation: Nigeria a case study. *Journal of Internet Banking and Commerce, 13*(2), 1–12.

Bhatt, S. (2021). An empirical study of factors affecting adoption of M-commerce in India. *Journal of Marketing Advances and Practices, 3*, 42–60.

Boadi, R. A., Boateng, R., Hinson, R., & Opoku, R. A. (2007). Preliminary insights into M-commerce adoption in Ghana. *Information Development, 23*(4), 253–265.

Boateng, R. (2011). Mobile phones and micro-trading activities – Conceptualizing the link, *info. Journal for Policy, Regulation and Strategy, 13*(5), 48–62.

Bounie, N., Adoue, F., Koning, M., & l'Hostis, A. (2019). What value do travelers put on connectivity to mobile phone and Internet networks in public transport? Empirical evidence from the Paris region. *Transportation Research Part A: Policy and Practice, 130*, 158–177.

CitiFMonline (2012). *Ghana's parliamentary proceedings globally accessible, CitiFM online*. Retrieved June 30, 2012, from http://citifmonline.com/index.php?id=1 .939855

Davis, F. D., Bagozzi, R. P., & Warshaw, P. R. (1989). User acceptance if computer technology: A comparison of two theoretical models. *Management Science, 35*(8), 982–1003.

Doe, J. K. (2020). *Stimulating the adoption of digital technologies in a developing country context. Firm Technology Adoption Model (F-TAM)* (Doctoral Thesis). Open Universiteit.

Eler, A. (2011). *Top 7 mobile commerce trends*. Read Write Web.

Ghana, M. T. N. (2012). *What is mobile money*. Retrieved July 21, 2012, from http://www.mobilemoney.com.gh/index.php/what-is-mobilemoney27

Gitau, L., & Nzuki, D. (2014). Analysis of determinants of m-commerce adoption by online consumers. *International Journal of Business, Humanities and Technology, 4*(3), 88–94.

Google Trader. (2012). *Ghana's marketplace for products and services, Google trader*. Retrieved June 30, 2012, from http://www.google.com.gh/local/trader

GSMA. (2011, November 9). *Africa now the world's second largest mobile market, reports GSMA*. Retrieved June 2012, from http://www.gsma.com/newsroom/africa-now-the-worlds-second-largest-mobile-market-reports-gsma/

Ibrahim, N. F., Hasan, N. H. M., Rusli, P. N. A., Shahreki, J., & Hasim, M. A. (2022). Technology acceptance model in E-wallet adoption among generation Z students: The Covid-19 endemic phase in Malaysia. *International Journal of Advanced Research in Technology and Innovation, 4*(4), 30–39.

Intelecon. (2005). *Nigerian demand study for the NCC. Part of a World Bank funded contract*. Presentation given to Nigeria Telecom Summit on 7 November.

International Telecommunications Union (ITU). (2010). *ICT statistics database*. ITU. Retrieved January 13, 2008, from http://www.itu.int/ITU-D/icteye/Indicators/Indicators.aspx

Jayanthi, R. M. (2020). Commerce–concept, future and its trend beyond 2020. *Digitalisation & Innovations in Business, 190*.

Jonker, J. (2003). M-commerce and m-payment. *Combining Technologies, 20*, 6–8.

Kagwe, W. (2009). *Kenyans to buy air, bus tickets through M-pesa, Nation Kenya*. Retrieved June 30, 2012, from http://www.nation.co.ke/business/news/-/1006 /675694/-/if8fn4z/-/index.html

Kim, J. W., Lee, B. H., Shaw, M. J., Chang, H. L., & Nelson, M. (2001). Application of decision-tree induction techniques to personalized advertisements on internet storefronts. *International Journal of Electronic Commerce, 5*(3), 45–62.

Laricchia. (2023, May 4). *Number of smartphone users by leading countries in 2022*. https://www.statista.com/statistics/748053/worldwide-top-countries-smart-phone-users/. Retrieved June 23, 2023, from https://www.statista.com/statistics /748053/worldwide-top-countries-smartphone-users/

Lopez, L. H. (2020). A closer look at direct carrier billing: Identifying the determi-nants of purchase and use of a mobile game. *International Journal of Online Marketing (IJOM), 10*(4), 18–40.

Lucas, G. A., Lunardi, G. L., & Dolci, D. B. (2023). From e-commerce to m-commerce: An analysis of the user's experience with different access platforms. *Electronic Commerce Research and Applications, 58*, 101240.

Michael, S., & David, S. (2003, March 5–8). *A model for small business new technology adoption: The case of mobile commerce*. Proceedings of 2003 ASBE Conference.

Milne, C. (2006). *Improving affordability of telecommunications: Cross-fertilisation between the developed and the developing world*. Telecommunications Policy Research Conference, George Mason University.

Mobile Content. (2012). *Mobile content Ghana products and services*. http://www.google.com.gh/local/trader http://www. Retrieved June 30, 2012, from mobile-content.com.gh/

Panos Brief. (2005). *Telephones and livelihoods: How telephones improve life for rural people in developing countries*. The Panos Institute.

Pedersen, P., Methlie, L., & Thorbjørnsen, H. (2002). Understanding mobile commerce end-user adoption: A triangulation perspective and suggestion for an exploratory service evaluation framework. In *proceedings of the 35th annual Hawaii international conference on system Sciences*, 8. IEEE.

Portio Research Mobile Factbook. (2012). *Portio research free mobile Factbook, portio. Research*. Retrieved June 2012, from http://www.portioresearch.com/en/free-mobile-factbook.aspx

Puiu, S., Demyen, S., Tănase, A. C., Vărzaru, A. A., & Bocean, C. G. (2022). Assessing the adoption of mobile technology for commerce by generation Z. *Electronics, 11*(6), 866.

Putri, M. F., Purwandari, B., & Hidayanto, A. N. (2020, November). What do affect customers to use mobile payment continually? A systematic literature review. In *2020 Fifth international conference on informatics and computing (ICIC)* (pp. 1–6). IEEE.

Rana, N. P., Barnard, D. J., Baabdullah, A. M., Rees, D., & Roderick, S. (2019). Exploring barriers of m-commerce adoption in SMEs in the UK: Developing a framework using ISM. *International Journal of Information Management, 44*, 141–153. http://www.readwriteweb.com/archives/top_7_mobile_commerce_trends_in_2011.ph

Reid, L. (2012). Need to know tablets. *Phones4U*. Retrieved February 20, 2012, from http://commchaptery.phones4u.co.uk/need-to-know-tablets/

Rogers, E. M. (1995). *Diffusion of innovations* (4th ed.). The Free Press. Rural People in Developing Countries, the Panos Institute.

Sey, A. (2009). Exploring mobile phone-sharing practices in Ghana. *Info, 11*(2), 66–78.

Shankar, V., Kalyanam, K., Setia, P., Golmohammadi, A., Tirunillai, S., Douglass, T., ... Waddoups, R. (2021). How technology is changing retail. *Journal of Retailing, 97*(1), 13–27.

Shrivastava, M., Prakash, D., & Ratna, V. V. (2019). M-commerce: Meaning, evolution, and growth. In *M-commerce*, Mithun Shrivastava, Devika Prakashand Vir Ved Ratna, (eds.), (pp. 3–27). Apple Academic Press.

Souter, D. (2005). *The economic impact of telecommunications on rural liveli-hoods and poverty reduction: A study of rural commchapteries in India (Gujarat), Mozambique and Tanzania.* Commonwealth Telecommunications Organisation.

Stanoevska-Slabeva, K. (2003). Towards a reference model for m-commerce applications. *Proceedings of ECIS Conference.* Naples.

Suebsin, C., & Gerdsri, N. (2009). Key factors driving the success of technology adoption: Case examples of ERP adoption. In *PICMET'09-2009 Portland International Conference on Management of Engineering & Technology,* 2638–2643. IEEE.

Turban, E., King, D., Lee, J., & Viehland, D. (2004). *Electronic Commerce: a managerial perspective 2004.* London, UK: Pearson Education.

Verisign. (2007). Mobile commerce services driving mobile commerce adoption: Best practices for a comprehensive, secure mobile commerce strategy. *Verisign.* Retrieved May 23, 2012, from http://www.verisign.com/static/DEV040159.pdf

Chapter 7

Ethical, Social, and Legal Issues in M-Commerce

Chapter Outline

- Introduction
- Ethical issues in m-commerce
- Social issues in m-commerce
- Legal issues in m-commerce
- M-commerce guidelines in security issues
- Emerging trends in mobile and m-commerce crime
- Case studies in m-commerce crime

Chapter Outcome

By the end of this chapter, the reader will be able to:

Analyse ethical issues in m-commerce:
- Examine and assess ethical dilemmas that may arise in the context of mobile commerce.

Evaluate social issues in m-commerce:
- Analyse the social implications and impacts of mobile commerce on individuals and communities.

DOI: 10.4324/9781003307457-7

Assess legal issues in m-commerce:
■ Evaluate the compliance of mobile commerce practices with existing legal standards.

Examine mobile commerce transactions:
■ Demonstrate a practical understanding of how transactions occur in the mobile commerce ecosystem.

Explore emerging trends in m-commerce crimes:
■ Identify potential threats and vulnerabilities in the evolving landscape of m-commerce crimes.

Familiarise yourself with guidelines for ensuring security in m-commerce:
■ Acquaint yourself with industry best practices and guidelines for enhancing security in mobile commerce.
■ Develop strategies and recommendations for securing m-commerce transactions and user data.

Introduction

As mobile technology continues to revolutionise the way we conduct business and interact with the digital world, the realm of mobile commerce, or m-commerce, has become a prominent force in shaping the global economy. However, the rapid evolution of m-commerce brings with it a host of ethical, social, and legal considerations that demand careful examination. This intersection of technology and commerce not only presents unprecedented opportunities for innovation but also raises important questions about privacy, security, and societal impact. For instance, Ghana, as part of its digitisation agenda, is seeking to build a robust digital ecosystem to contribute to achieving the country's massive socio-economic transformation programme (National Communications Authority, 2018). Hence, creating a safer cyber environment is critical to ensuring that Ghana's participation in the digital evolution is secured from the adverse vulnerabilities of internet use. Understanding the complementarities in the internet ecosystem allows policy implementation to focus on relevant drivers of the security and trustworthiness of internet use within the ecosystem. In line with this, exploring the ethical, social, and legal dimensions of m-commerce is crucial to understanding the broader implications of this transformative phenomenon. This would also provide a meaningful response to contextual challenges affecting the effective implementation of the regulatory framework within the internet ecosystem to boost user confidence.

From issues related to user privacy and data protection to the social impact of mobile commerce on diverse communities and the evolving legal frameworks governing mobile transactions, this chapter will delve into the multifaceted landscape that accompanies the proliferation of m-commerce. Whereas governments and other stakeholders in emerging markets and developing economies (EMDEs) attempt to implement policies to ensure a reliable and secure internet ecosystem in response to these difficulties, uncertainty persists over the effectiveness of the policies. Such gaps raise concerns regarding firms' and consumers' perceptions of the security and trustworthiness of the internet ecosystem in EMDEs. This chapter seeks to navigate the complex terrain where technology, business, and societal values intersect. By addressing the ethical considerations, social implications, and legal frameworks surrounding m-commerce, we aim to provide insights into the responsible development and deployment of mobile technologies that align with the principles of fairness, transparency, and societal well-being. As we embark on this exploration, we recognise the importance of fostering a balanced and informed dialogue that paves the way for a more ethical, socially responsible, and legally compliant future in the realm of m-commerce in EMDEs.

Ethics and Ethical Issues in M-commerce

Ethics is the branch of knowledge dealing with the appropriate course of action for man (Landauer & Rowlands, 2011). It normally answers the question, "What do I do?" On a more fundamental level, it is the study of right and wrong in human endeavours. Ethics is a necessity for human life and ensures the means for one to decide one's own course of action. Ethics act as principles of right and wrong that govern human behaviour. Moreover, without it, human action would be random and meaningless. However, a problem or any situation that requires a person or an organisation to choose between alternatives that must be assessed as right (ethical) or wrong (unethical) may also be considered an ethical issue. Ethical issues in information systems have become very important in our contemporary world due to the rise of electronic and mobile commerce activities.

Ethical, social, and political issues are closely connected in the information world, which includes that of mobiles. Ethical issues influence both social and political issues and have come to include mobile activities as well. For one, customer service has become the organisational function or service that attracts the largest ethical challenges in m-commerce. Moreover, the lack of training regarding internet usage has led many individuals to participate in conduct that questions their ethics. These ethical issues include information rights, confidentiality and privacy, and system quality (Laudon & Laudon, 2011).

Information Rights

Information rights refer to the rights mobile users and organisations have with respect to information that pertains to themselves. The questions asked are: what rights do mobile users and organisations have concerning the information made available or accessed through mobiles, and what can they protect?

For example, mobile users should be assured that their mobile information—names and mobile numbers—will not be sold or made available to a third-party institution without prior notice. In 2009, T-Mobile confirmed its biggest mobile phone customer data breach, when an employee stole and sold personal account details of mobile users to rival firms (Wray, 2009). It is imperative for organisations to take note of and protect the access, sharing, and use of information by employees and customers. Trading with some of these mobile devices becomes a problem if the right information is not sent to the right person. Hence, organisations providing mobile commerce should be more careful about the kind of information collected from customers and/or sent to them.

Confidentiality and Privacy

Most mobile devices (mobile phones, iPads, and PDAs) can be used symbolically to intimidate, deceive, or defraud victims. There have been several recent stories of movie celebrities' photos being leaked online, including those of Scarlett Johansson, Olivia Munn, and many others. The press repeatedly says that these celebrities' phones were "hacked." However, security experts explained that it is rare that a phone is "hacked." The emergence of different domains for working in cyberspace has not only made life more convenient and efficient but has also led to increased exposure to security threats. With the increased usage of mobile devices and social media, there has been an increased vulnerability to theft and all sorts of cybercrimes one may fall victim to (Mhlanga et al., 2021).

These mobile devices have made the invasion of privacy a great deal easier and potentially more dangerous. Some of the potential threats to privacy include the improper commercial use of computerised data (Chang, 2021), breaches of confidentiality caused by releasing confidential data to third parties (Nair & Tyagi, 2021), and the release of records to governmental agencies for investigative purposes (Shi et al., 2020). For example, some advertising networks have been secretly collecting mobile users' personal details as they visit their websites or download or use their applications. Some of these practices are not regulated or difficult to regulate; hence, a number of these companies go unpunished and repeat such unethical practices.

The challenge is how companies can ensure that mobile users have secure mobile accounts on their mobile phones. The continuous education of customers is a starting point. Other strategies may include disallowing the use of simple passwords on virtual accounts, establishing policies to enforce security measures on m-commerce platforms, and using multiple channels to confirm the identity of mobile users—biometrics, like fingerprints on computers. To some extent, the protection of privacy is also the responsibility of the consumer, not only that of the marketer or the marketing organisation.

System Quality

Sometimes ethical breaches can occur from system failure or a bug in a mobile application, software, or operating system (Suleman et al., 2021). How well a mobile device can function and to what extent it makes timely delivery is very important. In 2007, Google had to correct an error in the code of several of its services. The error exposed the address books of Gmail users to hackers. A hacker could copy all the entries in a Gmail user's address book, a potential treasure trove for spammers (Evers, 2015. This could easily happen on mobile devices since they have less security embedded in their operating systems.

Social Issues in M-Commerce

Social issues also raise security and legal issues. These concepts will enable you to understand the social and legal considerations when engaging in m-commerce activities. In technology, social issues can arise when a new product has an unexpected side-effect or unintended impact on a group of people (Coad et al., 2021). This can yield positive or negative consequences. For example, the rise in the use of mobile phones to send text messages has increased the demand for such phones. This provides employment for factory workers and enables people to keep in touch more easily, which means that there is less need for people to meet each other in person. However, in societies that thrive on close interpersonal relationships and communicating in person, the mobile device can be viewed as an influence on a traditional way of communicating, thus removing the need for people to meet physically or allowing them to be less interpersonal. Social issues arise from ethical issues as societies develop prospects or expectations in individuals about the correct course of action.

Despite their promise, mobiles have become a new aid in criminal and antisocial behaviour and have been used to facilitate assaults as well as harassment. Mobiles with texting capabilities and photo and video capabilities make it possible for businesses to have constant access to the internet, customers, and trading partners. However, much of this access is currently unsupervised. Some major social issues concerning mobile commerce include the upsurge of cybercrimes, unintended costs from viruses and malware, and identity theft.

Upsurge of Cybercrimes

Cybercrime refers to the use of computing devices and other forms of technology to perform criminal activities (Shah & Chudasama, 2021). Cybercrime has become one of the fastest-growing criminal activities on the planet. It covers a huge range of illegal activity, including financial scams, computer hacking, downloading pornographic images from the internet, virus attacks, stalking by e-mail, and creating websites that promote racial hatred (Kshetri, 2019). Cybercrime is also a common phenomenon in m-commerce. The fact that only a few users have a security solution on their mobile device to protect against attacks also makes it easier for cybercriminals to steal personal information, valuable corporate information, and money. Between 2021 and

2022, cybercrime attacks increased by about 125% (The Latest Cyber Crime Statistics (Updated June 2023) | AAG IT Support, 2023). In 2018, research by Norton Company indicated that 10% of adults experienced cybercrime on their mobile device in the year studied, 54% experienced malware or viruses, and 77% of travellers using free Wi-Fi also experienced cybercrime (Top 5 Cybercrimes in the U.S., From the Norton Cyber Security Insights Report, 2018). These issues have worried mobile users who patronise mobile banking.

Unintended Costs from Viruses and Malware

The mobile phone is nothing less than a simplified computer, and there have been numerous viruses released for mobile phones. Some only kill your battery as they scan for new victims, but others make phone calls to high-priced lines or send costly SMS messages without the owner's knowledge or consent. The point is that cell-phone viruses (and other forms of malware) are quite common and will only grow in popularity. We sometimes install software on our mobile phones through the internet. Some of this software may contain harmful codes that can cause problems with your mobile phones. If this same phone is used to transact business or purchase a product or service on a mobile website, then it is likely the information of the mobile user could become compromised. Hence, it is imperative to take note of the kind of software or mobile applications we download and install on our mobile phones. Failure to address issues with viruses and malware could lead to breaches of privacy and the theft of personal and business information. When the element of trust is exploited, mobile users are less likely to adopt m-commerce services.

Identity Theft

Identity theft is a crime in which a criminal obtains personal information, such as a passport number, bank account number, and address, to pose as someone else (Tahir, 2021). In a 2009 survey, the BBC reported that 4.2 million Britons store data on their mobiles that could be used for identity theft in the event it is stolen. Only 6 in 10 use a password to limit entry into their phones (BBC, 2009). The information can be used to obtain credit, bank statements, products, and services using the victims' names. It can also provide false credentials for immigration or other applications. One of the biggest problems with identity theft is that the crimes committed by the identity theft expert are often attributed to the victim. For example, if your mobile phone happens to be stolen, there are a lot of challenges that come with it. The information on the mobile is still valuable to an identity thief. He or she can use that information to make business transactions in your name. All charges may go into your account since it may be as if you are the real owner of the business transaction. This has become a major problem facing mobile usage in business transactions. Some mobile users avoid adopting m-commerce because of fears of identity theft.

Legal Issues in M-Commerce

The legality of every product is of great relevance to its existence. This provides a notion of the legal issues that must secure the application of mobile commerce in all marketing contexts. Mobile commerce law is simply the set of rules and guidelines governing mobile commerce activities in a country. The majority of the legal issues relating to mobile commerce are:

■ contracts for the sale of goods and services;
■ intellectual property.

Contracts for the sale of goods and services and intellectual property need international cooperation in well-directed conventions or treaties. The global legal institutions that develop and govern the law concerning mobile commerce include, not exhaustively:

■ UNCITRAL (United Nations Commission on International Trade Law)

This is the core legal body of the United Nations system in the field of international trade law. UNCITRAL's business is the modernisation and harmonisation of rules for international business. These include developing conventions, model laws, and rules that are acceptable worldwide, and organising regional and national seminars on uniform commercial law.

■ UNIDROIT (International Institute for the Unification of Private Law):
   Unidroit is an independent intergovernmental organisation whose purpose is to study the needs and methods for modernising, harmonising, and coordinating private and, in particular, commercial law between

countries and groups of countries and to formulate uniform law instruments, principles, and rules to achieve those objectives.

In Ghana, the national communication agency is the regulator of the telecommunications industry. Ghana has no mobile commerce law as yet, but there are electronic transaction laws. Ghana's Electronic Transaction Act 772 (2008) seeks to provide for and facilitate electronic communications and related transactions in the public interest, remove and prevent barriers to electronic communications and transactions, promote legal certainty and confidence, and provide a legal safe environment for the conduct of transactions with public and private bodies, institutions, and citizens. The Act covers electronic records, digital signatures, electronic signatures, consumer protection, cyber offences, and so on. Extracts from the Electronic Transactions Act are captured below on cyber offences:

Mobile Commerce Transaction

Under the Electronic Transactions law in Ghana, the requisite components for the formation of a contract in electronic transactions (including mobile transactions) include:

- An offer;
- An acceptance;
- An intention to be legally bound; and
- Consideration.

Components of a Mobile Commerce Contract

Offer and acceptance: This provides that an electronic record is deemed (unless the parties otherwise agree) to have been sent when it is accepted by an information system outside the control of the originator or of the person who sent the record on behalf of the originator.

Intention to be legally bound: This concerns whether computer autonomous programmes, for example, the sending of short messages or downloading of information via a mobile, can form the requisite "intention" to be legally bound and thereby consummate a contract.

Table 7.1   Extracts from the Electronic Transactions Act

Obtaining electronic payment medium falsely
A person who makes or causes to be made either directly or indirectly, a false representation to procure the issue of an electronic payment medium personally or to another person commits an offence and is liable on summary conviction to a fine of not more than five thousand penalty units or to a term of imprisonment of not more than ten years or to both.
Electronic trafficking
A person who is found in possession of any electronic related payment medium invoices, vouchers, sales drafts, or other representations of devices related to the manufacture or use of the device without lawful explanation commits the offence of electronic trafficking and is liable on summary conviction to a fine of not more than five thousand penalty units or a term of imprisonment of not more than ten years or to both.
General offence for fraudulent electronic fund transfer
A person who without authority, in the course of an electronic fund transfer, uses the personal or financial record or credit account numbers or electronic payment medium of another with intent to defraud an issuer or a creditor or who obtains money, goods, services, or anything fraudulently commits an offence and is liable on summary conviction to a fine of not more than five thousand penalty units or to a term of imprisonment of not more than ten years or to both.
General provision for cyber offences
Except as provided for in this Act, any offence under a law which is committed in whole or in part by use of an electronic medium or in electronic form is deemed to have been committed under that Act and the provisions of that Act shall apply,

Source: Authors (2024)

Consideration: A general offer includes the supply of goods or services, whether digitised or not, in exchange for payment. Payment could be made by electronic bank transfer, credit card payment, charged to the mobile user's monthly bills, and so on.

Intellectual property: The copyright law was amended, and anyone who knowingly possesses an infringing copy of a copyright work in business will commit a criminal offence. It includes the illegal copying of all copyrighted works, including sound recordings, musical works, and so on. Therefore, downloading the above without the consent of the copyright owner is illegal.

M-Commerce Guidelines for Security Issues

The most important element when dealing with m-commerce is security and privacy issues and how they can be dealt with so that customers to feel comfortable when using mobile phones. To attract customer usage of mobile commerce, there is a need to ensure the total quality of the security levels provided. This section elaborates on security and privacy issues relating to mobile commerce.

M-commerce Guidelines

M-commerce guidelines are general principles that foster a secure and safe environment for the conduct of m-commerce activities, thereby reinforcing the trust of consumers. They include the following:

Fair Business, Advertising, and Marketing Practices

M-commerce sets forth several general principles stating that businesses should not engage in practices that are likely to be deceptive, misleading, fraudulent, or unfair; that businesses marketing to consumers should not engage in practices that are likely to cause unreasonable risk of harm to consumers; and that businesses should present information about themselves and the goods or services they provide in a clear, conspicuous, accurate, and easily accessible manner.

Online Disclosures: Information about the Transaction

A business should provide sufficient information about the terms, conditions, and costs associated with a transaction to enable the consumer to make an informed decision about whether to enter into the transaction. The information must be clear, accurate, and easily accessible, and it must include an itemisation of total costs collected and/or imposed by the business.

Confirmation Process

There should be a way for consumers to review the purchase details and give express, informed, and deliberate consent to complete the transaction. It also states that consumers should be able to retain a complete and accurate record of their transactions. Finally, they should be able to cancel the transaction process before concluding it.

Dispute Resolution and Redress

Businesses should provide consumers with fair, effective, transparent, and internal mechanisms to address complaints. In this regard, the 2007 Convention on the Organisation for Economic Co-operation and Development (OECD) Recommendation on Consumer Dispute Resolution and Redress calls on the private sector to establish "effective processes for internal complaint handling, which provide consumers with the opportunity to resolve their complaints directly with the business concerned in a fair, effective, and timely manner without imposing a fee or charge for accessing or using these processes."

Unauthorised Mobile Use in M-commerce

The small size and functionality of mobile devices have made them attractive targets for thieves or criminals, who may be interested in

- re-using or re-selling the device;
- carrying out commercial transactions in a fraudulent or illegal way in the name of the legitimate owner;
- obtaining sensitive personal information.

The risk of theft is in many ways far higher than for standard computers, which are stationary, or bulkier portable computers, which are not carried around in public to the same degree. Building awareness of the risks of unauthorised use of mobile phones should help to lower the number of incidents. Stakeholders involved in mobile commerce should work together to provide information to consumers by

1. a) Promoting awareness of mobile theft and loss;
2. b) Outlining ways to protect mobile devices from loss and misuse; and
3. c) Advising on what consumers should do if they discover their device has been lost or is being misused.

To help deter unauthorised use, mobile operators and mobile device merchants could:

1. d) Assign random numbers as initial PIN codes;
2. e) Prompt consumers to change their default PIN code and set their own when they first use the device;

3. f) Advise consumers on installing security applications that erase data after several unsuccessful attempts.

Emerging Trends in Mobile and M-Commerce Crime

Mobile devices are increasingly becoming part of the everyday social and business activities of their users. This makes it quite easy for criminals to exploit them for their dubious activities. These and more are contributing to the trends in mobile and m-commerce crimes discussed below.

Financial Crimes

Considering that about 62% of online banking customers use their mobile phones to manage bank or credit card accounts, as compared to 39% of desktop users (Chugh, 2021), financial institutions seem to be the current target of criminals. These crimes are being carried out using simple mobile services like SMS and more complex viruses too. In Ghana, some users receive text messages to subscribe to a service or to redeem a prize, only for their airtime to be unknowingly transferred to the perpetrators.

Threats to the Business Enterprise

More businesses are adopting mobile technology because consumers need convenience and flexibility to access services without geographical restrictions. These devices allow employees to access information and/or connect to other employees and customers through mobile apps whose security may not have been thoroughly tested and passed for use in environments like the military, where information guarding is key. While an app could have a superficial use as a productivity tool (e.g., calendar), it may be designed to steal and transmit sensitive information stored on it to its creator.

Mobile Crime

Criminal Gang Activity

In addition to voice calls and text messaging, cybercriminals use social networking sites like Myspace, Facebook, Twitter, and YouTube. These tools are used to recruit new members and talk about their conquests. The tools are used to keep in touch even when they have been arrested and/or are on probation.

Victim Exploitation

Criminals use mobile devices to facilitate a variety of crimes against fellow humans. One important feature of mobile devices, which is geolocation or GPS (Global Positioning System) capability, is used to enhance their illegal operations. Criminals make friends with unsuspecting victims whose physical addresses are easily obtained using GPS on the devices they use to connect to mobile services, including social networks. For example, apps like Facebook allow criminals to see users' precise locations and the subject matter they are discussing. Such applications, when downloaded, could be sending other personal information to the creators.

Human Trafficking

Internet and mobile technology facilitate human trafficking, as has already been identified. Traffickers use mobile phones for communication and navigation. Mobile devices are also used to coordinate the recruitment and tracking of victims and their locations, respectively. Initial and ongoing contact with victims is also enhanced by mobile phones.

Activities

Section 1: Ethical Issues in M-commerce

Read the case study below and discuss two ethical issues in mobile commerce.

Case Study

Privacy Risk from **Ads in Apps**

Some advertising networks have been secretly collecting app users' personal details over the past year and now have access to millions of smartphones globally, according to US-based mobile security firm Lookout. These unregulated practices are on the rise, Lookout said on Monday as it unveiled the first industry guidelines on how application developers and advertisers could avoid raising consumer angst. Aggressive ad networks are much more prevalent than malicious applications. It is the most prevalent mobile privacy issue that exists, said Kevin Mahaffey, Lookouts technology chief and co-founder. Over 80 million apps have been downloaded that carry a form of invasive advertising—used by 5% of all free apps on Google's Android platform—that can take data from phones or install software without users' knowledge. Some more aggressive networks collect users email addresses or phone numbers without permission, while others install icons on home screens, track users' whereabouts, or push ads to the notification bar. Mobile devices have so far had limited appeal for writers of viruses and other malicious software, or malware, due to numerous small platforms and limited financial gains. But during the first quarter, the amount of malware on the popular Android platform jumped to 7,000 from 600, according to Intel's security software arm, McAfee. Lookout declined to name the most aggressive ad networks, hoping some of them would align practices to match the new guidelines, which include publishing details on their privacy policy and allowing consumers to avoid data collection. These guidelines make it clear that some practices are out-of-bounds. That's good news for both consumers and responsible businesses, said Jules Polonetsky, co-chair of the Future of Privacy Forum, a Washington-based thinktank focusing on responsible data handling practices. Many apps are ad-supported; there is nothing wrong with this, but users should know what their trade-off is. People want to have confidence and trust that they're not being compromised while on devices that have access to their most personal information, he said. The mobile experience is much more intimate and personal; a phone is an extension of you, not a distant publishing screen. The equivalent is someone whispering in your ear.

Review Questions

What do you understand by m-commerce crimes? How can they be resolved?

Case Studies on M-Commerce Crime

The section presents two case studies on ethical, social, and legal issues in m-commerce. It also presents questions that will guide readers in reviewing their understanding of the lessons provided in this unit.

Case Study

Anxiety over Mobile Money Fraud in Rwanda

Mobile commerce has been lauded as a great success story in carrying out financial transactions. It has also emerged as an effective tool to fight poverty, transforming the lives of thousands of Rwandans, mainly rural farmers who lack access to formal banking services. The recent upgrade to the mobile commerce platform now enables subscribers to pay for their electricity and water bills as well as access their bank accounts using mobile phones. The service is increasingly becoming popular in Rwanda. But it is also increasingly becoming exposed to fraud-related risks. This is contrary to the situation 2 years ago, when money transfers were the only service on the platform. The rising fraud rate, mainly in mobile money transfer services, is starting to worry subscribers, operators, and regulators of the platform. Official figures show that MTN Rwanda, the country's largest telecom operator by market share, has handled transactions worth Rwf65 billion through its mobile money service since 2010. It has 470,000 subscribers registered on the MTN Mobile Money service. TIGO, the second-largest operator, has 9127 subscribers on its TIGO Cash, with 1,917 transactions daily. The telecom regulator, Rwanda Utilities Regulatory Authority (RURA), says that mobile money fraud in the country has increased. RURA says most people are losing their money to fraudsters, calling for strict measures to contain the situation, which would ruin mobile banking amidst the drive to transform the country into a cashless economy. According to RURA, common fraud cases occur when a conman steals the pin number of a client and uses it to transfer money to their phones. The conman then throws away the card after accessing the money. Others swap the SIM cards of the targeted client and use them to give instructions to banks to authorise the payment of checks. Others use swapped numbers to call friends of the culprit and ask them to send money on their mobile account, and if another person or an agent gets to know your number, they can communicate with you to transfer your money. "That's why I'm always worried," says Giovanni Higiro, a subscriber.

In a bid to tackle the problem, telecom operators warn subscribers not to reply to anonymous messages instructing them (clients) to carry out transactions on their mobile money accounts or tricking them into thinking they have won money and need to pay a down payment to get their prize.

"Such SMS are aimed at cheating clients. We ask our clients not to reply to any of the messages," said Norman Munyampundu, Senior Manager for Customer Relations at MTN. Albert Kinuma, MTN Rwanda's Head of Mobile Banking, said, "Our mobile money is growing fast, and we are trying to educate our customers to always keep their PIN numbers safely and stop revealing them; this will help to reduce the current fraud cases."

Efforts to get a comment from TIGO were futile as Tongai Maramba, TIGO cash manager, refused to comment on the matter, saying that the parent company, MILLICOM, is listed on the stock exchange in Luxembourg and that TIGO is not independent enough to give out information without consent from the headquarters.

RURA hopes that its planned subscriber identification module (SIM) card registration project will make mobile commerce safer. The project first came to light in 2010. It also seeks to address other mobile phone crimes such as abusive calls and provocative messages, which many mobile users have been subjected to.

But this project might take longer, given the urgency of the problems at hand. Accordingly, to affect the card registration process, there must be a law ensuring that all mobile users are compelled to register their SIM cards and provide legal backing to operators against litigation in case they switch off floating numbers. This, therefore, will require the regulator to write a report that will be the basis for enacting the law.

According to RURA, this process has just begun. We are in the process of starting SIM card registration so that when a crime is committed, it is easier to know who has committed it. If you lose a card and it is used by a criminal, it will be easier to tell you are not the one who has committed the offence, Beata Mukangabo, Head of Corporate, Legal, and Industry Affairs Department at RURA, said, adding that the regulator will soon start sensitising people to register their SIM cards.

Under SIM card registration, the subscriber will be asked to provide details on their identification cards, which will be stored alongside the card details by the operator. In the event of a complaint, the SIM card is traced back using the stored information of the subscriber.

Source: Nyesiga (2012)

Case Study

Cell Phones: Easy ID Theft Targets

Cell phones are more powerful than ever, with innovations and features being unveiled continually. But, reports CBS News Business and Economics Correspondent Rebecca Jarvis, all that convenience could come with a cost. A recent survey shows 85% of American adults own cell phones, and many use them for much more than just making calls—for e-mail, instant messaging, Web access, shopping online, even banking, bill-paying, and much more.

But can cell phone users really be sure all their personal information is secure? Michael Gregg is what's known as a white-hat hacker. He helps companies and consumers keep valuable information safe. He says every phone's operating system has been hacked. The real concern, he told Jarvis, is that you start to have banking information, personal information, and other sorts of data on the cell phone. The hackers are always really one step ahead of everyone else because they're going where the money is. Whatever you're saying or doing may not be as private as you think.

Jarvis says it is happening across the country: identity theft, spying by cell phone—even major banks have been victimised. And no one is immune to having information snatched. Using just a laptop and a free WiFi access point, Gregg demonstrated how a hacker could spy on the iPhone of someone sitting on a park bench. When he visited Fandango to buy movie tickets, the site popped up on Gregg's screen. A hacker could use the trick to steal the iPhone user's credit card information. Another hacker's trick is referred to as caller ID spoofing, which makes it appear to a cell phone user that a call is from someone he or she knows when it's really from a hacker. "That," Greg explained to Jarvis, "could be used, for example, for me to make a call to you and pretend to be calling from your bank and ask for information, ask for personal information, a PIN number, and other types of data. Hackers can also easily break into and listen to voicemails left on some cell phones, especially if they're not protected by a password".

The bottom line: You can't afford to take cell phone security for granted. Cell phones, says Gregg, are really like minicomputers today, and the same kind of precautions you'd want to use when using a computer or laptop are the same type of precautions you'd want to use when using a cell phone or smartphone. When CBS News spoke to The Wireless Association, it acknowledged that, as devices have become more data-intensive, security is a challenge. But the organisation says the industry is constantly improving security features on wireless networks and devices to try to keep consumers safe. To help keep information secure, Jarvis suggests:

- Set up a voicemail password to make it harder for someone to break in.
- If you're going to shop or bank online, do it over a secure network. Free WiFi access points are much riskier.
- Don't download apps from unknown sources. Some apps have been accused of gathering personal information.

If you think you've been hacked, says Jarvis, contact the wireless carrier, bank, or credit card company and let them know your information may have been compromised. Don't contact them by e-mail or use the hacked phone to do that; use a different phone or visit in person.

Review Questions

1. What are the main ethical concerns associated with mobile commerce (m-commerce), and how do they impact consumer trust in mobile transactions?
2. Discuss the social implications of m-commerce. How has the rise of mobile commerce influenced consumer behaviour and interpersonal communication?
3. Outline the legal challenges that m-commerce presents. What laws and regulations are in place to address these challenges, and where are the gaps?
4. Describe some of the emerging trends in m-commerce crime. How are these affecting both consumers and businesses and what measures can be taken to mitigate these risks?

References

AAG, I. T. Services. (2023, February 6). The latest cyber crime statistics (updated June 2023). *AAG It Support*. https://aag-it.com/the-latest-cyber-crime-statistics/
BBC NEWS. (n.d.). Technology. Mobile users at risk of id theft. *BBC NEWS*. http://news.bbc.co.uk/2/hi/technology/7950263.stm

Chang, V. (2021). An ethical framework for big data and smart cities. *Technological Forecasting and Social Change, 165*, 120559.

Chugh, P. (2021). A study of customers' awareness with respect to mobile banking in Hisar. *International Journal of Information Movement, 5*(10), 11–17.

Coad, A., Nightingale, P., Stilgoe, J., & Vezzani, A. (2021). The dark side of innovation. *Industry and Innovation, 28*(1), 102–112.

Evers, A. (2015). Evaluating cloud automation as a service. Cyber Security Threats, 33.

Kshetri, N. (2019). Cybercrime and cybersecurity in Africa. *Journal of Global Information Technology Management, 22*(2), 77–81.

Landauer, J., & Rowlands, J. (2011). Definition of capitalism. *Importance of Philosophy.*

Laudon, K. C., & Laudon, J. P. (2011). *Essentials of management information systems.* Pearson.

Mhlanga, M. X., Maiti, R. R., & Hammer, B. (2021, March). Privacy and security matters related to use of mobile devices and social media. In *Southeastcon* (pp. 1–6). IEEE.

Nair, M. M., & Tyagi, A. K. (2021). Privacy: History, statistics, policy, laws, preservation and threat analysis. *Journal of Information Assurance & Security, 16*(1), 024–034.

National Communications Authority. (2018). *Our contributions in 2018 towards Ghana's digital agenda.* https://nca.org.gh/wp-content/uploads/2021/11/Key-NCA-Projects-2018.pdf

Nyesiga. (2012). *Anxiety over mobile money fraud.* https://allafrica.com/stories/201205220060.html.

Shah, A., & Chudasama, D. (2021). Investigating various approaches and ways to detect cybercrime. *Journal of Network Security, 9*(2), 12–20.

Shi, S., He, D., Li, L., Kumar, N., Khan, M. K., & Choo, K. K. R. (2020). Applications of blockchain in ensuring the security and privacy of electronic health record systems: A survey. *Computers and Security, 97*, 101966.

Suleman, M., Soomro, T. R., Ghazal, T. M., & Alshurideh, M. (2021). Combating against potentially harmful mobile apps. In *Proceedings of the international conference on artificial intelligence and computer vision (AICV2021)*, Aboul Ella Hassanien, Abdelkrim Haqiq, Peter J. Tonellato, Ladjel Bellatreche, Sam Goundar, Ahmad Taher Azar, Essaid Sabir, & Driss Bouzidi. (eds.), (pp. 154–173). Springer International Publishing.

Tahir, M. (2021, July). *Identity theft: Trends, detection and prevension.* London, United Kingdom. hal-03281803f

Top 5 Cybercrimes in the U.S., from the Norton Cyber Security Insights Report. (2018, August 8). https:///blog/online-scams/top-5-cybercrimes-in-america-norton-cyber-security-insights-report

Wray, J. A. (2009). *Mobile advertising engine.* A Senior Research Paper, Stetson University, Spring Term.

Chapter 8

Sociocultural and Ethical Aspects of Social Media Marketing

Chapter Outline

- Introduction
- Sociocultural issues in social media marketing
- Ethical issues in social media marketing
- Conclusion

Chapter Outcome

By the end of this chapter, the reader will be able to:

Demonstrate an understanding of the interaction between culture and social media:
- Analyse and articulate the dynamics of how culture influences and interacts with social media.
- Apply knowledge to interpret cultural nuances in various social media contexts.

Evaluate the maintenance of ethics in the social media space:
- Critically assess and analyse the ethical considerations and frameworks relevant to the social media environment.

DOI: 10.4324/9781003307457-8

■ Demonstrate the ability to recognise, evaluate, and respond to ethical dilemmas in social media.

Integrate the understanding of culture and ethics in the social media space:
■ Synthesise knowledge to understand how culture and ethics coexist and influence interactions within the social media space.
■ Apply principles of culture and ethics to navigate and engage effectively in diverse social media environments.

Introduction

Business ethics are an essential component of any business strategy, particularly in outbound communications like marketing. Social media marketing has witnessed an unpresented upsurge in recent times across the globe and has penetrated emerging markets such as Ghana. Social media adoption in marketing spans a wide spectrum of business and marketing operations, ranging from product and service idea generation to post-purchase follow-up service. In emerging economies, for example, social media marketing is adopted not only by large and small organisations but also by groups and individuals across different industries—extraction, manufacturing, and service industries. Both female and male smallholder artisans and celebrities also use social media marketing predominantly.

Observably, social media usage in marketing is targeted not only at the savvy youth and adult population but also at vulnerable children and the elderly population. The path of social media marketing knows no boundaries. It permeates the borders of every nation, opens up markets for emerging economies to the entire world, and draws customers (potential and real) from all over the world. As more and more individuals, groups, and organisations (small and large) rely more on social media marketing than on traditional marketing, unhealthy competition, which creates social and ethical concerns in the adoption of social media marketing, increases tremendously. Berman et al. (2018) acknowledge, "There are significant ethical implications in the adoption of technologies and social media platforms." According to them, ethical issues arise not only with respect to the privacy settings and confidentiality of data amassed by these applications and platforms but also in relation to the use of the data that is produced via social media for marketing purposes. Unfortunately, the literature on sociocultural and ethical issues associated with the use of social media in marketing, particularly from the perspective of emerging economies, is very scanty. This is because scholarship addressing the social and ethical dimensions of social media communication is inadvertently missing from the literature (Albarran, 2013).

Patino et al. (2012) attributed the inadequacy of studies on the ethical and social implications of social media adoption in marketing to the newness of the field of social media marketing and the quicker pace at which technology, driving social media, is moving faster than governments' responses in establishing guidelines and laws to manage social media platforms ethical issues. The urgent need for scholarly work addressing the ethical and social concerns of social media communication is thus warranted. This chapter is therefore developed to consider the sociocultural and ethical aspects of social media marketing, its adoption, and its usage. The chapter explains the sociocultural concerns of social media marketing, elaborates on the ethical issues in social media marketing, highlights the managerial implications of ethical considerations in social media marketing, and suggests some recommendations for enhancing ethical knowledge and practice of social media marketing.

Sociocultural Issues in Social Media Marketing

Culture defines the values, norms, beliefs, attitudes, and behaviours of individuals, groups, organisations, communities, and nations. Socially, the interactions between and among families, friends, and groups play a significant role in social media choice and usage, particularly in emerging markets. People live in communities and societies. They inherit some rituals and values and develop new beliefs, norms, and traditions over a period of time from the communities they live in. The set of beliefs, norms, values, attitudes, and behaviours they acquire influence their adoption and usage of social media. That is, the contents they consume from social media platforms, the interpretations they assign to social media posts, and the reactions they give to social media messages are functions of their culture. Therefore, people behave and develop values and norms as a consequence of interactions between other people and their material environment. Traditions, a component of culture, are also very crucial in the formation of the attitude and behaviour of customers. Culture thus influences how people perceive things on social media (Amin et al., 2017). This shows that cultural issues and customers' ethnic backgrounds impact their interpretations of social media content. Social media forms a new culture with different norms to create a strong urge to purchase in a convenient way. This supports Hoffman and Foder's (2010) claim that consumers, not marketers, are in charge of social media. Marketers should therefore be aware of the influence of sociocultural issues when they are planning to market their products and services through social media. A number of sociocultural issues have been identified as greatly impacting social media use in emerging economies. Amin et al. (2017) enumerated electronic consumer-to-customer interaction, convenience in shopping, preference in online shopping, freedom of speech or writing, addiction by users, big brands' advertisements, contents on social media, and the possibility of checking consumers' responses and feedback as some of the sociocultural concerns social media marketers in emerging markets face. The most influential factor, as they indicated, is electronic customer-to-customer interactions.

Electronic Customer-to-Customer Interaction

Electronic customer-to-customer interaction (e-CCI), according to Georgi and Mink (2013), is defined as any kind of individual or group interaction between customers encountered in the acquisition and consumption of goods and services via an electronic platform. It explains interactions between customers on a social media platform during the service encounter. Nicholls (2008) also states that e-CCI is the e-world equivalent of on-stage customer-to-customer interactions between customers of an e-service. It happens more or less accidentally to customers through their physical presence on social media platforms. There are virtual brand communities influencing the purchase decisions of customers. Virtual brand communities are an e-CCI platform, referring to a group of consumers that occur on the internet because of their interest in some brand or product (Muniz & O'Guinn, 2001). Interactions between users are core to social media and are particularly relevant as they form a key part of value creation and delivery. Social media marketers should therefore pay particular attention to its dynamics and quality. e-CCI platforms create different groups of customers who influence others and are in turn influenced by others. Georgi and Mink (2013) recognise help seekers, reactive helpers, proactive helpers, and physical customers, intellectual customers, and emotional customers as different groups of customers who interact on e-CCI platforms and are respectively influenced by others' attitudes and posts.

It is noted that e-CCI empowers customers (Georgi & Mink, 2013), compelling firms to see their "clients as partial organisational members;

customers as human resources; and customers as employees" (Georgi & Mink, 2013, p. 12). The very definition of social media supports this assertion. Social media is defined as "a group of internet-based applications that allow the creation and exchange of user-generated content" (Kaplan & Haenlein, 2010, p. 61). Whiting and Williams (2013) claim that social media includes a wide range of online information sources that customers create, disseminate, and use to inform one another about goods, services, and brands available in the market. The definitions clearly establish that the creation, circulation, and usage of social media content are in the hands of the customers, who, on a continual basis, educate one another about the offerings of an organisation through social networking, photo/picture sharing, video sharing, business networking, and microblogging. The social interactions between and among customers are major concerns for social media markets. As Georgi and Mink (2013) observe, e-CCI could have positive and negative impacts on the marketing efforts of the organisation. It is therefore exceptionally imperative that social media marketers pay critical attention to the content, security, hedonic, quantity, atmosphere, and convenience of e-CCI platforms, not only as a means of ensuring quality but also as an aid to value creation and delivery.

Ethical Issues in Social Media Marketing

Broadly, ethical issues are concerned with moral principles that govern or guide behaviour in society. According to Amin et al. (2017), the theory of conscience, which demonstrates a sense of right and wrong, underpins moral values and ethical thinking in society. This means that in the adoption and usage of social media in marketing, marketers and consumers alike have to be conscious and analytical about social media contents and behaviour. Vinjamuri (2011) advises that, ethically, marketers and consumers should avoid certain behaviours and practices while using social media marketing. For example, anonymous reviews about products, services, and ideas posted without involving or getting permission violate consumers' privacy and can harm a company's reputation. It should be avoided. Similarly, people on many social websites give their personal information, which becomes susceptible to misuse, particularly through disclosure to other websites, without the consent of the owner of the data or the people the data is about. Specifically, Amin et al. (2017) have identified several areas of ethical concern in emerging markets. The ethical issues of concern to the social marketer comprise leakage of private data; security of consumer data; fabricated negative reviews by rivals or negative word-of-mouth communication by users; misrepresentation of brands' data; presenting falsified contents, fake images and videos of products, spam messages, and fraudulent offers; and defamation of renowned brands and companies.

Knowing the Target Customers

It is argued that designing and implementing a successful social marketing campaign is about knowing who the target customers are. This requires an understanding of their needs, interests, preferences, and choices. To achieve this, social marketers aggressively seek demographic information about their potential customers. Unfortunately, the demographic information they gather is usually not only about the target customers but also about an array of people with varied needs, interests, tastes, and preferences that do not relate to the offerings of the organisation. The knowledge of organisations, therefore, about their target customers is foggy and hazy. As a result, the organisations are unable to clearly engage the customers with messages about products and services that are relevant to their lifestyle. This poses a threat to the organisations as it inundates the customers with unnecessary information and marketing campaigns, which make customers regard the messages of the organisation as nuisances. It is advised that before embarking on any social media marketing drive, companies should make sure that they know about their audience (preferences, interests, and choices) and have a complete demographic and psychographic overview of them (Maslow, 2018). This will help the companies refine their target audience, facilitate the development of anti-spam mechanisms, and segment the audience in order to send them relevant messages that will drive engagement.

Eliminating Bias

The adoption of social media in marketing relies on content posting and creating a hive of online followers on social media platforms. To keep their customers active, many organisations align themselves with trending but sensitive topics that are political, cultural, religious, economic, or social in nature. Different followers on social media platforms may have different tastes, preferences, opinions, and stances on these sensitive topical issues. Maintaining a balanced view on these issues to appeal to the varied groups of followers on social media can be daunting for organisations. By nature, these sensitive topics and various responses can alienate certain segments of the followers and, for that matter, the target customers. Pravina (2020) summarises that "one potentially biassed tweet can cause your brand to lose many followers and customers" and advises that organisations should steer away from sharing any political, cultural, or religious preferences, opinions, or stances. Social media businesses and marketers in emerging markets should therefore stay away from negative political, religious, ethnic, or any cultural bias that could be termed controversial, as a slight mistake can lead to a big social media marketing disaster.

Prioritising Privacy

Privacy issues are of major ethical concern in the use of social media in marketing. Social media marketing is about sharing information. Organisations are likely to use customer and user data to help inform the type of content they post and also gain important information about their followers' demographics. How the information is gathered and shared, and with whom it is shared, are sources of ethical concerns because privacy is very important for social media users. Maslow (2018) observes that some companies extract Facebook and LinkedIn data to build their email campaigns, breaching privacy protocols. He cautions that if a company leaks any personal information, this can lead to a tarnished reputation and backlash that can ruin the company. Social media marketers should therefore endeavour not to lash out at users, fans, or consumers on their social media accounts. Instead, they should maintain a strict and established set of privacy rules that will protect the people that interact and engage with their online platforms and ensure that the personal data of their individual clients remains secure and private.

Maintaining Transparency

Transparency explains the degree to which an organisation is open, truthful, and honest with its followers on social media platforms about its offerings. Organisations are always in a dilemma about the extent of disclosure of vital information about their products and services, particularly when the information has the potential to elicit negative responses from their followers. In many instances, some firms, for fear of customers' negative reactions and potential rejection of their products and services, either massage damaging information about their products and services to appear pleasant in the eyes of their clients or completely conceal the information from them. This

creates serious unethical social media usage in marketing and may pose reputational damage to companies. As Maslow (2018) notes, businesses really
pick up if organisations are honest with their followers. It is therefore recommended that businesses be honest and transparent with the content that they
post in their social media marketing campaigns. In addition, they should
disclose and provide disclaimers pertaining to the products, ideas, and even
people they support and endorse. Transparency is further enhanced if firms
are clear about their identity, values, and even philanthropic engagements.
Therefore, being transparent is not only ethical. It helps firms maintain a
positive image in the minds of their target customers. Companies using
social media marketing should therefore remain transparent, truthful, and
honest with their clients at all times.

Verifying Content

Social media platforms are flooded with unauthentic pieces of information. This complicates the functions of social media marketers with respect
to content sharing. Maslow (2018) asserts that any factual error may lead
to embarrassment and a negative perception of the brand. Therefore, it is
imperative that companies take on the responsibility of ensuring that the
content they share is correct and verifiable. That is, what a company shares
on its social marketing platforms should be authentic, easy to understand,
and correct. This is achieved if the company always verifies before sending out what it shares to prospects. Companies should always imagine the
impact of what they share before tweeting and retweeting. It is therefore
recommended that if a company is sharing some information that has been
acquired from a third party through a social media channel, it should give
clear disclaimers to avoid suspicions of conflict of interest. In addition, the
social marketer should ensure that appropriate terms and conditions are
established for both the use of the platform and for data collection, storage,
and sharing when creating a new platform (Berman et al., 2018).

Age-Based Concerns

Children and young people below the age of 18 are, in most cases, left out
of marketing communication via traditional media such as radio and television. In Ghana, for instance, advertisements relating to alcoholic beverages
are not permitted to be run on any radio or television station until after
20.00 GMT, by which time young people are expected to be asleep. This is

to protect young people from being exposed to alcohol at an early age until they reach the stage of discernment and are able to express their voluntary consent. Such restrictions are not available for the use of social media in marketing communications. Berman et al. (2018) explain that the age below which children legally should not access social media or need informed consent to use social media services varies according to the terms and conditions of the social media service and any relevant local legislation across emerging economies. This has implications for the legal age range that can and should be targeted for participation in marketing involving social media. The ethical concern in this regard is the lack of awareness of legal age requirements for children's participation in social media marketing.

Aside from the paucity of awareness or absence of a legal age requirement for participation in social media marketing, difficulties associated with verifying the age of users online (UNICEF Innocenti, 2011) are also recognised as a potential source of social media marketing ethical breaches. The difficulty of verifying participants' ages calls for significant reflection when considering the sensitivity of the social media content.

Berman et al. (2018) noted with confidence that children and young people below the age of majority may be legally entitled to have their data removed from social media servers and other databases containing this data, even if they previously provided consent for the use of their data or if their parent provided consent. The challenge with this right is the risk and the potential difficulty in identifying and removing the data from all databases. It is more complicated in emerging markets. In most emerging economies, the existence of regulations granting young people the right to have their consents expunged from the databases of social media organisations is virtually nonexistent. To ensure a high ethical standard in this regard, social marketers are encouraged to provide opt-out options on their social media platforms (Berman et al., 2018). Opt-out options, when created, should be made available to young people to allow their data to be removed from lists or forums and, more generally, from data collection on request. It is also recommended that consideration be given to the possibility of removing data on request from participants (Greenwood et al., 2016). It is acknowledged, however, that there may be instances where the removal of data from all databases is impossible. In these cases, Berman et al. (2018) suggested that young people should be made aware of this and be provided with the option of, at a minimum, removing their information or data from the site or page, if not from all databases (which may be unknown).

Parents and guardians do express their consent on behalf of their under-age wards, which affords young people the opportunity to participate in social media marketing platforms. The ethical issue with respect to parental consent is the challenge of its authentication. According to Berman et al. (2018), there is little guidance in pre-existing regulations in emerging markets regarding how marketers can and should authenticate parental consent when this is necessary by law or organisational terms and conditions for the sharing of data. It is thus incredibly difficult to verify whether the parent has, in reality, provided informed consent for and/or on behalf of their wards. In an attempt to address this ethical concern in emerging markets, Raymond et al. (2017) were of the opinion that social media marketers should adhere to relevant local, international, and organisational legal and ethical standards pertaining to data protection, storage, transfer, removal, and security.

Conclusion

Social media marketing is defined as marketing via a group of internet-based applications that allow customers to use online information gathered from platforms such as Facebook, Flickr, YouTube, LinkedIn, and Twitter to educate one another about the products, services, and brand availability in the marketplace (Kaplan & Haenlein, 2010; Whiting & Williams, 2013). Social media marketing has exorbitantly grown in usage and popularity across all sectors and corners of the world, including emerging markets. From children and youth to elderly people, billions of people have become fond of social media, and this has revolutionised the digital age of market-ing. As a result, countless companies around the globe have their accounts and pages on Facebook, Flickr, YouTube, LinkedIn, Twitter, and other social media platforms (Amin et al., 2017). Whiting and Williams (2013) attributed the upsurge in social media adoption and usage in marketing to its robust-ness in social interaction, information seeking, passing time, entertain-ment, relaxation, communicatory utility, convenience utility, expression of opinions, information sharing, and surveillance/knowledge about others. However, the use of social media marketing is characterised by sociocul-tural and ethical concerns. That is, as the adoption of social media market-ing increases, important ethical issues are raised. Social media marketing is perceived as anonymous, that is, crossing borders and cultures worldwide (Lipschultz, 2017) without permission. In this regard, Dahl (2018) argues that social media faces a lot of ethical dilemmas, which can be substantially more complex than even regulatory problems. From an interconnected perspective, Sandoval (2014) considers social media to be a monster, a phenomenon that describes the unethical and destructive tendencies of social media. Specifically, a number of sociocultural and ethical concerns have been raised about the use of social media marketing. Socioculturally, electronic consumer-to-customer interaction, convenience in shopping, preference in online shopping, freedom of speech or writing, addiction by users, big brands' advertisements, contents on social media, and the possibility of checking consumers' responses and feedback have been recognised as the sociocultural concerns social media marketers in emerging markets need to be mindful of (Amin et al., 2017). On the other hand, ethical issues of concern for social media marketers include leakage of private data; security of consumer data; fabricated negative reviews by rivals or negative word-of-mouth communication by users; misrepresentation of brands' data; presenting falsified contents, fake images and videos of products, spam messages, and fraudulent offers; and defamation of renowned brands and companies. It is therefore imperative that social media markets recognise the managing effects of the absence of and nonadherence to ethical standards and regulations in order to govern the ethical behaviour of social media markets and consumers.

Review Questions

1. Define mobile commerce (m-commerce) and discuss its various manifestations as a technology, a product, and a service. Refer to the definitions and categorisations to explain how m-commerce integrates these three elements.
2. What are the key features of mobile commerce that distinguish it from traditional commerce? Discuss the benefits of these features for both businesses and consumers.
3. Explain how mobile commerce and mobile business are intertwined. How do these concepts contribute to the various organisational functions such as financial management, marketing management, and customer relationship management?
4. Discuss the global trends in mobile commerce and the factors influencing its adoption. According to various cited researchers and studies

in the chapter, how do these trends and factors influence the use and development of m-commerce services in emerging markets?

References

Albarran, A. B. (Ed.). (2013). *The social media industries*. Routledge.

Amin, H., Qureshi, J. A., & Chandio, S. (2017). Cultural, ethical and legal considerations of using social media marketing in Karachi-Pakistan. *Journal of Independent Studies & Research: Management & Social Sciences & Economics*, *15*(2), 165–180. https://doi.org/10.31384/jisrmsse/2017.15.2.11

Berman, B., Evans, J. R., & Chatterjee, P. (2018). *Retail management: A strategic approach*. Pearson.

Dahl, S. (2018). *Social media marketing: Theories and applications*. Sage.

Georgi, D., & Mink, M. (2013). eCCIq: The quality of electronic customer-to-customer interaction. *Journal of Retailing and Consumer Services*, *20*(1), 11–19.

Greenwood, S., Perrin, A., & Duggan, M. (2016). Social media update 2016. *Pew Research Center*, *11*(2), 1–18.

Hoffman, D. L., & Fodor, M. (2010). Can you measure the ROI of your social media marketing? *MIT Sloan Management Review*, *52*(1), 41.

Kaplan, A. M., & Haenlein, M. (2010). Users of the world, unite! The challenges and opportunities of social media. *Business Horizons*, *53*(1), 59–68.

Lipschultz, J. H. (2017). *Social media communication: Concepts, practices, data, law and ethics*. Routledge.

Maslow, J. (2018). *4 Layers of ethics in social media marketing*. Retrieved June 30, 2020, from https://socialmediaexplorer.com/social-media-marketing/4-layers-of-ethics-in-social-media-marketing/

Muniz, A. M., & O'guinn, T. C. (2001). Brand community. *Journal of Consumer Research*, *27*(4), 412–432.

Nicholls, W. (2008, February 27). For two sisters, little cakes are a big hit. *Washington Post, F01*. Retrieved July 1, 2020, from http://www.washingtonpost.com/ wp-dyn/content/article/2008/02/26/ AR2008022600703.html

Patino, A., Pitta, D. A., & Quinones, R. (2012). Social media's emerging importance in market research. *Journal of Consumer Marketing*, *29*(3), 233–237.

Pravina, M. (2020). https://www.coursehero.com/file/75533797/PRAVINA-C00265706-BUSINESS-RESERACH-METHODSdocx/

Raymond, C. M., Frantzeskaki, N., Kabisch, N., Berry, P., Breil, M., Nita, M. R., ... Calfapietra, C. (2017). A framework for assessing and implementing the co-benefits of nature-based solutions in urban areas. *Environmental Science and Policy*, *77*, 15–24.

Sandoval, M. (2014). *From corporate to social media: Critical perspectives on corporate social responsibility in media and communication industries*. Routledge.

Unicef. (2011). *Child safety online: Global challenges and strategies*. UNICEF Innocenti Research Centre.

Vinjamuri, D. (2011). Ethics and the five deadly sins of social media. *Forbes. com.*

Whiting, A., & Williams, D. (2013). Why people use social media: A uses and gratifications approach. *Qualitative Market Research: An International Journal,* *16*(4), 362–369.

Chapter 9

Social Media Marketing Management: How to Penetrate Emerging Markets and Expand Your Customer Base

Chapter Outline

- Introduction
- Social media marketing and emerging markets
- The manufacturing sector and social media marketing
- Agribusiness and social media marketing
- Real estate and social media marketing
- Information and communication technology (ICT) sector and social media marketing
- Oil and gas and social media marketing
- Putting it all together

Chapter Outcome

By the end of this chapter, the reader will be able to:

DOI: 10.4324/9781003307457-9

Analyse the utilisation of social media in marketing strategies in emerging economies:
- Evaluate and interpret how emerging economies leverage social media within their marketing strategies.
- Apply insights to identify effective practices and challenges in utilising social media for marketing in emerging markets.

Examine the interplay between social media and marketing in emerging economies:
- Investigate and critically analyse the dynamic relationship and interactions between social media and marketing strategies in emerging economies.
- Synthesise the understanding to propose strategic recommendations for optimising this interplay.

Explore the application of social media in specific sectors of the economy:
- Investigate how social media is strategically employed in specific sectors of emerging economies.
- Apply sector-specific insights to develop targeted approaches for utilising social media in diverse economic domains.

Introduction

Social media serves as the virtual nexus of global interaction, and businesses are presented with unprecedented opportunities to expand their reach and connect with diverse markets. Many firms use social media to engage and interact with their customers without boundaries. Accordingly, social media provides avenues for firms to create value for their customers and other stakeholders. Felix et al. (2017) note that the effectiveness of social media marketing partly depends on the specific role consumers assign to companies and brands within the social media sphere. In this case, exploring the transformative power of social media as a strategic tool and platform for market penetration in emerging economies is of critical importance.

As businesses increasingly recognise the potency of social media marketing, the quest to understand the nuances of navigating emerging markets becomes essential. One benefit of social media is its ability to enable firms to reach out to many, irrespective of the industry. Hence, it is essential to formulate and execute effective social media strategies tailored to the unique dynamics of evolving markets. This chapter will provide marketers with the knowledge and tools needed to successfully extend their brand presence into untapped territories. With a focus on fostering meaningful connections, driving engagement, and cultivating customer loyalty, social media marketing management will serve as a compass for businesses seeking not only to enter but also to thrive in emerging markets. Firms need to take advantage of the increasing use of social media by various stakeholders to harness the full potential of this development and increase their customer base.

Social Media Marketing and Emerging Markets

Shah et al. (2020) have argued that social media engagement influences customer engagement and brand satisfaction among Muslim customers. Das and Pradip (2021) have also argued that new media is the best way to transform agricultural practices socially. It is a forum where all the farmers in the country can get together and address the issue of the agrarian crisis. Online social marketing (OSM) through WhatsApp is one of the best methods of behavioural change because different farmers can share their experiences of and emotions about the crisis and offer appropriate solutions to problems.

Raman et al. (2018) also argue that social media adoption assists in organisational innovation, and Tamilmani et al. (2018) also argue that social media in the context of emerging economies influences consumers and the organisations that adopt social media techniques. Salam et al. (2021) also argue that small- and medium-sized (SME) retailers adopted social marketing to varying degrees, and the perceived ease of use through perceived usefulness influenced SME retailers' attitudes towards the usage of social media marketing during the COVID-19 crisis. An important finding in that study was that business owners' education level influenced their perceptions of social media marketing.

Finally, Muhammad et al. (2023) have recently highlighted the significance of social media platforms like WhatsApp, TikTok, Pinterest, Viber, and Snapchat and their applications as promotional tools to inspire the purchase intentions of customers in this virtual age. In light of the foregoing benefits of social media adoption for the growth of firms in emerging markets, we focus in the last chapter on discussing ways in which social media marketing can be used as a tool for penetrating emerging markets and succeeding in those markets.

ESG Investing argued in a February 2022 article (https://esginvest.co/top-5-advanced-industries-in-emerging-markets/) that the top five industries in emerging markets are:

1. Information and communication technology;
2. Manufacturing;
3. Oil and gas;
4. Textiles and apparel;
5. Chemicals.

In this concluding chapter, we focus on social media marketing and emerging marketing penetration and consolidation around the following selected industries:

1. Manufacturing;
2. Agribusiness;
3. Real estate;
4. Information and communication technology;
5. Textiles and apparel;
6. Oil and gas.

In this concluding chapter, we examine the possibilities for businesses looking to expand into emerging economies from a sectorial perspective.

The Manufacturing Sector and Social Media Marketing

Social media marketing can play a significant role in the manufacturing sector, just as it does in many other industries. For businesses looking to expand into emerging economies, there are several ways in which social media marketing can benefit manufacturing companies. The first opportunity for businesses is the possibility of brand awareness. Social media platforms provide a powerful channel for manufacturers to build and promote their brands. By creating a strong online presence and sharing compelling content, manufacturers can increase brand awareness among their target audience.

Manufacturers can use social media to showcase their products and highlight their features and benefits. Visual platforms like Instagram and Pinterest are especially useful for showcasing product images. TikTok is also great for short-form content for product promotion as well. Sharing informative and educational content related to manufacturing processes, industry trends, and best practices can position a manufacturing company as an industry leader. This can be particularly effective on platforms like LinkedIn and YouTube, which support long-form content.

Social media marketing is also useful for recruitment and employer branding. It is important to note that employees are internal customers of every manufacturing form, and manufacturers can use social media to attract top talent by posting job openings, sharing company culture, and highlighting employee success stories. Social media can also be a useful feedback tool for allowing employees to share perspectives on issues that affect them, and likewise, social media can also serve as a feedback mechanism, allowing manufacturers to gather input from external customers and make improvements to their products and services.

Social media also provides a wealth of data and insights about customer preferences, industry trends, and competitor activities. Manufacturers can leverage this information to make informed business decisions, and this makes social media a crucial market research platform. Manufacturers can also use social media to identify and connect with potential partners, suppliers, and distributors, expanding their business networks.

Finally, social media platforms offer precise targeting options, allowing manufacturers to reach their ideal audience with tailored advertising, public relations, and related marketing communications campaigns.

To effectively utilise social media marketing in the manufacturing sector, companies should:

1. Define goals: Clearly outline what they aim to achieve through social media marketing, whether it's increased brand awareness, lead generation, or customer engagement.
2. Choose the right platforms: Identify the social media platforms that are most relevant to the target audience and industry. For business-to-business (B2B) manufacturing, LinkedIn and Twitter may be more effective, while visual platforms like Instagram and Pinterest could work well for business-to-customer (B2C) products.
3. Create quality content: Develop a content strategy that includes a mix of informative articles, videos, images, and user-generated content.
4. Engage consistently: Regularly update and engage with the audience to keep them interested and informed.

5. Monitor and analyse: Use analytics tools to measure the performance of social media campaigns and adjust strategies accordingly.
6. Comply with regulations: Be aware of industry-specific regulations, especially regarding the sharing of technical information and product specifications.

In conclusion, while the manufacturing sector may not be as naturally inclined towards social media as some other industries, it can still benefit significantly from a well-planned and executed social media marketing strategy. It can help manufacturers connect with their audience, build brand awareness, and ultimately drive business growth.

Agribusiness and Social Media Marketing

Social media marketing can be a powerful tool for agribusinesses, helping them connect with their target audience, promote products and services, share valuable information, and build brand awareness. Several emerging economies globally have vibrant agribusiness sectors, and there are several ways in which agribusinesses can effectively leverage social media marketing.

Agribusinesses can use social media to share educational content about farming practices, crop management, livestock care, and sustainable agriculture. This positions them as experts in the field and provides value to their audience. The educational content an agribusiness shares on social media can be short or long. Relatedly, social media can be used as product promotion vehicles, showcasing agricultural products, equipment, and services. Visual platforms like Instagram and Pinterest can be particularly effective for highlighting the visual aspects of farming and agribusiness.

Due to the complex ecosystems agribusinesses operate in, social media platforms can be used as a community-building vehicle where agribusinesses create and foster online communities or groups where farmers, ranchers, and agricultural enthusiasts can share their experiences, ask questions, and exchange information. Relatedly, social media platforms also serve as excellent customer engagement tools, because engaging with customers on social media can help agribusinesses build stronger relationships. Responding to comments, messages, and inquiries in a timely manner shows that the business values its customers.

To the extent that agriculture often follows seasonal cycles, agribusinesses can use social media to provide updates on planting seasons, harvest times, and weather-related information that can impact farming. For agribusinesses involved in livestock as well, social media can be used to advertise and facilitate livestock sales and auctions.

Other marketing uses for which agribusinesses can use social media include:

Market research: Social media provides a platform for agribusinesses to gather insights into market trends, customer preferences, and competitor activities. This data can inform business decisions.

Environmental stewardship: Highlighting sustainability efforts and eco-friendly practices through social media can resonate with consumers who are increasingly conscious of environmental issues.

Behind-the-scenes content: Offering a behind-the-scenes look at daily operations on the farm or within the agribusiness can humanise the brand and create a connection with the audience.

Advertising: Social media advertising platforms provide targeting options that can help agribusinesses reach specific demographics, geographic regions, and interests, making it easier to connect with potential customers.

To make the most of social media marketing in agribusiness, players in that sector should select appropriate platforms by choosing social media platforms that align with their target audiences. For instance, Facebook and YouTube are often effective for reaching a broad audience, while LinkedIn may be more suitable for B2B agribusinesses. They should also consider the following:

Create engaging content: Develop a content strategy that includes a mix of informative articles, videos, images, and user-generated content. Visual content that showcases the beauty of farms and agriculture can be particularly engaging.

Consistency: Regularly update your social media profiles with fresh content to keep your audience engaged.

Utilise hashtags: Use relevant hashtags to expand the reach of your posts to users interested in agriculture and related topics.

Measure and analyse: Use analytics tools to track the performance of your social media campaigns. This data can help you refine your strategy and improve results over time.

Ensure compliance: Ensure that any claims or information you share about your products and services comply with relevant regulations and standards in the agricultural industry.

Social media marketing offers numerous opportunities for agribusinesses to connect with their audience, share knowledge, and promote their products and services. By leveraging these platforms effectively, agribusinesses can build a strong online presence and penetrate and win in emerging markets.

Real Estate and Social Media Marketing

Social media marketing is a valuable tool for the real estate sector, helping professionals and companies promote properties, connect with potential buyers and sellers, and establish themselves as trusted experts in the industry. Here are several ways in which the real estate sector can effectively use social media marketing:

1. Property listings: Real estate agents and agencies can use social media platforms to showcase property listings. Visual platforms like Instagram, Facebook, and Pinterest are particularly effective for sharing images and videos of homes and commercial properties. This provides potential buyers with a visual preview of available properties.
2. Virtual tours: Live or recorded virtual property tours can be broadcast on platforms like Facebook Live or YouTube, allowing potential buyers to explore properties remotely. This is especially useful for international or long-distance buyers.
3. Market updates: Share regular updates on the local real estate market, including trends in property prices, mortgage rates, and other relevant information. This positions you as a knowledgeable resource.
4. Educational content: Create and share informative content on topics such as buying, selling, investing, and home improvement. This can include blog posts, how-to videos, and infographics.
5. Testimonials and success stories: Highlight satisfied clients and success stories through social media. These stories provide social proof of your expertise and the quality of your services.

6. Engage with the community: Interact with your local community on social media by participating in discussions, sharing local news, and supporting community events. This can help build a strong local reputation.

7. Paid advertising: Platforms like Facebook and Instagram offer targeted advertising options, allowing you to reach potential clients based on demographics, interests, and location.

8. Personal branding: Real estate professionals can use social media to build a personal brand. Share insights, tips, and your unique perspective on the market to establish credibility and trust.

9. Networking: Join real estate groups and communities on platforms like LinkedIn to connect with other professionals in the industry. Building a strong network can lead to valuable partnerships and referrals.

10. Customer service: Social media can be used to provide prompt responses to inquiries and comments from potential clients. It can be a real-time communication channel to address questions and concerns.

To make the most of social media marketing in the real estate sector:

11. Choose the right platforms: Focus on platforms that align with your target audience. Facebook, Instagram, LinkedIn, and Twitter are commonly used in the real estate industry.

12. Post quality visual content: Invest in professional-quality images and videos of properties. High-quality visuals can make a significant difference in attracting potential buyers.

13. Ensure consistency: Regularly update your social media profiles with fresh content to keep your audience engaged and informed.

14. Use hashtags: Incorporate relevant hashtags in your posts to increase discoverability. Local hashtags can be particularly effective.

15. Use analytics and tracking: Use analytics tools to monitor the performance of your social media campaigns. This data can help you refine your strategy and focus on what works best.

16. Ensure compliance: Ensure that your advertising and promotional content comply with real estate regulations and standards in your region.

Social media marketing can be a powerful tool for real estate professionals and companies to connect with clients, showcase properties, and establish themselves as trusted experts in the industry. When executed effectively, it can significantly contribute to the success and growth of your real estate business.

The Information and Communication Technology (ICT) Sector And Social Media Marketing

The Information and Communication Technology (ICT) sector is well-suited for social media marketing due to its digitally savvy audience and the dynamic nature of the industry. Here are several ways in which the ICT sector can effectively utilise social media marketing:

1. Product and service promotion: ICT companies can use social media platforms to showcase their latest products, software, and services. Visual platforms like Instagram and YouTube are great for product demos and tutorials.
2. Educational content: Share informative and educational content related to technology trends, industry insights, and how-to guides. This positions your company as an expert in the field and provides value to your audience.
3. Thought leadership: Build a reputation as a thought leader by sharing opinions, insights, and commentary on current industry developments, emerging technologies, and best practices. Platforms like LinkedIn are ideal for this purpose.
4. Customer support: Provide customer support and technical assistance through social media channels. Respond to inquiries and address concerns promptly, enhancing customer satisfaction.
5. Behind-the-scenes content: Give your audience a glimpse into your company's culture and operations by sharing behind-the-scenes content, such as employee interviews and office tours. This can humanise your brand.
6. Case studies and success stories: Highlight customer success stories and case studies to demonstrate the real-world impact of your products and services.
7. Webinars and live streams: Host webinars, live Q&A sessions, and virtual events to engage your audience in real time. These can be used to launch new products, discuss industry trends, or provide training.
8. User-generated content: Encourage customers and users to share their experiences with your products or services on social media. Repost user-generated content to build trust and authenticity.
9. Competitions and contests: Run online competitions or contests that engage your audience and encourage them to interact with your brand.

10. Paid advertising: Invest in targeted social media advertising to reach specific demographics, industries, or job titles relevant to your ICT products or services.

To effectively use social media marketing in the ICT sector:

11. Platform selection: Focus on platforms that are most relevant to your target audience. LinkedIn is crucial for B2B engagement, while platforms like Twitter and Facebook can work well for reaching a broader audience.
12. Content variety: Diversify your content by incorporating images, videos, infographics, articles, and interactive content like polls and quizzes.
13. Consistency: Maintain a consistent posting schedule to keep your audience engaged. Regular updates and interactions are key to building a strong online presence.
14. Analytics and metrics: Use analytics tools to track the performance of your social media campaigns. Adjust your strategy based on the data to optimise your results.
15. Community engagement: Actively engage with your audience by responding to comments, messages, and mentions. Building relationships with your followers can lead to increased brand loyalty.
16. Compliance: Be aware of regulations and standards that apply to your industry, especially regarding data privacy and cybersecurity if you handle sensitive information.

In conclusion, social media marketing is a valuable tool for the ICT sector to connect with tech-savvy audiences, showcase products and services, and establish thought leadership. When used strategically, social media can help ICT companies reach their marketing goals and stay competitive in a rapidly evolving industry.

Textile and Apparel Sector and Social Media Marketing

Social media marketing can be a powerful tool for the textile and apparel sector, helping companies in this industry showcase their products, connect with their target audience, and build brand awareness. Here are several ways in which the textile and apparel sector can effectively leverage social media marketing:

1. Product showcases: Use social media platforms to display your latest clothing and textile products. Visual platforms like Instagram and Pinterest are particularly effective for showcasing fashion items.
2. Fashion trends and styling: Share content about the latest fashion trends, styling tips, and outfit inspiration. You can use platforms like TikTok and Instagram Reels for short fashion videos.
3. Behind-the-scenes: Provide a behind-the-scenes look at your design process, manufacturing, and day-to-day operations. This adds a human touch to your brand and makes it more relatable.
4. User-generated content: Encourage customers to share photos of themselves wearing your products. Reposting user-generated content can build trust and authenticity.
5. Influencer collaborations: Partner with fashion influencers and bloggers to promote your products. Influencer marketing can expand your reach to a wider audience.
6. Seasonal campaigns: Plan and execute seasonal marketing campaigns for events like back-to-school, holidays, and fashion weeks. Social media is a great platform for announcing and promoting such campaigns.
7. Customer engagement: Engage with your audience by responding to comments, questions, and messages promptly. Encourage discussions about fashion and style.
8. Educational content: Create informative content about fabric care, sustainable fashion, and the manufacturing process. This positions your brand as knowledgeable and responsible.
9. Sales and promotions: Announce sales, discounts, and promotions through social media to incentivise purchases and attract bargain-hunting customers.
10. Sustainability initiatives: Highlight your company's sustainability efforts, such as eco-friendly materials, ethical manufacturing practices, and recycling programmes. Social media is a great platform to communicate your commitment to sustainability.

To effectively use social media marketing in the textile and apparel sectors:

11. Choose relevant platforms: Focus your efforts on platforms that align with your target demographic. Instagram, Facebook, and Pinterest are popular choices for fashion brands.

12. Visual content: Invest in high-quality photography and videography to showcase your products. Fashion is highly visual, so eye-catching visuals are crucial.

13. Content calendar: Plan and maintain a content calendar to ensure regular, consistent posting. Include themed posts for holidays, seasons, and special occasions.

14. Engagement metrics: Monitor engagement metrics like likes, shares, comments, and click-through rates to assess the success of your campaigns. Use these insights to refine your strategy.

15. Advertising: Consider using social media advertising to reach a broader audience and drive traffic to your website or online store.

16. Community building: Cultivate a loyal following by fostering a sense of community among your audience. Encourage discussions, feedback, and sharing among your followers.

17. Compliance: Be aware of any advertising and disclosure regulations related to the textile and apparel industry, especially when promoting sales or sustainability claims.

In summary, social media marketing is a valuable tool for the textile and apparel sectors to showcase products, engage with customers, and stay on top of fashion trends. When used effectively, it can enhance brand visibility, drive sales, and build a strong online presence in the highly competitive fashion industry.

Oil and Gas and Social Media Marketing

Social media marketing can be a valuable strategy for companies in the oil and gas industry, helping them connect with various stakeholders, share industry insights, promote their services, and enhance their brand presence. Here are several ways in which the oil and gas sector can effectively utilise social media marketing:

1. Industry updates: Share news and updates about the oil and gas industry, including market trends, regulatory changes, and technological advancements. This establishes your company as an authority in the industry.

2. Safety and sustainability: Highlight your commitment to safety and sustainability through social media. Share information about environmental practices, safety protocols, and corporate responsibility initiatives.
3. Project showcases: Showcase your company's ongoing projects and success stories. Visual platforms like Instagram and LinkedIn can be used to share images and videos of project developments.
4. Educational content: Create informative content about the oil and gas sector, explaining complex concepts, processes, and technologies. This helps your audience better understand the industry.
5. Thought leadership: Share opinions, insights, and commentary on relevant industry topics, such as energy policies, market volatility, and geopolitical factors. Use platforms like LinkedIn to establish thought leadership.
6. Community engagement: Actively engage with your audience, which may include industry professionals, investors, and local communities. Respond to comments, questions, and concerns to foster trust and transparency.
7. Recruitment: Use social media to attract talent by showcasing your company culture, job openings, and employee success stories.
8. Investor relations: Communicate with shareholders and potential investors by sharing financial updates, annual reports, and company performance. LinkedIn is a suitable platform for this purpose.
9. Crisis management: In the case of a crisis or emergency, social media can serve as a quick communication channel to address concerns, provide updates, and ensure public safety.
10. Paid advertising: Utilise social media advertising to reach a specific audience, such as investors or industry professionals, with targeted messages.

To effectively use social media marketing in the oil and gas industry:

11. Select relevant platforms: Identify the social media platforms most used by your target audience. LinkedIn is often essential for B2B engagement, while Twitter and Facebook can be effective for broader communication.
12. Content strategy: Develop a content strategy that includes a mix of written articles, videos, infographics, and data visualisations to cater to different learning preferences.

13. Visual storytelling: Utilise visuals like images and videos to make technical content more accessible and engaging.
14. Consistency: Maintain a consistent posting schedule to keep your audience engaged. Regular updates and interactions are key to building a strong online presence.
15. Analytics and metrics: Use analytics tools to monitor the performance of your social media campaigns. Adjust your strategy based on the data to optimise your results.
16. Compliance: Ensure that your content complies with industry regulations and standards, especially regarding safety and environmental claims.

In summary, while the oil and gas industry may not be as naturally aligned with social media marketing as some other sectors, it can still benefit significantly from a well-planned and executed strategy. Effective social media marketing can help oil and gas companies connect with stakeholders, promote their brand, and share important industry information.

Putting It All Together

Social media marketing is a powerful tool for customer acquisition when used strategically. It allows businesses to reach and engage with potential customers on platforms they already use and trust. Here are some effective strategies for using social media marketing to acquire customers:

1. **Define your target audience:**
   - Before you start any marketing campaign, it's essential to have a clear understanding of your ideal customer. Define demographics, interests, behaviours, and pain points to create highly targeted content.
2. **Choose the right social media platforms:**
   - Different social media platforms attract distinct user demographics. Choose platforms that align with your target audience. For example, Facebook and Instagram might be suitable for B2C businesses, while LinkedIn might be better for B2B.
3. **Create high-quality content:**
   - Produce valuable, engaging, and visually appealing content that addresses your audience's needs and interests. Content can include blog posts, videos, infographics, and more.

4. **Establish a consistent posting schedule:**
   - A consistent posting schedule will keep your audience engaged and informed. Consistency helps build trust and brand awareness.
5. **Use paid advertising:**
   - Social media advertising, such as Facebook ads and Instagram ads, allows you to target specific demographics, interests, and behaviours. Invest in paid advertising to reach a larger audience and generate leads.
6. **Run contests and giveaways:**
   - Hosting contests or giveaways can incentivise social media users to engage with your brand. Make sure the prize is relevant to your product or service to attract genuinely interested leads.
7. **Leverage influencers:**
   - Collaborate with social media influencers who align with your brand. Influencers can introduce your products or services to their followers, potentially leading to new customers.
8. **Utilise hashtags:**
   - Incorporate relevant and trending hashtags in your posts to increase visibility. Users searching for or following these hashtags may come across your content.
9. **Engage with your audience:**
   - Respond to comments, messages, and mentions promptly. Engaging with your audience shows that you value their input and are accessible.
10. **Use call-to-actions (CTAs):**
    - Encourage your social media audience to take action by using clear and compelling CTAs. For example, invite them to sign up for a newsletter, visit your website, or make a purchase.
11. **Landing pages and lead magnets:**
    - Create dedicated landing pages on your website for social media campaigns. Offer lead magnets, such as eBooks, webinars, or exclusive discounts, to encourage sign-ups and gather contact information.
12. **Track and analyse metrics:**
    - Regularly monitor the performance of your social media campaigns using analytics tools. Track metrics like engagement, click-through rates, conversions, and return on investment (ROI). Use this data to refine your strategies.

13. **Email marketing integration:**
    - Integrate social media with your email marketing efforts. Share content from your email campaigns on social media and encourage social media followers to subscribe to your email list.
14. **Customer reviews and testimonials:**
    - Showcase positive customer reviews and testimonials on your social media profiles. These provide social proof and build trust with potential customers.
15. **A/B testing:**
    - Experiment with different types of content, ad creatives, and targeting strategies. A/B testing helps you identify what resonates best with your audience.
16. **Implement retargeting:**
    - Retargeting campaigns can reach users who have shown interest in your products or visited your website but did not complete a desired action. This can help convert warm leads into customers.

Expanding your customer base in emerging markets through social media marketing management requires a well-thought-out strategy that considers the unique characteristics and challenges of these markets. Here's a step-by-step guide on how to penetrate emerging markets and grow your customer base through social media marketing:

1. **Conduct market research:**
   - Start by conducting thorough research to understand the specific characteristics of the emerging markets you're targeting. This includes demographic data, cultural norms, consumer behaviours, and economic conditions.
   - Identify the social media platforms that are most popular and widely used in these markets. It may not always be the same platforms as in your home market.
2. **Localise your content:**
   - Tailor your content to resonate with the local audience. This includes using the local language, incorporating cultural references, and addressing local issues and concerns.
   - Ensure that your content aligns with the values and preferences of the target market. What works in one market may not work in another.

3. **Understand the regulatory environment:**
   - Familiarise yourself with the local regulations and laws related to social media marketing and e-commerce in the target market. Compliance is essential to avoid legal issues.
4. **Build relationships:**
   - Establish relationships with local influencers and industry leaders who can help promote your brand to their followers. Influencer marketing can be particularly effective in emerging markets.
5. **Adapt your marketing strategy:**
   - Adjust your social media marketing strategy to accommodate the local internet infrastructure and access. Some emerging markets may have slower internet speeds or limited access to certain platforms.
6. **Offer local payment options:**
   - Ensure that your e-commerce platform supports local payment methods. Many emerging markets have unique payment preferences, such as mobile wallets or specific payment gateways.
7. **Offer customer support and engagement:**
   - Provide responsive customer support that is available in the local language and time zone. Engage with customers on social media and respond to inquiries and feedback promptly.
8. **Encourage user-generated content:**
   - Encourage user-generated content from your customers in the target market. Share their stories and experiences with your products or services. This can help build trust and authenticity.
9. **Form local partnerships:**
   - Consider forming partnerships with local businesses or organisations to enhance your market presence. Collaborations can help you reach a wider audience and establish credibility.
10. **Measure and analyse performance:**
    - Continuously monitor the performance of your social media marketing campaigns in the emerging market. Use analytics tools to track key metrics, such as engagement, conversions, and ROI.
    - Adjust your strategy based on the insights you gather. Be prepared to iterate and refine your approach as you learn more about the market.
11. **Test and experiment:**
    - Be open to experimenting with different content formats, ad campaigns, and marketing strategies. What works in one emerging market may not work in another, so be prepared to adapt and evolve.

12. **Establish long-term commitment:**
    ■ Entering emerging markets is often a long-term endeavour. It may take time to gain traction and establish a strong presence. Be patient and committed to your market expansion efforts.

Expanding into emerging markets through social media marketing management requires a deep understanding of local dynamics and a flexible approach. It's essential to be culturally sensitive, adapt to local preferences, and build trust with the target audience over time. Building a strong brand presence in these markets can lead to significant growth opportunities for your business.

Remember that customer acquisition is a continuous process. Social media marketing can help you attract new customers, but building lasting relationships and providing value will encourage customer retention and loyalty over time.

Review Questions

1. What social media approaches would you consider in seeking to succeed in the manufacturing sector of emerging markets?
2. What social media approaches would you consider in seeking to succeed in the oil and gas sector of emerging markets?
3. What social media approaches would you consider in seeking to succeed in the ICT sector of emerging markets?

References

Das, P., & Pradip, D. (2021). Usability and effectiveness of new media in agricultural learning and development: A case study on the southern states of India. *Journal of Social Marketing, 11*(4), 357–377. https://doi.org/10.1108/JSOCM-11-2019-0203

Felix, R., Rauschnabel, P. A., & Hinsch, C. (2017). Elements of strategic social media marketing: A holistic framework. *Journal of Business Research, 70*, 118–126.

Muhammad, A. M., Basha, M. B., & AlHafidh, G. (2023). Use of emerging social media platforms in reshaping the UAE Islamic banks' promotional strategies. *Journal of Islamic Marketing.* https://doi.org/10.1108/JIMA-01-2022-0015

Raman, R., & Menon, P. (2018). Using social media for innovation – Market segmentation of family firms. *International Journal of Innovation Science.* https://doi.org/10.1108/IJIS-08-2017-0078

Salam, M. T., Imtiaz, H., & Burhan, M. (2021). The perceptions of SME retailers towards the usage of social media marketing amid COVID-19 crisis. *Journal of Entrepreneurship in Emerging Economies, 13*(4), 58.

Shah, S. A. A., Sukmana, R., Fianto, B. A., Ahmad, M. A., Usman, I. U., & Mallah, W. A. (2020). Effects of halal social media and customer engagement on brand satisfaction of Muslim customer: Exploring the moderation of religiosity. *Journal of Islamic Marketing, 11*(6), 1671–1689. https://doi.org/10.1108/JIMA-06 -2019-0119

Tamilmani, K., Rana, N. P., Alryalat, M. A. A., Al-Khowaiter, W. A. A., & Dwivedi, Y. K. (2018). Social media research in the context of emerging markets: An analysis of extant literature from information systems perspective. *Journal of Advances in Management Research, 15*(2), 115–129. https://doi.org/10.1108/ JAMR-05-2017-0061

Index